Becoming Brilliant is an easy but important read for parents and educators seeking to understand the latest global research and thinking about the competencies today's children need to thrive in the 21st century.

—**Wendy Kopp,** *Founder of Teach For America and CEO and Cofounder, Teach For All, New York, NY*

A must-read for parents, educators, and policy makers. The authors do an outstanding job of illuminating the science behind how children learn. It's now our responsibility to take on the challenge to ask the much needed "what if" questions. Our children deserve enriching learning environments to build core competencies for their future success.

—**Rosemarie T. Truglio, PhD,** *Senior Vice President of Curriculum and Content, Sesame Workshop, New York, NY*

Golinkoff and Hirsh-Pasek provide a compelling argument for the core sets of skills our children need. This is an essential read for parents and anyone interested in how to best support our children.

—**Rebecca Winthrop, PhD,** *Director, The Center for Universal Education, The Brookings Institution, Washington, DC*

Combining the wise voice of experience with solid and compelling research on how we learn, *Becoming Brilliant* is the new "how to" raise a creative, strong, happy, and productive future—our children. I recommend this book for anyone looking to hone their perspective on the vital role we have as the caring adult in a young child's life. It grounds and guides decisions we all make in bringing up the next generation.

—**Susan H. Magsamen, MAS,** *Senior Advisor, Johns Hopkins University Science of Learning Institute and Brain Science Institute, Baltimore, MD, and Senior Vice President of Early Learning, Houghton Mifflin Harcourt*

BECOMING
BRILLIANT

BECOMING BRILLIANT

What Science Tells Us About Raising Successful Children

ROBERTA MICHNICK GOLINKOFF, PhD
KATHY HIRSH-PASEK, PhD

American Psychological Association • Washington, DC

First Printing March 2016
Second Printing July 2016

Published by
APA LifeTools
750 First Street, NE
Washington, DC 20002
www.apa.org

To order
APA Order Department
P.O. Box 92984
Washington, DC 20090-2984
Tel: (800) 374-2721;
Direct: (202) 336-5510
Fax: (202) 336-5502;
TDD/TTY: (202) 336-6123
Online: www.apa.org/pubs/books
E-mail: order@apa.org

In the U.K., Europe, Africa, and the Middle East, copies may be ordered from
American Psychological Association
3 Henrietta Street
Covent Garden, London
WC2E 8LU England

Typeset in Sabon by Circle Graphics, Inc., Columbia, MD

Printer: United Book Press, Baltimore, MD
Cover Designer: BookBaby, Pennsauken, NJ

The opinions and statements published are the responsibility of the authors, and such opinions and statements do not necessarily represent the policies of the American Psychological Association.

Library of Congress Cataloging-in-Publication Data

Names: Golinkoff, Roberta M., author. | Hirsh-Pasek, Kathy.
Title: Becoming brilliant : what science tells us about raising successful
   children / Roberta Michnick Golinkoff, PhD, and Kathy Hirsh-Pasek, PhD.
Description: First edition. | Washington, DC : American Psychological
   Association, [2016] | Series: LifeTools | Includes bibliographical
   references and index.
Identifiers: LCCN 2015045395 | ISBN 9781433822391 | ISBN 1433822393
Subjects: LCSH: Education—Parent participation. | Learning. | Child
   development. | Child psychology. | Success.
Classification: LCC LB1048.5 .G65 2016 | DDC 155.4/1315—dc23
LC record available at http://lccn.loc.gov/2015045395

British Library Cataloguing-in-Publication Data
A CIP record is available from the British Library.

Printed in the United States of America
First Edition

http://dx.doi.org/10.1037/14917-000

We dedicate this book to our future:
Ellie, Elio, Marina, Beau, Dominic, Lilah, Shai, Barbara,
and to children everywhere. Our goal is to make
education worthy of everyone's children and grandchildren.

CONTENTS

ACKNOWLEDGMENTS

Luck. How did we get so lucky? When we met at the University of Delaware lo those many years ago for an institute on the origins and growth of communication funded by the Carnegie Foundation and the Society for Research in Child Development, who could have predicted that we would be collaborating 35 years later? We feel so lucky to have each other to think with, to write with, to argue with, and to play and laugh with. But our luck continues. Each semester when we have a party for our labs (Roberta's at the University of Delaware; Kathy's at Temple University), we write "To the best lab ever" on the cake we invariably serve. And the funny thing is, it is always true. We have had wonderful students who have fine minds they share with us—both graduate and undergraduate—as well as postdoctoral fellows.

And our luck continues. We have five children between us, each of whom has unique and lovable gifts. They gave us the "on-the-ground" experience we needed to understand the trials and tribulations of parenthood. One of our books said, "To our children, delightful sources of inspiration and fatigue." The fatigue is gone! Now we have only the inspiring recollections. We also have a new, delicious fatigue from attending to our active (and of course, brilliant) grandchildren.

Our own children experienced a certain set of cultural circumstances and lived in a certain time. Our grandchildren—to whom this book is dedicated—have inherited a whole new world full of media and tablets and cell phones that did not exist 15 years ago. Like a galloping horse picking up speed, the pace of change we and our families are experiencing is ever increasing. But some things stay constant, despite the fact that there may be robots entering preschools: the need for children to be nurtured, to be made to feel safe, and to avoid trauma.

In this book, we share the work of our colleagues around the world about what is best for children and what they will need to be productive members of their community, good citizens of the world, responsible stewards of their own lives and destinies, and successful people to boot. The cacophony of child-rearing advice is becoming ever louder, and parents struggle to know whom to trust. Our answer is to trust the science of learning and developmental science, fields in which we are card-carrying members. The accumulated wisdom of the scientists in these fields is a tale that tells itself. This tale empowers parents to feel competent and comfortable in raising their children. As in our earlier book, *Einstein Never Used Flash Cards*, this book too encourages parents to "reflect, resist, and re-center" in the face of marketplace pitches about essential "educational" toys and apps and child-rearing "advice" from celebrities with few credentials.

But we did not get here on our own. We thank our colleagues far and wide for the magnificent insights and research findings that we have tried to weave into a coherent tapestry for our readers. We also thank the mentors we continue to carry in our heads who set a high bar for our research and reading of the science. Among them are Lila and Henry Gleitman of the University of Pennsylvania and George Suci and Eleanor Gibson of Cornell University. And we thank our funders and supporters without whom this work would have been impossible: Dr. Stan and Debra Lefkowitz, the National Institutes of Health, the National Science Foundation, the Institute of Education Sciences, the Bezos Family Foundation, and the William Penn Foundation. Kathy is also now a Senior Fellow of the Brookings Institution, and our discussion reflects conversations with Rebecca Winthrop at the Center for Universal Education.

Our own children—Jordan, Allison, Joshua, Benj, and Mikey— are our best critics and do not hesitate to tell us when they think we are wrong. Our stepchildren, Sasha, Ivin, and Chloe, are perfect sources of support and some are moles into the daily world of early childhood, as are the children we have gained from marriage: Laura, Liz, Dee, Meghan, and Barry. We are grateful to them all for their technical and intellectual reinforcement and for helping us see the world through their eyes. Bundles of energy and inspiration, our grandchildren continually add to our joy and challenge us to imagine what their futures will be like.

Our beloved and devoted husbands, Larry Ballen and Jeffrey Pasek, gave us constant and active encouragement, business acumen, and legal genius. In the olden days, behind every successful man was a woman. In today's world, women like us are lucky to have sensitive and brilliant men at our backs who are secret psychologists at heart.

Finally, there are a few special people without whom this book would never have been possible. Liz Edersheim, a dear friend, protégée of Peter Drucker, and author of several business books, including *The Definitive Drucker*, was a mentor for us. She helped us see how current trends in business were melding with those in education. It is imperative to envision an evidence-based educational system that makes contact with the workforce of the 21st century. All too often that link is never made.

Kathy's son Benj spent countless hours teaching us to write in a more engaging way. Thanks, Benj, for your patience and for showing us the power of using specific examples. We have so much more to learn.

Dr. Neha Mahajan worked tirelessly fleshing out the theory with us and helped spot any areas in which the logic was going astray. We could not have done this without her. Our proofreading team, composed of Natalie Brezack, Maya Marzouk, Jacob Schatz, Kate Margulis, and Jelani Medford, were fantastic and caught all kinds of unintended errors. We thank them greatly for their efforts.

Thanks also go to good friends who read through versions of this book and who gave us invaluable feedback. Cyd Weisman, educator and writer extraordinaire; Ruth Pinkenson Feldman, a visionary in early education; and Shelly Kessler, a brilliant consultant who is quickly mastering the field of early education, all read earlier drafts of this work and helped us make our ideas less obscure. Ellen Galinsky, head of the Families and Work Institute in New York, provided us with conversation on innumerable occasions that sparked our thinking.

Kathy owes much to her dearest friend, Marcia Taylor, who also offered sage advice as we wrestled through the ideas that would use science to shape a new report card for the 21st century. In Marcia, we found a good listener with practical questions that grounded us. She forced us to think beyond what we wanted to say and to think about how the theory would make contact with a real education system.

Our editor, Susan Herman of American Psychological Association Books, was extremely helpful to us in asking us to clarify and explain our sometimes inchoate thoughts. Thanks for sticking by us, Susan! And big thanks go to Jennifer Gamble and Rebecca Winthrop from the Brookings Institution for coming up with the title: *Becoming Brilliant*. It does indeed take a village to write a book!

Finally, we thank our readers, who continue to indulge us and read our prose. We think this is because they know how much we care about them and the individuals who will create our future—our children.

BECOMING
BRILLIANT

INTRODUCTION

What if . . . ? That question became the title of a comic book series Marvel published in the late 1970s and early 1980s. In this popular series, Uatu, who observed alternative realities from his lunar abode, asked questions such as, What if Spiderman joined the Fantastic Four? Issues in the *What If* series turned the characters' lives upside down, killing them off in alternative realities and sometimes having a superhero choose a life of crime. It ignored the rules the characters normally lived by and created wild worlds from a totally different angle.

In this book, we invite you to play with the idea of *what if* as it relates to your children's learning and success. What if we could create a world in which the educational system matched what we know about how children learn? What if school actually offered programs that matched the demands of the future world that our children will inhabit?

It's easy to complain about the problems of parenting and schooling. We've been there ourselves! As parents, we lived with the anxieties about our children's education in and out of school. We sweated over each math test and over the topic sentences in our fifth grader's Martin Luther King Jr. essay. Were we providing enough time at home for our kids to practice those tricky fractions? Maybe their topic sentence didn't conform to the textbook example—would the teacher give them more opportunities to get it right? Luckily, the kids turned out okay.

As scientists, and during our own years of raising children and beyond, we've had a lot of time to examine what works in education. Our hope for this book is that it will help you move beyond the anxieties and get a glimpse of what really works. We show you the pockets of excellence—there are some wonderful schools and classrooms out there that we can learn from. We share the latest hype, the latest data, and the latest evidence-based practices that allow your children to reach their fullest potential—intellectually and socially—in a complex global 21st-century world.

WHAT IF A SCHOOL COULD BECOME A RAINFOREST?

We visited Friends' Central School outside of Philadelphia on the day that the students in Grades 2, 3, and 4 were studying the rainforest. The rainforest was *everywhere*—stuffed animals climbed paper trees with broad green leaves, rippled crepe paper on the floor represented flowing streams. We entered Indonesia in Ms. Papino's second-grade classroom and New Guinea down the hall—complete with walls adorned with children's valiant attempts at primitive masks. The masks had signage—as at a museum—that highlighted a bit about the creators and the history of the places from which the masks originated. Mr. Briggs's fourth graders were using math and reading skills to build a boat that would take them on a journey to Treasure Island. The scene is rich in content learning as information seeps through the vine-covered hallways and children use their burgeoning skills for an authentic purpose: to read written directions, make measurement calculations, and to write a paragraph about their boat-building plan.

But—and this is critical—children are learning more than just their ABCs and 123s in this rain forest. Five other 21st-century skills pop out of the thick foliage—skills that, together with *content*, we call the 6Cs. We've identified the 6Cs as the key skills that will help all children become the thinkers and entrepreneurs of tomorrow. These skills will also help children become contributing members of their communities and good citizens as they forge a fulfilling personal life. *Collaboration* comes in the form of boat-building partners who work in concert, consulting with one another to fabricate a boat that can last through a virtual trip. *Communication* enters through the books the children write to describe what they will find when they arrive at Treasure Island. *Content* includes the measurement, the geography that surrounds the forest, the science that emerges in the study of the ant-eating echidna and the mountain weasel. *Critical thinking* makes the boat possible as the students gently evaluate each other's boat-building plans for stability, speed, and seaworthiness. One plan based on the directions might work, but another will surely fail. *Creativity* abounds as engaged students come up with novel ideas, some of which garner laughter. Should they paint the boat with green monsters to ward off evil spirits? Or put lions and tigers on flags to keep pirates away? *Confidence* oozes when students tear up plans and start over, recognizing that they had to think more about the boat's materials and what to take along.

Perhaps most stunning is that every summer the Friends' School faculty rethinks how to deliver the rich content of the curriculum in a new and engaging way. They ask themselves how they can transform a traditional classroom of right-angled walls into rainforests, mountain villages, and themes like "flight" so that they and their students can learn the basics through the 6Cs. The teachers themselves become excited students in a theme-based environment that raises them out of the confines of their desks. Here they are constructing new knowledge and entering into an expansive and vibrant educational arena. Here, in this kind of a classroom, we meet what Professor John Bruer, an expert in the developing brain, called *knowledge transformers* rather than just *knowledge digesters*.

WHAT IF ALL STUDENTS HAD THE CHANCE
TO MAKE A RAINFOREST AT SCHOOL?

What if all schools could design classrooms that fostered the 6Cs? What if our report cards for each individual child looked at their progress as they moved through the levels of learning in each of the 6Cs? What if parent–teacher conferences focused on the 6Cs— content, collaboration, communication, critical thinking, creativity, and confidence—in addition to how your child did on the last test? What if the report card you received gave you a fuller profile of your child's strengths and weaknesses?

A report card based on the 6Cs captures the skill set that kids growing up in the 21st century must have for success. How does it differ from the report card of a standard straight-A student? Although we all want our children to achieve, each child is more than just his or her grades. People whose skill set is limited to content sometimes do wonderfully in school but never seem to get anywhere on the job. When that new spot opens up at the plant, will anyone think of them for the management position? (Maybe they lack the ability to collaborate.) Or when their laboratory has to develop a new method, they run in the other direction (maybe due to a lack of creativity?). Looking through the lens of the 6Cs, we get a more complete picture of our children's strengths and weaknesses.

Consider what your own 6Cs profile might look like. What strengths do you have that you can celebrate? What areas can you develop even more? How do you communicate about your own skills, or lack thereof, to your child?

We ask you as you read this book to think differently and to ask, "What if?" What if our schools and homes integrated the 6Cs as a suite of skills that will help children to be socially adept, flexible thinkers who take joy in a lifetime of learning? "What if" is a phrase we hope you will think of often as you read this book because we have designed it to help you consider how learning can be different—for us and for our children.

WHY DID WE WRITE THIS BOOK?

Every year for the past 4 decades, babies, toddlers, and preschoolers have marched into our laboratories with their parents in tow. Our laboratories are the places where *children teach adults* how they learn language, how they master number skills, and how they learn to read. The information children share—some even before they utter their first words—becomes the fodder for books like this one. We used data from our learning labs and others around the country to write our books, *How Babies Talk* and *Einstein Never Used Flashcards*. Children themselves have helped us fill the wide gap in what we actually know.

Working with other scientists around the globe, we have uncovered many new features in the fascinating landscape that is child development, and we are now poised to share that knowledge so that educators and innovators can design the best possible programs, toys, apps, and classrooms for all children. Although the world beyond the ivory tower stresses the importance of teaching children content, content, and more content, we see a broader vision for our children that includes the mastery of many skills and competencies. We understand that robots can memorize the facts, but only children have the potential to socialize, be good citizens, think, and create. With years of research at our fingertips, hundreds of published papers behind us, and 13 books to our names, it is time to share the collective wisdom from the science of learning and to embrace a new way of thinking about thinking: the 6Cs. And share we do—in our *Huffington Post* blog; on a blog for the Brookings Institution; in our tweets (@kathyandRo1); by offering our consulting services for companies like Disney, LEGO, K'Nex, Crayola, and Fisher Price; by serving on the board for nonprofit organizations for children such as Choices, Frontiers of Innovation, Alliance for Childhood, Jumpstart, and children's museums; and now in this book. We also share our work through our attendance at academic conferences and speeches we give to professional and lay audiences around the world. Sometimes in the pages of this book we take you with us to these venues, sharing our excitement and how much these events teach us. Describing some of our experiences in communicating and sharing our latest scientific findings, interacting with leaders in our field, and learning from others' presentations allows you to be a "fly on the wall," seeing these events through our eyes.

Scientists like us have to come out of our academic closets. With our peers, we are poised to weigh in on the issues of the day that concern children. If scientists do not share what we know, the void will be filled by those with little experience or with values that are more in line with the marketplace than with the betterment of children. Just as the fast food industry fills us with empty calories, what we call the "learning industry" has convinced many among us that the memorization of content is all that is needed for learning success and joyful lives.

We wrote this book because we are parents and grandparents. We raised five children, and we know how hard it is to sift through the many options available to families. We know that feeling when every time you look at your smartphone you think, Seriously? Can there really be more products for improving children's intelligence? Are these people kidding—attaching a tablet to a potty chair? Although we often dismiss the worst of what we see, we know that many families feel at a loss when deciding what their children *really* need. Here we offer a set of guiding principles so that you can ensure your children develop all the skills they need to reach their potential and still be happy and well-adjusted.

A SNEAK PREVIEW

Success. We all want our children to achieve it so that they can fulfill their potential. But how exactly do we define success? Chapter 1 explores our assumptions about success and examines how we might define it in a 21st century, global world. Is the current education system preparing our children for success in this climate? We join many who think it is not. But we need solutions, not more complaints.

In this book, we rethink education in and out of school that is inspired by the science of learning. Chapter 2 begins our quest by describing how we got into this educational quagmire and by pointing the way forward. Chapter 3 explores the educational question from a "glocal" perspective by reflecting on how global scientific solutions can be molded to fit local educational problems. Chapter 4 suggests that what counts as education in and out of school will have to address the needs of a dynamic, international workforce. Educational systems that prepare children for success will have to embrace not only "hard" skills like reading and mathematics but also the so-called "soft skills" that are the bedrock for these academic achievements. What are these glocal competencies informed by science and consistent with the needs of the workplace? Chapters 5 through 10 lay bare a scientific answer to this question. On the basis of the latest evidence from child development, we chart a solution with what we call the 6Cs: collaboration, communication, content, critical thinking, creative innovation, and confidence. These competencies reflect how children grow and learn.

Chapter 11 demonstrates how these competencies fit together into a unified system that becomes a framework for education and a potential new report card for the 21st century. Dotted throughout, the "Taking Action" sections allow you to bring the learning home with concrete examples that explore where you are as a learner and how you can best help your child achieve his or her fullest potential.

Using these techniques, we think that all children can be successful and can profit from the tools suggested by the science of how children learn.

CONSIDER THE POSSIBILITIES

What if this book inspires you to sponsor your school's next Teacher Appreciation Day? What if it helps you organize your thoughts about how children learn so that you can present them to your local PTA? What if what you learn here helps you choose a better school for your child? What if the evidence we present here is exactly what you need to write that letter you've wanted to write to your school board or congressional representative? What if the 6Cs offer you a whole new, helpful framework for bringing academic lessons to life at home?

We hope that these and many more *what ifs* will come to mind as you read this book. Thanks for reading!

CHAPTER I

REDEFINING SUCCESS IN THE 21ST CENTURY

Really? A football-sized, turtle-shaped night-light designed (so the package says) to help babies sleep better? And it's *proven* to reduce fear? This is no ordinary turtle night-light! This turtle night-light projects the constellations in the night sky onto the nursery room ceiling so that babies can learn to identify Orion's belt as they drift into dreaming of milk and succulent pacifiers. The guests at Robert and Stephanie's baby shower ooh and aah.

Though their daughter will not arrive for 2 more months, Robert and Stephanie's educator, physician, and lawyer friends have brought a panoply of presents that promise to make her the next generation's Madeleine Albright or Hillary Clinton. After admiring the turtle, Stephanie tears into a shiny purple and white striped bag with a lavender bow and pulls out a plush toy peacock with the color of every plume labeled in three languages so that the baby's young eyes will be exposed to written samples of English, Spanish, and Mandarin even before she can talk.

These so-called educational toys are everywhere. And plastered on the boxes lies the implicit message that advertisers want to sell to parents and our society at large: Without the ABCs or 123s in every box, our children will be doomed to failure. Mastery of facts at an early age, they claim, leads to bigger and better brains, and better brains lead to better jobs with higher earnings and more discretionary wealth. There are actually toys out there like *Brainy Baby* that boast a separate DVD for the right brain and the left, even though neuroscientists have all but debunked the theory that a person, let alone a baby, can be right-brained or left-brained. Then there is the multimillion-dollar revenue from products like *Your Baby Can Read*. Those of us who study early language and literacy are known to talk back to the television when ads like that come on. "No, your baby CAN'T read!" we retort. Like the beloved stuffed animal in Margery Williams's *Velveteen Rabbit* or Woody in the movie *Toy Story*, the classic toys have moved to the back shelf. Parents don't want to buy a Slinky or a package of Play-Doh that doesn't have obvious educational value. As parents, we pass by the spatial learning embedded in forming clay and constructing train sets. We whiz by the storytelling and language learning that naturally envelops us when playing with toy castles where we encounter crenellations and knights in shining armor who must traverse the moat. We want to optimize the learning potential of our child's every waking moment. Who wouldn't want a fast-food learning recipe straight from the box that will set your child's trajectory for study at the Ivy Leagues?

The problem is that filling heads with facts is not the secret to success in a world where facts are literally at our fingertips. With Google and Wikipedia a click away, every one of us can easily access the answer to virtually any question in a matter of seconds. Certainly there are some things we still need to memorize, such as the alphabet and the multiplication tables. But the real issue confronting the modern child (or the modern parent) is how we sort through, prioritize, and make use of all the information that's coming at us on a daily basis. The great jobs in Fortune 500 companies, now and in the future, are likely to go to people who have thinking skills that cannot be taught through memorization.

So what are those abilities that employers see, and how do we infuse the culture with a more solid measure of success? That is the core question that we ask in this book. We have all heard the clarion cries by groups like The National Committee on Excellence in Education, warning that our country's economic preeminence is in danger because we are not teaching the children well. We also have heard frightening projections, such as those from the National Center on Education and the Economy, quipping that American classrooms were preparing children for the workforce of 1953! But what are we to do about it? In this book, we examine this issue from the perspective of scientists who study how children learn. Our goal is to ask two simple questions: First, what would you count as success for your child? And second, how should we prepare children to meet those goals in ways that are sensitive to your culture and your life? We hope to put a new definition of learning and education in your hands so that you can make informed choices as you nurture your children on various paths toward success. As you might have already gathered, we also argue that real learning will not come in the form of turtle night-lights or multilanguage mobiles—even if a huge learning industry wants you to believe that it will. It will also not come from simply doing well on a test that measures your child's mastery of factoids. As the United Nations Secretary-General's Global Initiative on Education suggested,

> The world faces global challenges, which require global solutions. These interconnected global challenges call for far-reaching changes in how we think and act for the dignity of fellow human beings. It is not enough for education to produce individuals who can read, write and count. Education must be transformative and bring shared values to life. . . . Education must also be relevant in answering the big questions of the day.[1]

Creating a core set of values and outcomes has become a lightning rod issue in discussions of education around the globe. Whether it is Wendy Kopp and her team at Teach for All or *Sesame Street* or the global education initiative at the Brookings Institution or even the New York Academy of Science that is embracing a global perspective, conversation is centered on the skills all children need to succeed in a 21st-century world and how to deliver those skills in a culturally sensitive way. Consider an analogy: There is no limit to the cultural variation in clothing design despite the fact that clothes are constrained by having openings for two arms and two legs. So too, in a shrinking world where geographic boundaries are porous, today's demands constrain the kinds of skills children in Western societies will need to succeed, despite the fact that they may come with different emphases to suit the local flavor. Given rapidly changing technology, these skills are different from the ones our parents and grandparents needed to make their way. Put simply, the educational approaches that dominate the world stage have not yet caught up to these goals. Despite the fact that organizations around the world question current practices, most schools are operating in a way that is antithetical to these new goals.

The Province of Ontario in Canada has been in the forefront of thinking about what these common skills might be. A mission statement defines what is believed to be the shared goals we hold for our children as they navigate the 21st century. Ontario is looking to create environments that will support the development of "happy, healthy children and youth today . . . caring, creative, responsible adults tomorrow."[2] We might embellish this a tad by suggesting that society thrives when we craft environments, in and out of school, that support happy, healthy, thinking, caring, and social children who become collaborative, creative, competent, and responsible citizens tomorrow. If these words capture a set of shared values, or come even close, then the challenge is determining how we achieve these goals. This is our book's mission.

REIMAGINING EDUCATION IN AND OUT OF SCHOOL: THE 6Cs

How do we achieve this lofty mission? Ironically, the answer to this question comes from a surprising source: the children themselves and the science of how children learn. The study of how children learn offers us a window into an integrative and systemic set of skills that can produce the outcomes we want for our children. As mentioned in the Introduction, we call the following skills the 6Cs: collaboration, communication, content, critical thinking, creative innovation, and confidence.

From the first moments of life, infants demonstrate nascent *collaboration* as they enter into the community of their family and navigate how to snuggle with different family members. Collaboration comes to include the ways in which we learn our cultural patterns, the ways we shift our responses for different people, the ways we learn to take turns, the ways we learn to build our Lego bricks and our experiences together, and the way we develop the social self-control that enables true collaboration to occur. As humans, we are innately sensitive to other people; it's programmed by evolution. We are social beings at our very core. Working in teams is at the center of new business models and is even how many of us learn to learn. Collaboration, resting as it does on self-control, is a core skill and is one that is fundamental to being socially competent as a child and as an adult.

Built on the foundation of collaboration is *communication.* Babies in the presence of adoring adults will carry on entire "conversations" through coos and grunts even before they utter their first words. Like Bamm-Bamm in the *Flintstones* cartoon, they babble away in perfect cadence and use their talent for attracting other people to communicate their wants and needs. Think how effective that 10-month-old can be as he looks at a favorite toy, uses the "royal point," and grunts commandingly. Using their inborn social foundation, children piece together their first communities. As they do, they become "speakers" and listeners in a melody of conversations through which they learn about their present and come to entertain fictional worlds of unicorns and tooth fairies. Reading, writing, and that all but lost art of listening germinate from these early encounters between parents and their infants. Strong communication skills are related to better health and to strong academic skills.[3]

Content is one, but *only* one, of the six skills central to children's development. It is what we reap from communication—how we learn information about people, places, things, and events around us. It is also how we learn to learn: the strategies and approaches we take when we encounter new information. Babies are building content as they learn that floors are to crawl on and walls are impermeable. There was a time not so long ago when researchers thought babies looked on their world as a place of "blooming, buzzing confusion."[4] Nothing could be further from the truth. Babies are making sense of the many patterns they hear in the language that passes their ears and by just 8 months of age are performing statistical analyses on the sentences they hear. Eight months! The beginnings of word learning in the 8-month-old become the entry point for the vocabulary of the 2- and 3-year-old who is on the highway toward literacy.[5] In their first year, children are little physicists learning about the properties of objects and master sociologists who imitate us and watch closely what it means to be a member of the species.[6] The 3- and 4-year-olds sorting shapes and counting their raisins are developing a sense of number and geometry en route to mathematical thinking.[7] But reading and math are not all there is to content. These children are also learning to learn, building strong memories when they play card games and find the square in a game of "I Spy."

Howard Gardner, professor of cognition and education at the Harvard Graduate School of Education, suggested that content has to be expansive and to include truth, beauty, and goodness.[8] In an interconnected world, aesthetics and morality are not mere accessories to letters and numbers. They are essential for appreciating the amazing ring we see around the moon on a cloudy night and for giving our seat to the old man on the bus. We live in an information age, where we are barraged with new data and must quickly and effectively take in masses of new content if we are to survive. It is the mastery of content, and the ability to quickly and strategically incorporate new information, that offers the foundation for thinking, the stuff we need to know to be critical thinkers and creative innovators.

Professor Deanna Kuhn of Columbia University developed an entire theory of *critical thinking* that moves among stages of development, from the "seeing is believing" of the 4-year-old to the thoughtful weighing of evidence of the jury member who has to decide whether Rebecca really pulled the trigger.[9] Anyone who has witnessed the political circuses of the last decade or so, however, knows that this critical thinking is not developmentally secure even in adults. We live in an era of exploding information. Eric Schmidt, the CEO of Google, calculated that every 2 days we create as much information as we did from the dawn of civilization up until 2003.[10] And business leaders tell us that knowledge is doubling every 2 years.[11] Thus, even if we memorize every fact known to civilization now, in just 2 1/2 years we will know but 50% of what we know today, and in just 5 years we will be down to 25%.

The critical thinker who can take a step back and reflect on what is wanted, what the question is that needs to be answered, will be the person all look to in this new era. That person will have what scientists call *executive function skills*: the ability to inhibit old solutions to problems and to rapidly shift to a new approach, as well as the ability to craft the plan needed to make that problem a thing of the past. Critical thinking is all about focus: Digging in deep and holding the relevant facts in mind enables solutions.

Creative innovation is born from content and critical thinking. Children are naturally free-flowing creative thinkers with few inhibitions. Stick figures drawn on colored construction paper? Why, it's a family portrait! Making swirls in the mashed potatoes? Three-year-old Dennis sees ocean waves! But the research on creativity demonstrates that the long road to creative innovation embraces content rather than skirts it. The truly creative artist has learned the classical techniques, and the creative inventor is often a well-trained engineer or electrician. Creative ideas do not emerge fully formed from nothing, and the science of learning is starting to chart the processes that move us from those initial scribbles on paper to mastering drawing and then thinking outside the box to design the Freedom Tower that occupies the World Trade Center site.

The work world is ever changing. It is estimated that graduates today will hold 10 jobs in their lifetime and that eight of those jobs have not yet been invented. Pity the poor photographer who could not adapt to digital cameras or the publisher who thought books had to be printed on paper. In a knowledge-driven economy, workers are constantly faced with new problems and shifting product needs. Take, as an example, the sheer number of iPad covers available for a product market that was only invented in April of 2010. No wonder the business executives in the Partnership for 21st Century Skills survey called for a more creative and flexible workforce. An IBM study released in May 2010 reported that creativity and management of complexity were the two key characteristics most prized by 1,500 global CEOs.[12]

Sometimes creative solutions work—as when we use our favorite oversized book as a doorstop—and sometimes they don't and our efforts fall flat. Having the *confidence* to persevere enables us to overcome our failures and not throw in the proverbial towel. Having the self-regulation not to flip out when the first solution doesn't work will be important for persevering. All too often we meet children who are not allowed on jungle gyms because they might fall and children who are rewarded for the right answer but not encouraged to try solving the problem another way. The learning sciences are investigating the teachings that underlie this fear of failure. We don't want our youngsters to touch a hot stove or to walk into the middle of a busy street. Yet, Edison could not have invented electricity without the drive to explore and the confidence to test new ideas. In the era of the knowledge worker, economic viability relies on having the confidence to take informed risks.

WHY DO WE NEED THE 6Cs?

If you are willing to look at children's education and development from the point of view of a learning scientist, we demonstrate how you can help your kids become well-adjusted critical thinkers who might even create the next iPad or write the next great American novel. The 6Cs are the road maps toward success. They are not *isolated competencies*. Like having both a belt and suspenders, the 6Cs, taken together, improve our chances for success because each skill is constructed on the others. As you can see in Table 1.1, these skills build from left to right (you cannot communicate if no one is home) and from bottom to top.

We invite you to refer back to this summary of the 6Cs as often as you need to and use it to quiz yourself. As you read on you might ask yourself, What stage of critical thinking has my child reached so far? Or, How might I invite my child to use the sewing supplies with me? Or perhaps, What boundaries should I set, and which ones should I let go of, so my teen will feel confident in her newfound driving skills? You can also use the grid as a tool to quickly evaluate the assignments your child brings home from school. Does that history report ask for more than just dates and names and places and lists of raw materials? What might your fourth grader learn from

TABLE 1.1. Four Levels of Mastery for Each of the 6 Cs

	Collaboration	Communication	Content	Critical Thinking	Creative Innovation	Confidence
Level 4	Building it together	Tell a joint story	Expertise	Evidence	Vision	Dare to fail
Level 3	Back and forth	Dialogue	Making connections	Opinions	Voice	Calculated risks
Level 2	Side by side	Show and tell	Wide breadth/ Shallow understanding	Truths differ	Means–end	Where do I stand?
Level 1	On my own	Raw emotion	Early learning/ Situation specific	Seeing is believing	Experimentation	Barrel on

building a model of Mission Santa Barbara, for instance, that she might not otherwise learn if she simply printed off some photos of it from the Internet? Let's say she is doing an Internet search on the California missions—can you bump the critical thinking or content learning up a notch by asking her what search terms she used or why some sources of information are more reliable than others?

With the 6Cs and their gradations as shown previously, we have used the latest science to create a new report card for lifelong learning that moves beyond a narrow focus on content and can help us move all children toward achieving the shared values that define success in our time. Perhaps, just perhaps, we won't need that turtle night-light or that multilingual mobile. Perhaps it is time to broaden our vision of what constitutes success and of how our children's education can help them achieve it.

THE LEARNING INDUSTRY AND THE LEARNING SCIENCES: HOW EDUCATIONAL REFORM SENT US IN THE WRONG DIRECTION

Why would we ever think that filling little heads with factoids available on educational toys would prepare them—even a little bit—for success? In many ways, our laser focus on the mastery of content has been increasing for decades. With content as king, there is room for little else, especially when high-stakes evaluations loom. Somewhere along the line, we forgot that being happy and social and a good person are also key ingredients to our children's future. How did we get to this place where we view children as passive objects of instruction, where their social selves became secondary to what facts they could spew? The story actually begins in the mid 20th century when the United States was in a "cold war" with the then Soviet Union—a war that promoted educational reform.

OUCH: THE RUSSIANS ARE WINNING

On October 4, 1957, *The New York Times* headline read, "Soviet Union Launches Sputnik Satellite." This historical event had huge consequences for all of us and sparked American school reform on an unprecedented level. That 184-pound piece of floating metal that was only the size of a beach ball had become the symbol, the proof, that the Russians were winning the space race. "The Russians," it was argued, "beat us into space because they had better schools."[1] That was the story at the time, and this was about more than a race into space, it was about a race to the future and about world dominance. By 1958, just a year later, Congress passed the National Defense Education Act to improve students' academic achievement.[2] The rush to buttress education, especially in math and the sciences, led to the "new math," of the 1960s—which even our teachers struggled to understand. And it would find a current voice in the renewed emphasis on STEM—science, technology, engineering, and mathematics.

How can we alter the trajectory for millions of American children so that they can become the developers of the next generation of Sputniks? A small but powerful document published in 1983 answered that question by warning the country that we were *A Nation at Risk*. Penned by leading scientists, policymakers, and educators, the chilling opening began this way:

> Our Nation is at risk. Our once unchallenged preeminence in commerce, industry, science, and technological innovation is being overtaken by competitors throughout the world. . . . What was unimaginable a generation ago has begun to occur—others are matching and surpassing our educational attainments.[3]

Eleven years later, under President Clinton, the recommendations of *A Nation at Risk* became the initiative called the *Goals 2000: Educate America Act*, signed into law on March 31, 1994.[4] To be competitive in the new world, we were told, we had to achieve high levels of competency in literacy, mathematics, and science by the year 2000. Among the mandates were that "United States students will be first in the world in mathematics and science achievement" (Goal 4) and "Every adult American will be literate and will possess the knowledge and skills necessary to compete in a global economy and exercise the rights and responsibilities of citizenship"

(Goal 5).[5] It was a tall charge. In the United States, each state had its own set of standards and goals. Reaching national standards was kind of like herding cats. President Clinton's term came and went without any real signs of educational improvement.

It was in this historical context that the George W. Bush administration declared a new and sweeping range of educational reforms. Many previous presidents had considered themselves the "education" president, but the Bush administration's signature legislation, No Child Left Behind, was to be the most sweeping of all reforms—an overhaul that would put school accountability and children's learning at the core of the national agenda. Learning scientists were called together to chart the direction for the educational overhaul. The conference rooms we inhabited as participants in this conversation were pregnant with the possibility that learning scientists would finally work hand in hand with policymakers to help reduce the achievement gap. But as time marched on and political pressure to do something quickly took the upper hand, NCLB, as the law was affectionately called, became laden with ready-made tests that narrowly measured outcomes in selected subjects like reading and math, often leaving behind the question of whether kids could use what they had learned in math to measure out the ingredients for brownies or write a sentence that showed what the word *critical* meant. There was little mention about how to best use our science to craft deeper learning or improve teacher preparation.

Despite scientists' best efforts, available tests were dusted off and brought out of dented file drawers for immediate use. American children would be trained to focus on literacy and math (forget about science and art) and parrot answers on short bubble tests that did not take up too much classroom time. In the state of Pennsylvania, students take 2 weeks off from their regular curriculum to learn how to pass the Pennsylvania System of State Assessments test appropriate for their grade. Starting at Grade 3, these tests continue through high school. There are even numerous reports in *The New York Times* of crying, anxiety, and stomachaches among fourth graders taking the high-stakes tests.[6] As Stanford education professor Linda Darling-Hammond said on July 30, 2011, to attendees at a Save the Children march in Washington, DC,

> Many people are asking, "Why are we here?" . . . We are here because we want to prepare our children for the 21st century world they are entering, not for an endless series of multiple choice tests that increasingly deflect us from our mission to teach them well.[7]

Please understand that scientists like ourselves are not against accountability or even against tests that examine real learning. But we have to ask a central question: Accountability for what? What counts as success in school or in life? And did the tests that were available measure those skills? Did they teach teachers how to harness the skills that children need to be happy, healthy, thinking, caring, and social people? We are sympathetic to those like Diane Ravitch, an educational history professor at New York University who was a chief architect of the accountability movement for President Bush. She and her team wanted to do right by kids and to close that persistent achievement gap between low- and middle-income children. President Bush and his team were well-intentioned, but even Ravitch, in her 2010 book titled *The Death and Life of the Great American School System: How Testing and Choice Are Undermining Education*, apologized to the nation for being wrong.[8]

Alas, the reforms continue. NCLB was a colossal failure. Reforms continue in the meantime. Children who were 4 years old and in preschool in 2001 when NCLB was introduced took the Programme for International Student Assessment (PISA) tests 11 years later as high school 15-year-olds. How did they do? One might think that with all of that educational preparation, they would outclass students from other industrialized nations. America's math score ranks at a paltry 30th, a full 13 slots behind Slovenia. In reading, we are 20th, behind Finland, Poland, and Japan. And in science we are only 23rd![9] Memorization of factoids will not get you a good score on the PISA, nor will it prepare you for real success in the 21st century.

Today, the educational reform movement has become the drive toward what the Obama administration calls the *Common Core*. There are many wonderful features in this well-intentioned set of benchmarks that children should achieve to be well educated. At least the blueprint for the Common Core includes reading, math, science, and the arts, hoping to broaden the palette of what children should know. At least the Common Core notes that social skills are also key to success and that those learning-to-learn skills such as critical thinking and problem solving are key components of a 21st-century mind.

But here's the rub: Introduced in the mind-set of narrowly defined outcomes for success, even solid initiatives like Common Core are being misinterpreted. The benchmarks became the outcomes and the test makers and curriculum developers are seeking ways to script learning toward these outcomes and test directly for them. At the time of this writing, 43 states in the United States have adopted these standards, yet many decry that they too are misguided. Referring to teach-to-the-test practices that continue even when the benchmarks for learning are worthwhile, writer David Kohn opined in *The New York Times*,

> That kind of education will fail to produce people who can discover and innovate, and will merely produce people who are likely to be passive consumers of information, followers rather than inventors. Which kind of citizen do we want for the 21st century?[10]

ENTER A CULTURE OF TESTING: LEARNING INDUSTRY TRUMPS LEARNING SCIENCES

By the early 2000s, the fact that American children were behind their international peers in academic outcomes had startled the country. Terms such as *PISA scores* and *achievement gap* were part of everyday parlance and, frankly, we Americans were scared. There is nothing like fear to motivate the economy. Then, in 2005, Thomas Friedman's *The World is Flat* came on the market, with the thesis that in our new "flattened" world, no company would offer lifetime employment and that the United States needed a relentless emphasis on science and engineering. *Tough Choices or Tough Times* came out in 2007, and we were barraged with messages that we needed to shove facts into children's heads if they were to be prepared for the workforce of tomorrow.[11]

For the first time, companies like Kaplan that used to tutor children who had problems with the SATs and that then expanded to tutoring school-age children for school became hubs for preparing children so that they would be ahead of their peers. Between Kaplan and Junior Kumon, the preschool tutoring business is flourishing.[12]

Testing companies were also profiting. With narrowly defined outcomes for success, such as knowing the capital of Kansas is Topeka, it was easy to proliferate tests that could be approved and used to test for NCLB standards or Common Core guidelines. Those guidelines were being written in stone, and tests and curricula designed to foster learning in reading and math had become an multibillion-dollar industry, or as a commentator quipped, "There's gold in them there tests."[13]

Finally, there were those so-called educational toys. Toymakers responded with "edutainment" (a term coined by Alissa Quart in her 2006 article "Extreme Parenting" in *The Atlantic*[14]). Today this includes not only flashcards but also games, mobiles, and yep—that turtle night-light. Educational toys are a multibillion-dollar business. In 2009 alone, so-called educational toys outsold traditional toys![15]

In addition to the toys, there are countless "educational apps" and media that can drill your children on numbers and letters as they travel in cars and on subways and buses so that they will be fully prepared to take those bubble tests in the future. Whether on smartphones, tablets, or computers, our youngest kids are glued to the Internet at least 4 hours a day (the equivalent of a part-time job), and 8-year-olds and above are stationed in front of screens for 8 hours a day.[16] We now have educational television geared to our youngest citizens 24/7 on channels such as Sprout.

Put simply, the marketplace ran to fill the void inadvertently created by the educational establishment. If we start drilling our children early and often, so the argument goes, we can better prepare them for success in school and beyond. Though there are some clear counter examples in programming like *Sesame Street*, *Blues Clues*, and *Mister Rogers' Neighborhood*, among others, much of what appeared in that market was uninformed by the latest science of how kids really learn. Rather, the marketplace, seeing an opening, burst forth to satisfy parental hunger to better prepare even younger children for later success on these tests. If testing focused on narrowly defined outcomes was to be the measure of success, then children who memorized the material to be learned or tested were by definition successful. One could argue that the learning industry is shaping society's definition of success and that the learning sciences have been largely muffled in the discussion of how to best prepare children for real success in and out of school.

THE ROAD AHEAD

Learning scientists have not given up. In 2004, the National Science Foundation began a project called the Science of Learning Centers that would fund applied research capable of moving learning science from the lab to our schools and to our living rooms. An army of scientists is involved, collecting evidence about how children learn best—about how brains process the written word, about how spatial skills like map reading feed into mathematical learning, and about how the inability to stop yourself from making impulsive decisions can impair learning. Those of us who study how kids learn in high-tech worlds with avatars and in low-tech environments like parks have much to share with the learning industry. And, most important for our economy and our children's future, the findings that flow from our work are completely consistent with the needs expressed by the business community. But our education right now—the education brought to us by the learning industry—could not be further from this vision. With scripted texts, many teachers—despite their concerns—must be on page 3 on Tuesday and page 6 by Wednesday.

The irony of the press to test pushed by the learning industry is that we are not educating but eradicating our future. One of our most prized (and lamentable) examples of this problem is that of the young Teach for America volunteer we knew who had been placed in the Philadelphia school system and called us to lament the fact that she had been asked to teach adjectives. "Nothing wrong with adjectives," we said. "How about having some fun with 'red trucks' or 'happy students'? Do they know nouns?" "No," she said, "but this is Thursday. It's adjective day."

Time magazine was right when it suggested that Rip Van Winkle would feel totally at home in the modern school because our schools simply have not changed much in the last 100 years, despite the fact that there have been extensive attempts at school reform.[17]

So, what would it take to embrace a fuller vision of success and to help our children learn and socialize in ways that are more in line with what we know from learning science? What would it take to help all children be happy, healthy, thinking, caring, and sociable children who enjoy learning and who move toward becoming collaborative, creative, competent, and responsible citizens of tomorrow? And how do we do this given that we are trapped inside a worldview driven by educational reform and the learning industry? Management consultant Elizabeth Haas Edersheim, a protégée of Peter Drucker (who is generally considered the father of modern management), once told us that it would mean doing a *green field experiment*—one in which you start literally with only a green field and ask what you might build today if you had no constraints.[18] Drucker's advice has been central to moving business models onto the global stage.

Perhaps we can do the same thing with education. In fact, some countries are already moving in that direction. Let's take a look at how they're doing it and how we might do it better.

CHAPTER 3

THE SKILLS NEEDED FOR SUCCESS ARE GLOBAL

Jim Heckman, a Nobel laureate and professor of economics at the University of Chicago, put it bluntly, "No Child Left Behind became the ultimate pathology."[1] He was speaking at the Brookings Institution Global Education Summit to a group concerned with the needs of the changing international workforce. Stephan Turnipseed from the 21st Century Partnership explained why we are in "deep trouble." In 2015, there were 7.2 billion people on the planet, 40% of whom were connected to the Internet on 25 billion devices, all of which can talk to one another, yielding tremendous productivity. By 2020, there will be 11.5 billion people, and more than 50% will be connected on over 50 billion devices. The pace of technological change is the same in Africa as it is in the United States. Across the globe, robots will be telling humans what to do. Only people who are creative and collaborative will be able to go beyond what a well-designed robot could achieve. Turnipseed went on to say that today's academic manufacturing system does what it was designed to do: The ability to learn and succeed with a single body of knowledge is just not the world we live in today.

Around the world, countries are seeing these warning signs. Their economic futures in this global world demand a 21st-century educational system. Despite the fact that these countries are remarkably diverse and have very different political systems, they are instituting educational changes that are worth learning about. Some are having an impact on their students' future success *now*. Diverse places like Singapore, Finland, Canada, and Uruguay are changing. Places that didn't value creativity before—like China and Singapore—now recognize that to be competitive they must nurture their children's ability to innovate and solve new problems. Otherwise, make way for the robots.

Organizations from Wendy Kopp's Teach for All and the New York National Academy for Science are thinking globally. They recognize that the skills kids in Thailand need will be the same ones needed by the kids in Slovenia. For example, Teach for All (http://teachforall.org/en) is thinking hard about *outcomes*: What do children around the world need to know? Rob Simmons, a public health expert at Jefferson University, coined the term *glocal* to capture how the same skill set will be taught in different ways depending on the culture (personal communication, July 2015). And the New York Academy of Sciences (despite its state-specific name) has created a Global STEM Alliance that is focused on "designing solutions to the world's greatest challenges, and developing the critical STEM skills necessary for the future of both themselves and their countries."[2] As Dr. Nancy Zimpher, chancellor of the The State University of New York, stated on their website, "To meet increasing global demand for a more technically savvy, highly skilled workforce, it's critical to use today's top technology and innovative thinking in our classrooms."[3]

HEADWAY IN SINGAPORE

The small but powerful city-state of Singapore hears this message loud and clear. We received an unexpected e-mail from a guy named Brian Caswell, one of the founders of a company called Mind-Champs. He had read our book *Einstein Never Used Flashcards*[4] and wanted to talk. We were skeptical. MindChamps sounded a bit like the learning industry propaganda we are fighting against. Singapore, after all, is the place where it's illegal to chew gum in the street! Why would they want to talk to us?

It turns out that our snap judgments were wrong. The Ministry of Education in Singapore was feeling the winds of change and understood that innovation would be the key to Singapore's economic success in the next decades. When Singapore looks north and east it sees a looming Chinese economy, to the north and west, a vibrant Indian economy. To prosper, its children need to do more than excel on international assessments; they need to make breakthroughs. The children of Singapore had long been weaned from the bottle of innovation, but in a benevolent dictatorship, changing the rules in an instant is not a problem. Singapore was erecting a new system to guarantee that it was educating not only a smart workforce but also a creative one.

The Ministry of Education wants the product of Singapore schools to develop

> a good sense of self-awareness, a sound moral compass, and the necessary skills and knowledge to take on challenges of the future. He is responsible to his family, community and nation. He appreciates the beauty of the world around him, possesses a healthy mind and body, and has a zest for life.[5]

Wow! While policymakers in the United States were taking music, art, and recess out of our schools to make more time for reading drills, Singapore was declaring those "extras" essential to educating the next generation of thinkers. The Ministry of Education realized that the 4- and 5-year-olds in their preschools today would be the workforce of the future and that to remain a modern-day economic miracle, they would have to train those children to be critical thinkers and creative innovators.

The founders of MindChamps had jumped on the bandwagon and were betting that they could create a new educational model built on learning science that would address Singapore's new definition of success. The website of Singapore's Ministry of Education tells the world what they now value:

> We want to nurture young Singaporeans who ask questions and look for answers, and who are willing to think in new ways, solve new problems and create new opportunities for the future. And, equally important, we want to help our young to build up a set of sound values so that they have the strength of character and resilience to deal with life's inevitable setbacks without being unduly discouraged, and so that they have the willingness to work hard to achieve their dreams.[6]

No wonder the folks at MindChamps think they can prepare the next generation for economic success in Singapore.

FINLAND LEADS THE PACK

In the 1970s, at the same time that the United States began to recognize that our education system was in need of an overhaul, the Finns were ramping up their own plans for their educational future. According to a report from the Organization for Economic Co-Operation and Development (the folks who administer those international Programme for International Student Assessment [PISA] tests that are the yardstick of international brainpower), only 5% of Finnish workers were involved in research and development in 1991; by 2003 that number had risen to 20%. And, "by 2001 Finland's ranking in the World Economic Forum's global competitiveness index had climbed from 15th to 1st, and it has remained at or near the top in these rankings ever since."[7]

What was the special sauce Finns were eating? In his 2010 book, *Finnish Lessons: What the World Can Learn From Educational Change in Finland*, author Pasi Sahlberg diagnosed the secret.[8] Winner of the prestigious Grawemeyer Award in 2013 for innovative ideas, Sahlberg is the director general of the Centre for International Mobility and Cooperation in the Finnish Ministry of Education and Culture. An insider to the process of creating the revolution in his own country, he is also a superstar in conveying the Finnish success story. From a U.S. perspective, it's hard to believe that for Finnish 7- and 8-year-olds, the road to success is packaged in a 4-hour school day with no homework and no tests!

So what's up? Articles about the Finnish miracle credit the fact that teachers are paid and respected as top professionals, that they collectively design the curricula without resorting to ready-made scripted lessons, and that as a consequence, they feel completely responsible for the success or failure of the children in their charge. But there is more. The schools reward creativity and inclusiveness and they work to make the students feel like a central part of the wider society that extends beyond the school walls. The Finnish kids are playing and applying what they know while American kids are stressed and cramming for the test.

But are you thinking that we can't possibly compare Finland with a country the size of the United States? If so, you are experiencing what Samuel Abrams writing in the *New Republic* referred to as the *reflexive critique*: "The reflexive critique of comparing the Finnish and U.S. educational systems is to say that Finland's PISA results are consequences of the country being a much smaller, more homogeneous nation (5.3 million people, only 4 percent of whom are foreign-born)."[9] This is not the reason for Finland's success. Next door, Norway (also small, with 4.8 million people), with similar homogeneity (only 10% foreign-born), does not reach the heights that Finland does. Norway takes an approach similar to that of the United States: salaries are not great ("Teachers with 15 years of experience earn only 70 percent of what fellow university graduates make"[10]), minimal education for teachers is fine, and since 2004, Norway has instituted a national system of standardized testing.

THE MAPLE LEAF ROCKS: OH, CANADA

Another case in point is the large country just north of our border. Canadians, too, best us on international tests despite the fact they are similar to the United States on any number of dimensions. But, unlike the United States, Canada has been educating kids on the basis of the findings of the learning sciences for the past decade. And although Canadians are not known for jumping up and down and waving the flag (unless it's at a hockey game), they proudly claim fifth place in international test scores for math, literacy, and science.[11]

We were in Canada for the rollout of Ontario's new early educational initiative. Issued on June 15, 2009, a report on Ontario's early learning program detailed how "a universal preschool program, taught by educators trained in early childhood development and schooled in the importance of learning-based play, will improve school readiness."[12] Putting play at the center of their educational agenda is exactly what learning scientists advocate; unfortunately, it's antithetical to the way most Western countries pour information wholesale into the minds of young children.

We were invited to Canada to calm the fears about the havoc this new program might create and to offer reassurance that this attention to playful learning in the early years might actually have value. When we went in 2009, we were greeted by skeptics. When we returned in 2010 and in 2011, the teachers were believers. Professor Stuart Shanker from York University in Toronto penned it this way in his visionary report *Every Child, Every Opportunity*: "The goal here is not to replicate the sort of teacher-directed program that characterizes grade school; *it is to create an environment of child-directed activity that mobilizes the child's interest and imagination.* (emphasis added)"[13] We have much to learn from our neighbors to the north.

URUGUAY'S EXPERIMENT

Now if you think that Finland and Canada are unlikely places to find enviable educational reform, pop over to a Latin American country: Uruguay. With a population of just over 3 million people, they are trying an experiment that leaps into the digital universe. In the last 7 years, the government has distributed more than half a million laptops to the nation's children and teachers. The program is dubbed CEIBAL, an acronym that stands for Basic Informative Educative Connectivity for Online Learning (*Conectividad Educativa Informatica Basica para el Aprendizaje en Linea*). The name is associated with the ceibo tree, which bears Uruguay's national flower. Designed to distribute technology, to promote knowledge, and to generate social equality, the program populates laptops with books, educational materials, and games that all families can use and enjoy (see http://laptop.org/en/children/countries/uruguay.shtml). Scientists in South America designed games that children play to spur their love of learning and intellectual curiosity. Computer games are great for children if their content is created with learning science principles as a guide.[14] While children are learning content, they do so in a fun, engaged, and collaborative way, with teachers and parents at their side. Uruguay's top learning scientists have created apps that they can keep improving through research.

The country is a model for how to connect an entire population to the cloud. Every park, library, and school is wired. And as the kids read and play, every keystroke from all of those interactions on the laptop are uploaded so that teachers and scientists can tell how the "play" translates into learning. The hope is that this learning will fuel Uruguay's economic success in the international marketplace. José Mujica, the president of Uruguay, known for continuing to tend to his farm clad in denim even while operating on the international stage, has created a national educational movement. The outcomes? Well, this program is very much a work in progress, but a scientific evaluation team published a paper showing that a program similar to CEIBAL delivered in Argentina increased students' reading and math scores. In particular, apps designed to help kids have more self-control were found to be effective.[15] This is a promising result for the more expansive program in Uruguay. When we visited Uruguay in 2014, there was an energy and excitement about education that was downright palpable. The whole country seems vested in creating a learning community. Nationwide mathematical competitions that were thought to only interest a few hundred people had thousands of participants. This was a country bursting with learning potential. And though they were often using the laptops to work on math, reading, and science, many of the kids were also having fun while they pushed through intellectual problem spaces.

A number of countries are becoming mindful of educating children in a way that will propel them to the top of the economic ladder in the years to come—in a way that respects and encourages real thinking mixed with high doses of creativity and innovation. These same countries are putting a high priority on community, investing more in younger kids, and allowing more time for active playful exploration of information. They also value their teachers and adopt a teacher/scholar model of education in which the teachers view themselves as learning alongside the children. In other words, teachers are no longer tasked with pouring knowledge into the children's empty heads; they are constructing knowledge together with children.

BACK TO THE FUTURE IN SINGAPORE

And so we return to Singapore. Out of context, it did seem odd for MindChamps to talk to two professors who tout the promise of playful learning. But in the larger climate of educational reform that is sweeping across the globe and of redefining success for our children, perhaps we did offer a new and refreshing conversation. Our mantra endorsed active engagement, meaningful learning, and social interaction in our homes, in our schools, and in our communities. The folks at MindChamps wanted to harness that science and to shape it into a new force to prepare children for success in a world dominated by technological advances, a world where learning "stuff" is not enough.

In Heckman's address to the Global Education Summit, he encouraged us to drop the idea that we can measure success by a single score on a standardized test—even a test as highly regarded as the PISA.[16] Instead, he challenged us to derive a set of skills that children will need to prosper in the world. We take this challenge seriously; the rest of the book describes the solution we offer. Fully recognizing that social skills and personal happiness are also key to success, we share what the learning sciences tell us about how to rear children to succeed in the 21st century. The changes other countries are making, and the new world we live in, demand that we reinvent our education system so that it instills not just the ABCs but also the 6Cs. The 6Cs provide a suite of so-called hard and "soft skills" that can offer a profile of children's competencies as they approach the society of tomorrow.

CHAPTER 4

HARD SKILLS AND "SOFT SKILLS": FINDING THE PERFECT BALANCE

"'Soft skills' are centrally important for human capital development and workforce success. A growing evidence base shows that these skills rival academic or technical skills in their ability to predict employment and earnings, among other outcomes."[1] This opening from the Child Trends Report on *Workforce Connections* released in June 2015 speaks to our need to move beyond what have been called *hard skills* and to also embrace "*soft skills*." *Hard skills* are the measurable outcomes that are easy to identify, test, and track across time. School subjects that appear on traditional report cards fit neatly into the hard skill camp—think math, reading, and typing. In the workplace, they might be skills such as computer programming, machine operation, and knowledge of specific scientific techniques.

Although the alternative is called "*soft skills*," they are anything but. We use the term in this chapter only to make contact with how others have discussed them. We fully recognize that this term is unfortunate because these skills are the bedrock for hard skills. What have been called "*soft skills*" include collaboration, the ability to regulate your emotions (not flipping out when that meeting doesn't go your way), and executive function. *Executive function* is a fancy term for being flexible in your thinking or finding another way to solve a pesky problem without perseverating. Focusing your attention on balancing your checkbook even when your kids are blasting their music right outside your door is another way you use your executive function. These terms apply across occupations whether you are a janitor, an attorney, or a physician, and we revisit them in Chapter 7. They are harder to identify and harder to measure, though the business community and social scientists have made enormous progress in this area.[2] In fact, the more we learn about the role of interpersonal relationships and social acumen in young children and adults, the more we realize that these so-called "soft skills" are not soft at all, but rather are more predictive of academic success than are the hard skills.

When you review the business and social science literatures, you find a plethora of terms that fall under the definition of "soft skills." Among them are adaptability, autonomy, communication skills, creativity, cultural sensitivity, empathy, higher order thinking skills, integrity, planfulness, positive attitude, professionalism, resilience, self-control, self-motivation, social skills, teamwork skills, responsibility, leadership, learning to learn skills, persuasiveness, organization, initiative, character, goal orientation, and so forth. No one would deny that these skills are important, and we all know them when we see them. Despite the fact that these are seen as key factors for success in the workplace, in school, and beyond, we are still fixated on the hard skills.

A beautiful illustration comes from a column written by Jacques Steinberg, an educational editor for *The New York Times*. On September 11, 2009, Steinberg asked whether we would be willing to write an essay for the paper's blog *The Choice*.[3] Just 2 days earlier, William R. Fitzsimmons, director of admissions and financial aid at Harvard College, had made a guest appearance answering readers' questions about getting into college. The *Times* editors were shocked by the 1,000+ questions and comments they received from concerned parents laying bare their worries and strategies for ensuring their children's admission to an elite institution—even though some of those children were only 5 years old. Steinberg believed that the parents' e-mails revealed a degree of anxiety about their children's future that begged for expert analysis.

WHAT PARENTS ARE ASKING: HARD SKILLS RULE

One of our favorite questions came from a mom who wrote to Dean Fitzsimmons:

> My daughter has a 3.9 cumulative average, is a ranked tennis doubles champion, has published two volumes of poetry—and not the kind that rhymes, but the sophisticated, esoteric non-rhyming kind—spent last July building a schoolhouse for disadvantaged Guatemalan children, and cures leukemia on weekends. She's about to start Middle School, and I want to know what extra clubs she should join to give her a leg-up in the Harvard admission process.[4]

Then there were the questions from Nidhi, who wanted the inside scoop for her 5- and 7-year-olds, and from Ian, who sought answers for maximizing the chances of future admission for his third grader. Chethana was already sculpting her fifth grader to become a Dartmouth groupie by buying him all the college's paraphernalia available online, and Esther wondered whether splurging for a private education for her Dakota would magically swing open the gates to Princeton.

Others focused on high school students, providing Dean Fitzsimmons with what amounted to public back-door applications. "What does my kid, a varsity athlete with a 4.0—wink wink, hint hint—need to do to be part of the class of 2014?" We even met the newly minted father, Ken, who wondered whether he should send his baby's APGAR score (the health rating scale used at birth on newborns) to ensure a spot in the class of 2026. We hoped his question was tongue-in-cheek, but we weren't sure.

What began as a forum for discussing the opaque college admissions process had quickly morphed into a Dear Abby session on how to package and brand children for Harvard. Adopting the "empty vessel" approach to parenting, these parents (and hundreds more like them) were convinced that if they just fed the right facts (hard skills) into their children's pliable minds, their children would enter the halls of success that would pave the way to a six-figure salary and a secure Vanguard account.

Of course, the real headline news is that all these questions and comments provided a glimpse into a distorted portrait of success. Although we agree that hard skills are important for our children, they are just one piece of who they become. If we truly embrace the broader definition of success we have offered, then whether our children become good people and people who are good to others is also part of the equation. No one wants their children to achieve by traditional standards and be miserable. Hail to the marketers—the learning industry—that has caricatured children as commodities and grades as the primary route to a bright future. Although we certainly applaud those kids who win the spelling and geography bees, the true winners of the next generation will be those who can sift through mountains of information and cull just what they need to invent solutions for, say, a lighter, less gas-guzzling car. The information sifters think of learning as a way to come up with multiple equations for possible ways to solve an engineering problem or three possible ideas for building a more efficient supermarket cart. They know how to find the gold in the intellectual rubble and, to borrow from GPS lingo, to "recalculate" when they make a wrong turn. Business leaders and educators are saying just that! There's a mismatch between what we are teaching and what kids need for success in a 21st-century global world.

Business leaders, as well as leaders in many industries, are looking for thinkers and problem solvers, not fact grinders. Scientists, academicians (like us), lawyers, and people in all walks of life

from service jobs to the health sector, have t
to interpret them and come up with new c
our lawyer friends put it,

> I need graduates who can read a legal case, think through the
> arguments, and then analyze the potential consequences for the
> client. Instead, I have to walk the new lawyers through every step
> of the assignment as if they were assembling an IKEA bookcase.

Elizabeth Edersheim and Peter Drucker talked about these new
kinds of people as *knowledge workers*,[5] the ones who created the
iPad that revolutionized the way we think about touch screens and
who are now developing the nanotechnologies projected to overcome limits in our biology.[6] Deaf people can now hear with cochlear
implants; paraplegics with no arm control can type messages on a
keyboard using eye movements. At the heart of the value delivered
from knowledge work is innovation, which, as Drucker defined it, is
the act that endows resources with a new capacity to create wealth.

Business thinker and bestselling author Daniel Pink put it this
way in *A Whole New Mind*:

> The last few decades have belonged to a certain kind of per-
> son with a certain kind of mind—computer programmers who
> could crank code, lawyers who could craft contracts, MBAs
> who could crunch numbers. *But the keys to the kingdom are
> changing hands. The future belongs to a very different kind of
> person with a very different kind of mind—creators and empa-
> thizers, pattern recognizers and meaning makers* [emphasis
> added]. These people—artists, inventors, designers, storytellers,
> caregivers, consolers, big picture thinkers—will now reap soci-
> ety's richest rewards and share its greatest joys.[7]

One of Pink's central messages is that we need more creative thinkers, more innovators, in all the jobs people do. Without us noticing,

many of today's jobs have morphed into occupations that didn't used to require information sifting. Take sales jobs. Selling copiers? New copiers come on the market all the time, and customers now have the capability to read tons of information that compare copiers online. A copier salesperson who doesn't keep up will lose that sale to a competing company. The same is true in science: Stop reading and interpreting the new findings from labs working on the same problems and your lab will be left in the dust.

In Pink's 2009 book, *Drive*, he suggested that the "carrot and stick" kind of motivation—giving money or material rewards—worked successfully in the 20th century but often produced the opposite of the results it was intended to achieve.[8] Instead of trying to motivate people from the outside with rewards, Pink argued that the ability to learn and create new things and to improve our world is the motivation that really matters. That comes from the inside!

But Pink is not the only one rethinking the suite of skills our children will need for success in the era of the knowledge worker. In April and May of 2006, a report titled *Are They Really Ready to Work?* was issued by a collaborative group including The Conference Board, Corporate Voices for Working Families, Partnership for 21st Century Skills, and the Society for Human Resource Management.[9] More than 400 employers were asked what skills they considered most important and whether high school, 2-year college, or 4-year college graduates had these desired skills. It is interesting that the top five ranked skills were oral communication, teamwork, professionalism, written communication, and critical thinking or problem solving. And 81% of responders also considered creativity and innovation very important. The report quoted J. Willard Marriott Jr., Chairman and CEO of Marriott International Inc., as saying,

> To succeed in today's workplace, young people need more than basic reading and math skills. They need substantial content knowledge and information technology skills; advanced think-

ing skills, flexibility to adapt to change; and interpersonal skills
to succeed in multi-cultural, cross-function teams.[10]

Only 24% of current 4-year college graduates were rated as excellent in the skills needed for success in today's world.

The 2005 *National Study of Employers* released by the Family and Work Institute found similar results.[11] Their conclusion was that neither teaching to the test nor having preschool children sit in rows and fill out worksheets will create the skill set and diverse thinking styles needed to conquer 21st-century challenges. According to the report, solitary workers should not be our model for educational environments or of future success when all types of workplaces are becoming a patchwork of problem solving with associates spanning the globe.

A Forbes article in 2013 reviewed the suite of skills that college graduates would need to be successful in the workplace.[12] Topping the list from the survey by the National Association of Colleges and Employers was ability to work in a team and ability to make decisions and solve problems.

What is clear is that those who wrote to Steinberg about his column were not on the same page as the employers, scientists, and educators when thinking about how to groom children for the world of tomorrow. It is critical to outline a set of skills that include both hard and soft skills—and some that seem to bridge both—that can be embraced by schools and parents to cultivate in their children. This is the direction that many took as they sketched out what has become known as *21st-century skills*.

A PROLIFERATION OF SKILLS: CHARTING THE LANDSCAPE

As it turned out, 2009 was a watershed year—perhaps a kind of quiet tipping point. In 2009, the iPhone was but 2 years old, YouTube turned 4, and Facebook was 5. A new generation of learners was growing up with access to information literally at their fingertips.

49

Business, science, art, transportation—virtually any field you can name—is moving deftly across geographic boundaries, and our ways of learning and processing information are morphing overnight. For the first time in our memory, business leaders who think about their requirements for employees and child psychologists are talking the same language and looking for the same benchmarks. Only our school system seems to be stuck somewhere in the agrarian societies of past centuries.

Also in 2009, the Partnership for 21st Century Skills published *A Framework for 21st Century Learning,* which included a Common Core toolkit, a book, and a teacher's manual for professional training.[13] On the basis of their business survey, the Partnership outlined their 3Rs and 4Cs approach. The 3Rs are the standard stock of reading, 'riting, and 'rithmetic. No self-respecting learning approach can leave these behind. But our current educational approach usually stops there.

The *Framework,* however, moved beyond the basics to posit four more Cs—critical thinking, communication, collaboration, and creativity—and added to these learning skills life and career skills as well as information, media, and technology skills, such as information and media literacy.[14]

That same year, we published a child psychology book, *A Mandate for Playful Learning in Preschool,*[15] that advocated the value of play as a metaphor for the kind of active, engaged, and meaningful learning that occurs when a child masters counting by playing Chutes and Ladders and when he understands stories through the tales of King Arthur and his valiant knights. Our book celebrated the science of learning in action and concluded with what we called the 5Cs—a skill set for the 21st century designed in the lab for the living room. These included collaboration (or how children learn to work together and see from another's point of view), communication (speaking and listening), content (reading, writing, and math *along with* history, science, and the arts), critical thinking, and creative innovation. Surprising to some but not to us, many of these skills develop as kids are playing in the sandbox.

By the time we wrote that essay for *The New York Times*[16] in late 2009, the 5Cs had morphed into the 6Cs, and having the confidence to take risks rounded out the developmental repertoire. About 40 additional Cs, including culture, character, charisma, and clarity, had been recommended to us as we made the rounds with our work through Utah, London, Thailand, and other states and countries around the world. In the end, we stuck with those Cs that were related to learning, were scientifically valid, and were malleable in the sense that they would be applicable to real kids who live in real homes and go to real schools.

Amazingly, the term *21st-century skills* has grown exponentially since then. It was first mentioned in 2009, and now in 2015, we get 72,600,000 Google search results on this term in just 30 seconds. Promoting 21st-century skills has become something of a cottage industry—or perhaps a very large industry.

Among the important contributions to this growing field was Ellen Galinsky's *Mind in the Making*, a superb book that appeared in 2010 outlining seven essential life skills for success in the modern world.[17] This book, carefully rooted in science, has been deeply influential because it puts the latest science in the hands of educators and families and poses directly the question "What kind of person do I want my child to be?"

Also notable were timely books by Pellegrino and Hilton (2012; *Education for Life and Work*) and by Laura Greenstein (2012; *Assessing 21st Century Skills: A Guide to Evaluating Mastery and Authentic Learning*) that offer tools for assessing students' achievement in a variety of skills, as well as research-based ideas on how to adapt the Common Core for the 21st century. Their themes are remarkably similar in that both recognize that problem solving, critical thinking, communication, and self-management must augment a traditional school curriculum and all must be measurable.

The Organization for Economic Co-Operation and Development, composed of 34 democracies with market economies as well as more than 70 nonmember economies, issued a report in 2015 that also outlined a series of malleable skills that prepare our children for success. Among the skills they highlighted were the "soft skills." They wrote, "Social and emotional skills do not play a role in isolation, they interact with cognitive skills, cross-fertilise, and further enhance children's likelihood of achieving positive outcomes later in life."[18] All of these initiatives have one thing in common. They go beyond supporting the notion that mastering hard skills alone will pave the road to success. Today's children require a suite of skills that will include "soft skills." As talent management strategist Dorothy Dalton deftly wrote, "Hard skills are the foundation of a successful career. But soft skills are the cement."[19]

Though progress has been made, we are left with a conundrum: How do we sort through the piles of skills and determine which are most crucial for success in our time? Rather than viewing skills in isolation, might there be a way to integrate and define these aptitudes such that they foster coherent curriculum design, positive classroom and family experiences, and good assessments of skill achievement? As suggested by Jay Mathews in *The Washington Post*, if we are unable to do so, lists of 21st-century skills will become nothing more than "the latest doomed pedagogical fad."[20]

A HEALTHY MIX OF HARD AND SOFT SKILLS: THE 6Cs

Here, we rise to this challenge, suggesting that advances in the science of learning can help address these issues by revealing a systemic suite of skills informed by empirical research and modeled in an education framework.

Our skill set, the 6Cs, consists of six skills that address the following needs: collaboration, communication, content, critical thinking, creative innovation, and confidence. The 6Cs differ from extant models. First, our model is *born from the science of learning* and rooted in decades of research in child development. Using this research allows us to condense long lists of desirable attributes into a few key interrelated skills that develop recursively, scaffolding and building on one another. Second, our skills are *malleable.* Anyone can achieve new levels within each skill, and no one will ever completely master each skill in all content areas. These skills are not traits nor are they to be achieved once and checked off a list. Third, our skills *focus on the learner*, rather than the teacher or parent. Our model highlights not only what can be learned but also the ways in which children learn. Fourth, the skills are *adaptable to many contexts*, an important consideration because children only spend about 20% of their time in school.[21] It is thus our obligation to inform parents about the potential for learning in informal settings from living rooms to libraries.

A BROADER VISION OF SUCCESS

The parents who wrote to Dean Fitzsimmons had a clear vision of what they had to do to ensure their children's success. It was simple: hard skills, hard skills, and then more hard skills. At the end of the day, these kids might be really smart, learning the techniques they need to play on the pro tennis circuit and signing up to help those disadvantaged children in a far away land. But these kids are also stressed out. In a 2000 column, Fitzsimmons was quoted as saying,

> Unless something changes we are going to lose a lot of them . . . too many of them are going to experience one form or another of burn out, and that would be a tragedy . . . the fabric of family life has just been destroyed.[22]

This is because children can no longer take time off with their families. That trip to the beach has given way to early school soccer practice.

Drawing from the research in the learning sciences and the long lists of potential 21st-century skills, we use the process of how children naturally develop to weave a web of skills that can promote healthy and productive lives. This model borrows many of the themes that have been broadcast over the last decade, but it casts the skills in a new light by encouraging families to help their children develop these skills outside the context of school. Schools today mostly teach the hard skills. It takes more than hard skills to foster a child who is happy and productive. The Cs we selected are tools children can use to enrich their personal and professional lives, tools that can serve our kids throughout their lives as they continually improve and expand.

A recent study published in the *American Journal of Public Health* illustrated how crucial the "soft skills" really are. The researchers followed 753 children who were in kindergarten in the 1990s for 20 years until they turned 25.[23] What factors would account for how children turned out 20 years later? Are you thinking IQ must be what really matters? Or family socioeconomic background? Get ready to hear something that might shock you: Kindergarten students who were socially competent and did things such as sharing, cooperating, or helping other kids were more likely to attain higher education and well-paying jobs than those who were less socially competent. Neither race nor gender mattered—indeed, the researchers' fancy statistics controlled for the children's demographic characteristics. When the researchers combined their measures of social competence to place kids on a 5-point scale, some really interesting findings emerged: For every single point of increase in social skills, children were twice as likely to go to college and 46% more likely to have a full-time job at the age of 25. Dale Carnegie was right all along: Social skills matter, and they matter a lot—even when you are in kindergarten.[24] Social skills predict children's successful lives and careers in adulthood. What this means is that we are going to have to think about education—in and out of school—in a more holistic way. Children are far more than the grades they earn.

The 6Cs drive us toward the broader vision of success that can support happy, healthy, thinking, caring, and social children. So let's explore the 6Cs in depth now to get a clearer picture of how we can mold those collaborative, creative, competent, and responsible citizens of tomorrow.

1

CHAPTER 5

COLLABORATION: NO ONE CAN FIDDLE A SYMPHONY

Never doubt that a small group of thoughtful committed citizens can change the world; indeed, it's the only thing that ever has.
—Margaret Mead, American anthropologist, cited in Nancy C. Lutkehaus, *Margaret Mead: The Making of an American Icon*

BLINK! In the time it takes us to open our eyes, another educational app has been added to the Apple Store inventory, another parody music video has popped up on YouTube, and more features have been added to the latest addictive online game. Do your children have their eyes glued to a screen right now, or are they on the cusp of begging you for screen time for the 14th time today? What is the effect of all this screen time on our kids? And what might they be missing?

Patricia Greenfield, a professor at UCLA, asked just this question. She looked at the social skills of sixth graders who were headed out to a weeklong camping experience that prohibited any use of screen media. Now that is a survival test. She compared these campers with kids who spent their normal days in classrooms and at home. Both groups were tested before camp started to see how they did at reading others' facial expressions and emotions. Though both groups looked the same at the beginning of the study, the group that went to the nature camp came back better at reading those social skills than the group that had stayed home with their screens and televisions. Face-to-face interaction with real people made a difference.

Whether it's with your life partner or your coworker in Switzerland, collaboration—in person or online—is essential to how humans learn, how they accomplish tasks, and how they improve their own performance. John does great graphics, but Sally puts things pithily; together they up each other's ante and write a great paper. Collaboration is the ultimate soft skill that all other skills build on because when we enter the world alone and incompetent, the first thing we do is to make contact with other humans.

History and the learning sciences support the role that other people play in fueling our learning. In Socrates' time, learning resembled more of the back and forth of a tennis match than a listen-and-passively-swallow-all-facts-given approach. Indeed, in every epoch people have learned best from interaction with their peers or supportive adults. Ancient Jewish education had students study holy texts in pairs called *hevruta*. This "debate-as-learning" approach is still used today in the yeshivas of Brooklyn and in the temples of Jerusalem. More recently, anthropologists watch the learning that occurs as movements spread through our society and become common agendas many of us share. Take the civil rights movement or how we are "going green" or learning as a culture to respect differences in sexual orientation. None of these mass movements could have happened if we simply marched side by side without growing together with common themes and messages. Collaboration is at the heart of these changes because by working in teams we build community and mutual respect. These in turn rest on social–emotional control so that we can regulate our impulses and not just do anything we feel like doing.

Why? Because from the earliest ages we learn from people. Especially when those other people—parents, caregivers, teachers, friends, and coworkers—are sensitive and responsive to what we want to know. Seven-year-old Josh is excited to be playing a collaborative board game with his buds. In the context of a game where his competitive juices are rising, he learns the words *hyena* and *flamingo*. Laura at 24 months is more likely to learn the word *slug* when we walk alongside her and she discovers one on the sidewalk. And budding lawyers learn to think like lawyers when they sit with a respected colleague and build a more complex argument together.

Today, sophisticated computer technology—tablets, smartphones—is already having a dramatic effect on communication between parents and children.[1] Go to any fast-food restaurant and you will observe the phenomenon for yourself. Out of 55 parents, 40 were on a cell phone or tablet when eating with their kids. Not only did they talk less with their kids than they might have, but 73% were totally absorbed with their devices, staring down and virtually ignoring anything but the screen.

But the digital world also offers a boon for individualized learning. Middle school and high school kids are now mastering algebra through the Khan Academy, where the blackboard examples of just how you solve for $a^2 + b^2 = c^2$ are carefully illustrated in a series of online lessons that can be tailored to students' strengths and weaknesses. Don't these digital devices overcome the need for a *hevruta* or for working alongside others? We don't think so. Of course, people can learn from online instruction; there is no denying that. That kind of learning is just the beginning, though. We will always need people to discuss the material with if we are to adopt a critical stance and not just swallow it whole. Is the text the whole truth? Aren't there limits to what we have learned, circumstances in which that lesson does not apply? The challenge for those of us who work in the field is to create social educational media that capitalizes on how we really learn, which is from people. We are— as Barbra Streisand would tell us—people who need people.

Professor Michael Tomasello highlighted our dependence on people in his research on chimpanzees. Our furry cousins travel in groups. And though humans share 99% of their genes, chimps don't go to school or develop strong apprenticeships with their elders. Why? Mike suggested it is because humans are *ultra social.*[2]

In his lab at the Max Planck Institute in Leipzig, Germany, Michael (now at Duke University) and his students ask what apes know and how they learn best. Mike is unpacking our evolutionary heritage as he watches our cousins find hidden food. A sneak peek at the research featured on his website begins to tell the collaboration story. It begins with a fact that should come as no surprise. Chimps are smart, *Planet of the Apes* smart. Mike and his collaborators gave a 2-year-old *Homo sapiens* and a young *Pan troglodyte* a series of tests to see how each thought about the physical and social world. Chimps were pretty good at the physics part of his studies; they looked just like the 2-year-olds in figuring out that a rolling ball would emerge from behind a barrier. But social skills? None could hold jobs as priests, psychologists, or bartenders.

Take collaborating to find food. In one activity, the ape and the toddler had to look for a reward under one of two overturned yellow buckets placed side by side about a foot apart. A graduate student sitting opposite the child or chimp would first look directly into the chimp's or child's eyes and then point and look to the winning bucket. Would toddlers and chimps follow the graduate student's obvious point and eye gaze to find their delectable treat? Following another's perspective is a first step in social reasoning; collaboration depends on it. You might think that Zulu the chimp, 21 years young, would consider this a no-brainer. To us, it is as if the graduate student is screaming, "LOOK UNDER THE LEFT BUCKET FOR A BANANA SLICE!" But as obvious as it seems to us, Zulu, with her vast social experience with other chimps and with humans, didn't take the clue. Two-year-old Irving, who hasn't played with more than 10 kids in his whole short life, went directly for the bucket with the payoff.

Apes get an *F* in collaboration and working with others. Apes are just not as good as we are at connecting the social dots. As anthropologist Kim Hill added, humans are not special because of their big brains. That's not the reason we can build rocket ships—no individual can. We have rockets because 10,000 individuals cooperate in producing the information.[3]

This human feature of working and learning together—collaboration—has huge benefits. Even Michael's book titles tell that story: *Why We Cooperate* and *The Cultural Origins of Human Cognition*.[4,5] Human collaboration is the basis for the very behaviors that make us stand out among the animal kingdom. Human language offers a great example. The fact that people talk means the placement of our larynx makes us much more likely to choke on our food than other animals. This is clearly evolutionarily crazy. Yet the choking hazard is outweighed by the fact that language is a huge evolutionary advantage. Where shall we hunt today? How many mammoths were there? Should we take enough provisions for 2 days? Can you imagine trying to have a "discussion" of these questions without language? Whether it is building villages, killing dinner, ordering groceries, or putting out fires, language, a distinctly human ability, likely evolved from our need to collaborate and work together. Humans are collaborators from the get go.

Michael pushed this argument to the limit. Collaboration, he wrote, is the basis for all human culture: "This new mode of understanding other persons [and collaborating with other people] changed the nature of all types of social interactions . . . so that a unique form of cultural evolution began to take place over historical time."[6]

No one has to reinvent the wheel or rediscover fire. Rather than dealing with the same problems anew in each generation, our shared knowledge and cultural practices, originally developed through collaboration, can be passed on from generation to generation. The "ratchet effect," as Michael said, continually changes the environment in which children grow up. Just think skyscrapers, toasters, and flash mobs. None were with us 200 years ago; all needed collaboration for their creation. The ability to collaborate is not just important for learning in classrooms or for global commerce. It is arguably the very foundation on which the human experience is built. Everything we do is influenced by our living in the social soup. And every child—except perhaps those children labeled *autistic*—has the advantage of being ultra social from birth.

Though babies and 2-year-olds can charm the pants off the meanest curmudgeon, they still have a lot to learn. Just ask any parent or preschool teacher. A pleasant playground collaboration can turn into a flailing conflagration in a matter of moments. Remember that section on our report cards: "Works and plays well with others"? It turns out that section captures something genuinely crucial to our success—in our personal relationships as well as with our colleagues in the workplace.

In business, in science, and in virtually any profession, collaboration is the new normal—it embraces a set of "soft skills" that we need to master if we are to be successful. National Public Radio interviewed Jeff Winter, who recruits techies for Apple and IBM. There are tons of people with great programming skills. But, Winter said, their social skills are holding them back. As he put it, "The ones that aren't nice though, they don't get their Zuck," referring to Mark Zuckerberg, who started Facebook.[7] In other words, you won't get the chance to make your mark if your social skills drag you down. If you don't have the soft skill of getting along with people, you can't be empathic and keep from saying anything that pops into your head.

In fact, social control is the foundation for collaboration. Researchers have found that differences in self-control as early as age 7 can predict how much time people are unemployed 4 decades later.[8] Being unable to control your impulses and emotional expression leads to conflict and makes collaboration almost impossible.

These more recent findings parallel those found in a follow-up from the classic marshmallow test. Children who could wait for the experimenter before eating the prized marshmallows when they were 4 years old had higher SAT scores when they were applying for college—indeed, those scores were higher by over 200 points.[9]

How do kids learn to collaborate? The science of learning has suggested that we progress through a series of four levels. Fortunately, as with all the 6Cs, collaboration is a malleable skill. We may be born to be social, but that doesn't mean we were born with the self-control necessary for collaboration. The elements that go into successful collaborations are learned and can be explicitly taught. Working and playing well with others is a crucial life skill. In the learning sciences, people call this self-regulation or self-control.

LEVEL 1: ON MY OWN

Screaming out of control, baby Olivia just won't go to sleep. Cowering in the living room wondering whether to don earphones or blast the television, Olivia's parents don't know what to do. Sometimes Olivia has "conversations" with them, delightfully going back and forth while cooing and gurgling. Babies are born social, but they don't know how to self-regulate. It's our job as parents to help Olivia get a grip. Collaboration is a skill that we refine throughout our lives, but that starts with the self-regulation that keeps us from getting hysterical each time something goes wrong. Olivia's parents will scaffold the development of her self-regulation by comforting her and distracting her ("Oh, look at the birdie!") until she learns to do this for herself. Unless we learn to self-regulate and, later on, to express our opinions in respectful ways and really hear what others are saying, collaboration will be impossible.

Just as painters stand on a scaffold outside a tall building to extend their reach, adults provide scaffolding for younger children to help them interact and take turns. When 24-month-old Solly needs help in inserting that triangle in the shape sorter, Dad rotates the sorter so that the triangle fits neatly in the upright position. When Solly's baby brother insists on having his toy at dinner, Dad starts to sing "Row, Row, Row Your Boat" and the baby is charmed into silence.

Level 1 is like playing a hidden figures game in a *Highlights* magazine. You don't even notice those budding moments of collaboration and the important role parents are playing in supporting self-regulation. These everyday interactions offer opportunities to help children adopt more mature behaviors. It is in these little moments when parents assist kids to overcome their frustrations and help them turn to other choices that self-regulation and then the capacity to collaborate are born.

Parents scaffold their children in all domains. Sensitive parents scaffold children and offer them other ways to express their feelings, ways that children don't think of on their own. In Level 1, it is mostly the parent helping the child; the child doesn't even realize the role his or her parent is playing. But lower levels are necessary building blocks for the upper levels. In the beginning it is the parent who has the burden for crafting the collaboration and the social control; little by little the child takes more and more of the responsibility.

In Andy Meltzoff's baby lab, 14-month-old Ruthie watches closely as a man she hasn't seen before tries repeatedly to put a string of beads into a vase with a narrow opening.[10] He finally gives up and pushes it over to the baby. Ruthie picks up the beads and plops them right into the vase—even though she never actually saw him do this. Ruthie figured out what the man was trying to do and performed a kind of mind-meld. This kind of "mind reading" will be the basis for Ruthie's future collaborations with others—and the basis for understanding their emotions.

Despite their burgeoning sensitivity to the people around them, babies don't really collaborate with others to achieve goals. This is partly because their goals are pretty local ("I want that!") and certainly not long term. No baby could plan a trip with you or collaborate in any realistic way about who to invite to their playgroup. Babies don't even have some of the communication devices we take for granted.

Sadly, we see Level 1 in many, though not all, of the nation's classrooms. Children are increasingly encouraged to sit on their own, not speaking to or working with others, and little to no collaboration is encouraged.

Believe it or not, there are adults in every walk of life who are still at Level 1. In 1991, management consultant Geary Rummler is credited with inventing the term *silo syndrome*.[11] Now a hackneyed phrase, it was designed to capture how units within a corporation can develop their own cultures. They can even have difficulty talking to each other—clear Level 1 behavior. Turf guarding ("We do engineering and don't need your ideas, thank you") is an outgrowth of silo syndrome. And if you have silo syndrome you are much less likely to innovate; after all, who is thinking big picture? It's all about your own unit. Would you want to be part of an organization in which walking into another department felt like invading alien territory? Or would you rather be at a company like Toyota where team members at every level participate in making decisions together? Level 1 silo syndrome, to quote management consultant Evan Rosen, "breeds insular thinking, redundancy, and suboptimal decision-making."[12] Want to transform your organization from a noncollaborative set of independent units to one that functions as a well-oiled community of team players? Again, we borrow from the research on children. Parental scaffolding morphs into management coaches who facilitate that change.

Talking about suboptimal decision-making brings Hurricane Katrina to mind. *Time Magazine* reported that when Governor

Kathleen Babineaux of Louisiana called the White House on the day Katrina hit, neither President George Bush nor his chief of staff was available. There was no effective network in place—all the players were operating in their own silos. In fact, Michael Brown, head of FEMA (Federal Emergency Management Agency), thought everything was going swell! Silo syndrome was written all over this disaster and it cost people their lives and disrupted families forever.[13] When communities large and small fail to collaborate, natural disasters morph into massive disasters that could have been avoided or at least mitigated. Lack of collaboration among government agencies created an unparalleled situation in New Orleans that we will be hearing about for years.

LEVEL 2: SIDE BY SIDE

In Level 1, as a toddler, Solly leaned on his dad to insert his triangle in his shape sorter and to control his emotions. Now at Level 2, the roots of collaboration are sprouting. Solly works more on his own and has budding respect for the needs of others (at least a little bit). *Side by side* is an advance over *on my own*. Toddlers know that they can use others as tools to get things done. Collaboration isn't finely honed, but it is well on its way. Jump forward a couple of years and we can see the progress.

Daniel and Cynthia—3-year-olds—are in the sandbox with their shovels and buckets and castle molds. They play along quietly together not really acknowledging each other until Daniel can't find his castle mold. He looks over at Cynthia, "You got my castle?" and she reaches under the sand to grasp a red plastic corner peeking out and pulls the castle out smiling, "Here!" she says triumphantly. Every now and then they might come together for a few moments to pat something down and smooth out the sand, but there is no real collaboration on a common, overarching task. No planning is involved, just momentary joining to get a little job done. No surprise that scientists call this *parallel play*. But let's see what is positive here. Playing separately demands that the children maintain their own space and not invade each other's castles. At least they are controlling their impulses that much.

At this level, children realize that others have goals and desires that might be different from their own. Toddlers and even chimpanzees are eager to help adults carry out their plans.[14,15,16,17] Felix Warneken, a Harvard professor, put 3-year-olds in a collaborative problem-solving situation. Would kids work together on an apparatus to receive gummy bears and stickers? Would they share the spoils? Indeed, they did—even when one 3-year-old could have grabbed all the goodies for himself. At age 3, children seem motivated to share their spoils equally. Chimps in the same experiment couldn't collaborate because it was every chimp for itself (Level 1). Warneken and his colleagues wrote, "Human children present a striking contrast to chimpanzees, whose collaboration is severely constrained by their tendency to compete over the spoils of collaborative efforts."[18]

Day care and preschool environments can heighten or dampen children's collaborative attempts. Even young children can learn to work together if the adults that surround them give them tasks to do together. "Jack and Larry—can you please put away those blocks neatly in the block corner, putting the same kinds together?" Jack and Larry enjoy pleasing the teacher and arranging the blocks by category—long bricks with long bricks, half moons with half moons—it's right up their alley. When they return from their mission, Ms. Jonquil holds them up as a model for the class, "Larry and Jack worked so well together in putting the blocks away! I heard no bickering at all!" Classrooms that expect collaboration and social control from kids often get it.

Kids seem to want to share. But we might be dampening this natural urge with parallel play on electronic devices that are increasingly consuming children's (and our) free time. Even adolescents can collaborate at a low level. Kids can sit in the same room with a group of friends and be texting each other rather than talking! Joel Bakan, a parent, wrote an op-ed in *The New York Times* on August 22, 2011, and was worried:

> When I sit with my two teenagers, and they are a million miles away, absorbed by the titillating roil of online social life, the addictive pull of video games and virtual worlds, as they stare endlessly at video clips and digital pictures of themselves and their friends, it feels like something is wrong.[19]

How will kids learn to take each other's perspective and to identify each other's feelings if they are glued to Angry Birds and Draw Something?

Many learning environments are the embodiment of side-by-side learning, even though students have outgrown parallel play in the sandbox. From preschool on, many children sit in rows of desks doing worksheets next to each other but without interacting or cooperating with one another. If a child gets sent home with homework each night in the form of worksheets, this is a tip-off that kids are likely doing their own thing and not talking with each other.

Working together really builds understanding. If Chris and Diego got to solve fraction addition problems together and talk about which steps to follow and why, they would understand fractions better. When Diego explains to Chris why he adds the numerators, he is moving beyond being a mere calculator to being a problem solver. In fact, this is what the Common Core urges kids to do in math.

Even if school has kids working solo, there are other venues where kids can get the scaffolding they need to build collaboration. Watch a kiddie soccer game and notice that the kids wearing the blue and green shirts all just start running to one or the other goal without any attention to who is on their team or what they are doing. Each of them has a singular mind-set: "Kick ball into goal"—even if it is the wrong goal! It takes patient coaches to help children understand that they are part of a team, not just playing on their own. It takes an even more patient coach to teach children the self-control they need to let someone other than themselves kick the ball. Here again, we see the need for self-control and scaffolding as key features for collaboration.

Ever play Candyland—and then play Candyland again and again? Although parents may be ready to tear their hair out, their children are learning to take turns and wait until one finishes before the other launches. We all remember when these concepts were foreign to our children; they needed to learn to play board games and we were key in that mix—the scaffolds to collaboration. The solo experience of working on a computer game, although great for those moments when a parent is on a long-distance call, are not breeding the back and forth kids need for success.

Level 2 side-by-side collaboration is great for the sandbox, but it is pretty shallow. On a town council in a "main line" community in suburban Philadelphia, we see this side-by-side mentality all the time. The town needs a facelift, downtrodden from years of heavy use and worn-out buildings. Committees are formed to address the problem and each has laser focus—one will prettify the train station, another the township building, and yet another the parking lot structure (can you really make a parking lot attractive to the eye?). Everyone comes to the meeting excited about his or her plans. Alas, the newly imaged train station seems to have no architectural connection to the township building, and all show disgust with the parking structure. No one gave a whit of thought to the *total plan*. Each of the groups is working separately toward the same goal with no thought of getting the design coordinated in any way. This is Level 2—marching side by side toward a common goal but not

69

really working together. Fortunately, Levels 3 and 4 represent a big advance over Levels 1 and 2.

LEVEL 3: BACK AND FORTH

By age 4, Daniel and Cynthia eagerly share their buckets and molds in the sandbox, ask each other questions about what the other is doing, and hold conversations about digging to China. They engage in give-and-take behavior and comment on each other's progress: "Oh that shovel is bad; try this one!" Cynthia freely volunteers. In Level 3, children pursue their loosely defined common interests. But at least they are aware that there are "other" interests. They show a level of self-control (well sometimes at least) in that they don't bash each other's sand creations. Back in 1932, Parten called this *associative play.* You know you are seeing Level 3 when children appear more interested in one another than in the toys they are playing with. Side-by-side Level 2 children are together but function as independent agents; if they were adults we might think they were angry at each other (or just on their cell phones) because little interaction takes place. Children engaged in the back-and-forth of Level 3 collaboration actually talk to each other and work together, "Cynthia, can I help you build the tower?" Daniel even knows what she is trying to achieve!

Psychologists have cool ways to study and measure collaboration. Picture four children between 6 and 10 years old playing a game in which each gets to pull a string. Each child's string is attached to the same pen that is itself anchored in a holder to keep it in contact with a square game board. The board is divided into quadrants and a circle has been drawn in each one. The goal of the game is to get the pen to travel and mark through each of the four circles drawn on the board. In this game, collaboration is essential.

Unless they are manipulating those strings together, children can't possibly get the pen to mark through each of the circles. But the children have to figure that part out for themselves. Each child sits at a corner of the board excitedly holding his or her string. If they can get the pen to mark through all four circles, they each get a little paper bag with prizes in it. How did they do? Great!

But then the researchers changed the rules: Now children would be rewarded *individually* by how many times each could get the pen to go through the circle in their *own* quadrant. Say goodbye to collaboration! Mayhem ensued. Kids pulled their own string toward themselves and never realized that if they worked together and took turns, they could all be winners. The children reverted to Level 1—they each wanted the same outcome, and there was lots of back-and-forth, but collaboration occurred only by accident.

There is one more wrinkle to this story: Culture matters. Growing up a "country mouse" in a collective society—like in a kibbutz in Israel—might make you more likely to collaborate than if you were raised as a "city mouse," where it's more important to do things independently. The scene we just watched involved city kids. The same experiment was run with country kids. The country children, growing up on a collectivist kibbutz, got loads of mystery prize bags because they agreed to take turns and help each other. Want kids to collaborate? Have them learn that you get more prizes by helping each other than going it alone.

Back and forth can enliven learning in the classroom too. Teacher Myrna Baker is a dyed-in-the-wool "New Yawka" sitting in front of her third-grade inner city class as her kids work together. Roald Dahl's *James and the Giant Peach*[20] is the focus of the children's team meetings. How do the kids turn a key scene in the story into a skit? Should they pick the scene when the wizard gave James Henry Trotter (the little boy who is the protagonist) the magic bag with the magic seeds that started the whole adventure? Or should they pick the scene when a mass of seagulls lifts James and the giant peach skyward? Jamal and Shevon sound like Siskel and Ebert reviewing a movie. They use lots of complex language ("It's important because . . .") and if–then statements ("But if that didn't happen, there'd be no story!") and argue like pros. But are they learning more than if they didn't work together to discuss the story?

Robert Slavin of Johns Hopkins University and the Johnson brothers at the University of Minnesota showed that back-and-forth discussions increase learning over the usual sitting-in-your-seat competitive kind of learning. Competition has only a couple of "winners," whereas collaboration yields more. Collaboration expands language skills and encourages kids like Jamal and Shevon to express their ideas. Listening to others' ideas and learning debate skills can be handy in life—with your spouse as well as on the job. Even shy children (remember that kid in elementary school who never spoke up?) are more likely to talk and take risks in small groups—and are more likely to be heard.

But would the kids have learned just as much if each kid read the book alone and followed up with that old classic, the book report? Nope. The whole meaning of the story takes front and center in this debate. Jamal realizes that the man who gave James the bag was a "wizard"—now there's a cool adult occupation—and a good new vocabulary item! And Shevon never thought about how a bunch of birds flying above the clouds made the story turn out. Billy is quietly noticing how much his friends know and thinking that next time he's going to really pay attention while he reads.

These examples demonstrate the power of collaborative learning. In a way, this kind of success emerges because the scaffolding is now implicit in the task we ask the children to do, whether it is in a string game or in reading in a classroom. Setting up these environments to foster collaboration not only encourages social skills but also breeds better outcomes for kids.

The story of collaborative learning, however, is not just for kids. The prestigious journal *Science* published an article by three physicists: Louis Deslauriers, Ellen Schelew, and Carl Weiman of the University of British Columbia.[21] They got tired of the traditional way physics is taught: in lectures. And they weren't convinced that students were really learning. They tried something new, something that paid off big. One group of over 200 students heard standard 3-hour lectures in quantum mechanics from a highly experienced lecturer who actually received great course evaluations.

The other group of students got a "green" postdoctoral fellow to be available to answer their questions during the class. This group spent virtually the whole class working in teams to practice "thinking scientifically." Take Saul and Miranda. They sit next to each other by chance and become a team today. Neither one is quite sure of what *entropy* is. But the professor passes out a series of challenging questions and problems to provoke them to think like physicists. As they talk over the questions little glimmers of understanding arise and their faces alternate between happy and sober. Finally, after they are pretty sure they understand the problems, they independently write a response to the questions and turn them in. Saul and Miranda's achievement soared under the new method. And no surprise, in a questionnaire given at the end of the semester, Saul and Miranda both reported that they liked physics. Wouldn't you like physics more if you got to practice it with a buddy instead of sitting still during a long, unresponsive lecture? Getting Saul and Miranda involved and talking to each other makes a huge difference in their understanding—and over a very short time! Saul and Miranda are social animals. As learning science (and the ancient practice of studying in a *hevruta*) has shown, Saul and Miranda are just like the rest of us: We love to learn from others.

Collaboration at Level 3 can also be found in the office. Back and forth characterizes many of our business and work exchanges.

Panic! Your hard drive crashes, and you decide to take it in for repair at the local technology superstore. It doesn't take long for Adam, the minimally trained "specialist" at the help desk, to realize that your computer's malady is above his pay grade. In today's globalized world, Adam is not flying solo. With a quick e-mail to Bangalore, trained help is just 8,000 miles away. Level 3 collaboration allows Adam to relay information to an Indian technician. With knowledge specific to your computer's failures, that technician can offer customized instruction to Adam on how to get you back on the keys. Adam can only be successful in his job in Philadelphia if he can talk to Sura in Bangalore. And Sura can only be successful if there are enough Adams from Philadelphia and other distant parts to contact him. It's like assembling a puzzle: They each have their information and they trade it to accomplish a common goal. Your hard drive lives!

Think about what it takes to collaborate in the business environment. Michael Schrage wrote the book *Shared Minds: New Technologies of Collaboration.*[22] In these days of exploding information (we'll discuss that more when we talk about critical thinking), no one can master it all. That's why building on each other's strengths can be so powerful in collaborative relationships. There are ways to make collaborations work at a high level, but not all businesses follow this path.[23] *Defining the goal* of the collaboration is obviously the first step. Do we want to build a better widget or to figure out how to make the widget we have cost less? *Who* should collaborate is the next question. Collaboration thrives on differences in opinion, not similarities. As Schrage said, collaboration is shared creation and works best when two or more individuals with complementary skills interact to create something or some idea that wasn't there before they began. In the words of a CEO, "Having a few beers together is not collaboration. Collaboration is a discipline."[24]

Creating the space and time for collaboration is huge. Schrage thinks our personal computers get in the way and inhibit sharing new ideas—aside from the distraction of that new e-mail that just came in. And hearing someone say, "You have 30 minutes to solve the problem together" is like saying, "We don't really value collaboration, but knock yourself out anyway." Collaboration works best when leaders aren't just paying lip service to the concept.

Parents can encourage Level 3 collaboration at home too by inviting their children to join them in projects. Time to stack the firewood! Let's all do it together. Unpacking the groceries? Why spare kids the trouble when helping you is collaborating and implicitly teaching them about the importance of working together? In school, joint projects fit the bill. Creating a diorama together to capture a scene in the book we read—that's a fun and collaborative project.

True collaboration—Level 4—is essential for fueling change and growth. But at least in Level 3, people go back and forth toward a common goal. As Casey Stengel, legendary former manager of the Brooklyn Dodgers said, "Gettin' good players is easy. Gettin' 'em to play together is the hard part."[25]

LEVEL 4: BUILDING IT TOGETHER

Hewlett and Packard. Lerner and Loewe. Watson and Crick. Abbott and Costello. Masters and Johnson. What do these pairs of names have in common? These super successful collaborations left their mark on the world and made them household names. Obviously, not all collaborations reach this level. Not everyone has to be a star. Moe and Molly's local luncheonette can be born of a great collaboration too. Yet Lerner and Loewe or Masters and Johnson are unlikely to have had the impact they had working alone.

Whether the area is musical theatre, the biology of sex, or good food and service, there are some universal characteristics that underlie these collaborations: First, these pairs all had a clear goal: bringing new office products to market, writing successful Broadway

75

shows, uncovering the structure of DNA, making the world laugh, or discovering how sex really worked. There has to be a shared passion about the importance of the goal and wanting to reach it—almost at all costs. Second, trust between the collaborators is necessary. In real collaborations, partners can disagree and dispute vehemently. Often, great joint ideas are born in their debates. After he won the Nobel Prize with Watson for discovering the structure of DNA, Crick said, "Politeness is the poison of all good collaboration in science."[26]

Finally, the input of each member must be valued and there must be a sense of joint responsibility for the product that emerges. This also involves having respect for one another and the self-control to let each person speak his or her mind. Unless Nancy believes that she was part of the process and contributed to the outcome, she won't feel any ownership in the product. Without these elements, collaborations dissolve. The pairs listed earlier collaborated for years. The authors of this book have been collaborating for over 35 years. It's kind of like being married!

How did all these collaborations develop? Like most skills we prize, they have their origins in childhood. Remember Dan and Cynthia? At Level 4, we see what Parten called *collaborative play.*[27] They plan together, define rules, and assign roles to each other. "Let's build Queen Elsa's castle," Cynthia says enthusiastically, after having seen the Disney movie *Frozen.* "OK," Dan says, "but then we have to build a big wall to keep the invaders out." Cynthia: "I'll be Queen Elsa; you be the Olaf the snowman." Dan agrees—although reluctantly—and thinks about the weird motions he can try with his body to capture snowman Olaf's elasticity.

Some schools rise to Level 4 collaboration. Enter a room filled with paper airplanes hanging at all heights. Then walk down the hall to the classroom-sized model of Amelia Earhart's plane or to the communications center that transmits Morse code messages to budding pilots and navigators in the far-off dining hall. Sounds impossible. This is the reality at the Friends' Central School in the suburbs of Philadelphia, where teachers collectively choose and teach school-wide themes each year. Science classes explore what *thermo-dynamic* means, and children in art class work intently over draw-ings of what the world would look like if people could fly like birds. This project-based learning (we wish we'd had more of it ourselves) is a collaborative nirvana for learning. Children work for a long time together in a serious way on a specific authentic topic, asking ques-tions that push their joint inquiry along. Authentic problems are real problems—like the Wright brothers' struggle to achieve flight.

Level 4 collaboration can be found in the most amazing places. Five people get up on a stage with no script. Welcome to improv! Mary, a petite blonde, bellows to the audience, "Who are we?" And a guy in a red shirt hollers, "Construction workers!" The group is off! According to Malcolm Gladwell, author of *Blink!*, there is only one inviolable rule in improv: "*Never* say no."[28] "Never say no" means building on whatever comes out of the mouth of your fellow actors. John says, "I am trying not to tear my pantyhose on these PVC pipes." Mary can't say, "That makes no sense!" Instead, Mary builds on his statement: "Try laying concrete in spike heels!" This is why Level 4 is "building it together"—improv actors share the overarching grand plan of working together to create a great performance.

Improv works best when people know each other well. If work-ing with colleagues for a long time on the same problem sounds a lot like what you might do in industry or in a science lab, you're right on! This is exactly how new ideas are born and evaluated. In the best Level 4 style, communities (in business, in science, in engineering, and many others) solve problems together. Organizations that col-laborate at Level 4 rarely have management offer solutions from the top down; instead, solutions percolate from the bottom up as groups work together to find answers.

One of the best examples of collaboration comes from open source programming and from something we use almost every day: Wikipedia. Wikipedia exemplifies *building it together*: "As of June 2012, Wikipedia includes over 22 million freely usable articles in 284 languages, written by over 34 million registered users and countless anonymous contributors worldwide"[29] With that many people collaborating on one product, it is not surprising that Wikipedia is often our destination to find the answer to just about anything.

We learned on Wikipedia (where else!) that it was launched on January 15, 2001. Don Tapscott and Anthony Williams wrote a book inspired by Wikipedia called *Wikinomics: How Mass Collaboration Changes Everything*.[30] This is the new reality that Tapscott talked about with Tom Peters, another business maven.[31] Tapscott said that Wikipedia inspires *radical collaboration*. He talked about how his neighbor, now a billionaire named Rod McEwen, created another example of radical collaboration. McEwen literally owned a gold mine and wanted to mine the gold. But when his geologists checked out the property they couldn't say whether it still had gold or how much there was. McEwen then went public: He published his geological data on the web and created a contest. The winner would get half a million dollars if he or she could tell McEwen whether his property had gold. Tapscott said *no one* in the mining biz ever publishes their geological data—it's their intellectual property. But McEwen saw the potential of the Internet and broke the rules to create a collaboration with anyone in the world to find his gold. And gold he found. The market value of his company increased from $90 million to $10 billion.

The collaborative oomph behind Wikipedia inspires people to leave their comfort zone and invite the world in to solve a problem. Tapscott also told the story of Procter and Gamble (P&G) and Lafley, its CEO. Seven thousand researchers inside P&G were not enough to keep the innovation engine going, so Lafley appealed to the "ideagora"—*agora* being the Greek word for marketplace. When P&G needed a molecule to wash away a red wine stain, it asked the world of chemists in the ether to find the answer. It worked. In fact, Lafley said "connect and develop" is P&G's slogan, and "PFE" or "proudly found elsewhere" shows how valued this strategy is. Concepts from the ideagora have no stigma attached to them; in fact, companies that use this strategy lead the field, as the IBM study mentioned in Chapter 1 showed.[32]

This is, of course, exactly what Peter Drucker predicted. With knowledge abounding, Drucker looked into his crystal ball and saw that key to future business success was collaboration *outside* the company and with those who in a past life would have been called *competitors*. Take Dell computer. Liz Edersheim, Drucker's anointed biographer, said that Dell is "a pioneer of collaboration."[33] Dell became known for helping customers put together their own computers by using the components built by other companies. This turned into gold as Dell began working closely with huge companies like Boeing to plan for their network needs. Drucker told Edersheim that we now live in a "LEGO world." Companies are working across geographical and business boundaries to join their people LEGO, product LEGO, and idea LEGO and then pull them apart and reassemble them into a new Lego structure to start all over again.

Bringing folks together to work on a common goal is just what Lisa Guernsey had in mind by pulling the digital media community together in two conferences. Guernsey began to move the field from Level 2 to Level 4 collaboration. Competitors sat together to think about the future of the app universe and to learn about possibilities and what might become industry standards. There was also talk of building a new platform to develop and review educational programming. This move toward a collaborative stance does not rob the free marketplace, bind individual scholars or businesses, or discourage creativity. Instead, it harnesses the talents of all of these groups. As PBS, *Sesame Street*, and others proceed, they do so in a culture of innovation that will benefit all.

How can parents support their children's development of Level 4 collaboration? Parents can look at their kids' schools to see if joint projects are encouraged or if kids are always working alone (desks in rows or in circles?). If collaboration is encouraged, it means that kids understand there is a common goal and can explain it to you when you ask and that the input of each group member is valued. After-school programs should be encouraging collaboration too because kids are often starved for interacting with their peers by the time they arrive at aftercare.

Collaboration is a team sport. Just as we cannot win the football game if we always run and never pass, we cannot become successful in the global economy if we do not learn to build things together and see things from other perspectives. Once we've established that we can work together, we do so by setting up strong lines of communication that allow us to build a common vocabulary and hear one another's narratives.

TAKING ACTION

How do you know collaboration when you see it?

In Yourself

All of us could be better collaborators. Take a look at the levels and ask, Where do I fall and how might I move up the proverbial ladder of collaboration? Am I one of those drivers who rushes through the yellow without letting that car on the left into my lane? Did I ever make a decision about a vacation plan when I know my partner should have been consulted? In tennis matches, in basketball games and in life, many of us go for the shot rather than letting our partners get the glory. Even in team sports there are those who always have to be the MVP.

Our children are watching us. We are their models. If we take a moment to reflect on our own actions, we can change the little behaviors—we can let the lady with the heavy packages go through the door first—and we can become just a little more collaborative with others. We can even give our children more voice in the process. Do you really care if she is wearing stripes with plaid if you allowed her to pick the outfit for herself?

In Your Child

Sharing is hard. Children's lack of self-control often gets in the way. After all, it's tough to get off that swing when you are having such a good time. How do we help them see that playing with others is even more fun? How do we nurture sharing and taking turns? We can start by taking turns with them—rolling a ball back and forth, taking turns in that board game, and playing catch. No one wants to play catch alone! And if we showed our children how to do it, they could see the benefits of sharing and taking turns with their friends. The Brio train layout you design with friends is always a little more complex and intricate than the one you design by yourself.

The first step toward creating more sophisticated collaboration is by identifying opportunities for turn taking and sharing. Then by scaffolding our child's behavior ("It would be so nice to let Alvin have the next turn") and reflecting on what they did, we reward positive social behavior: "Wow, you were such a good sharer. Thanks for letting Alvin put that piece in the puzzle." There are an infinite number of teachable moments that present themselves for encouraging children to work with others rather than going it alone.

In the Places You Go

We are often asked how to know which schools are the best for helping a child to succeed. Because collaboration can be nurtured, there are some things to look for when you peek inside a school. Find out if each child is glued to his desk and only allowed to move freely with a hall pass. Are the children constructing things together and is their collaborative work prominently displayed? Is there a block corner? Is there a dress up corner where multiple children can convene to engage in pretend play? For older kids, ask if there are projects they do together or if everything is solo. If these elements are present in the school, it might well be a place that encourages collaboration. If not, and your child must go there, there are lots of ways that your family can encourage collaboration.

How about afterschool activities? The best afterschool activities are organized and planful, but they also allow—in fact, foster—collaboration. Team sports might fall into this category. We say "might" because in recent years some team sports have suffered from overzealous coaching as if "winning at all cost" was all that mattered. Take soccer. Is the coach encouraging kids to work together or are they just clumping together as in the soccer games described earlier? Once kids can understand the position names in organized sports, they have to learn to use even finer self-control to fulfill their roles. Defenders on the soccer field are supposed to stop the potential goals coming in from the opposing team. The forward shoots the goals. Knowing your assignments helps the team succeed.

How about drama class? Long a staple for encouraging kids to literally get into another's shoes, drama fosters collaboration because kids have to talk to each other and work together when putting on plays. How about ballet class or music class? Any place where kids are performing together encourages collaboration. This occurs in service projects: Some schools require kids to figure out how to do service for their community. This helps them realize they need to collaborate on a larger scale and that they too have an important place in the world.

How Do We Create Environments That Foster Collaboration?

Once you know about the arc of development, you can design environments and contexts that spark collaboration. One example comes from a children's museum that had a bucket hanging from a large crane. To pick up anything in the bucket, you needed to have one person putting things in the bucket and one operating the crane. Even though the kids did not know one another, they formed a team so that they could move the gray (light weight) boulders from place to place in the bucket. Collaboration was built into the activity.

In our college classes, we foster collaboration by writing group activities into the syllabus. Our students have to do group-based presentations of primary research and they are encouraged to even study in groups to prepare for the exams. Why? You learn more this way than when you go it alone. You produce a better product.

Now none of this precludes us from having downtime or from being independent. It just means that just as we seek moments to grow rugged individualism, we must also seek moments to grow our social skills. We often believe that we should focus on the content, the learning of facts, and that the social stuff will take care of itself. However, these "soft skills" take practice, too, and there are plenty of opportunities to move our children from being the independent soul to one who also embraces the chance to build something as a part of a team.

THE ROAD TO SUCCESS

Collaboration is critical to many of the outcomes we want for our kids. Happiness requires friendships and self-control. Research has suggested that people who feel like they belong and have social companions are healthier and more fulfilled individuals. Cognitive skills also need collaboration so that the weaknesses I have are balanced out by the strengths you have. This is why collaborations often—though not always—yield better outcomes than working solo. And finally, being part of a community fuels what we as individuals do best: thinking about how our place in the world makes a difference for others.

CHAPTER 6

COMMUNICATION:
LINES OF CONNECTION

The single biggest problem in communication is the illusion that it has taken place.

—George Bernard Shaw,
cited in Marlene Caroselli,
Leadership Skills for Managers

There has been a seismic shift in the education our children need if they are to ride the information highway. Moving from the age of technology to the age of information parallels historic shifts that we have seen before, when society leaped from an oral system to one influenced by Gutenberg's printing press. The change mirrors that which our great-grandparents witnessed in the industrial revolution of the late 1800s. In the 20th century, the world began to get smaller. Trains and planes connected people across oceans and allowed goods to move freely from coast to coast. Now, in the 21st century, the world is the size of a walnut.

Communication now routinely takes place across geographic boundaries. It is the grease that allows the new paradigm of international commerce to advance. When business leaders cry out for workers with better communication skills, they focus on two primary areas: speaking and writing. Employers assume all workers can use a computer, but can those workers communicate what they have found there? Speaking and writing are becoming lost arts. On receiving the "Family of Man" Award in 1964, Edward R. Murrow said, "The newest computer can merely compound, at speed, the oldest problem in the relations between human beings, and in the end the communicator will be confronted with the old problem, of what to say and how to say it."[1]

As Joseph Priestley (1733–1804), the person credited with the discovery of oxygen, once said, "The more elaborate our means of communication, the less we communicate."[2] If only Priestly had been around to see Facebook, Tumblr, and Twitter! Humans are hungry for communication and connection. We keep inventing new ways to communicate. Many of us can't refrain from talking on our cell phones when we drive, even though we know that even "hands-free" cell phone usage isn't safe when driving. Clifford Nass, a sociology professor at Stanford University who studies electronic distraction, wrote that when we drive we are typically alone. This is tough on fundamentally social animals. "The ring of a phone or the ping of a text becomes a promise of human connection, which is like catnip to humans."[3]

Talk about catnip! Ninety-five percent of people between the ages of 18 and 24 sent or received an average of 109.5 text messages a day in 2011, according to the Pew Research Center's Internet and American Life Project.[4] Texting is great for sharing quick bits of information ("Running 10 minutes late" and "Forgot socks!"), and we use it all the time.

Communication is irresistible. It undoubtedly contributed to our evolutionary survival. But remember the woman who took a face-first flop into a fountain while texting? Accidents like this are happening to adults more and more frequently and to children on the playground as their parents engage with their communication devices.[5] Communication has overpowering appeal. The cruelest way to punish human beings is to put them into isolation—for children, we call this a *time-out.*

Effective communication is the fuel that propels collaboration. Paradoxically, at the same time, communication is built squarely on the foundation of collaboration because without someone to tell your stories to, there'd be no need to communicate. Stories abound that speak to the importance of communication—even above and beyond mere collaboration. Take the story (and delicious alliteration in the headline) reported in Lisa Grossman's *Wired* column "Metric Math Mistake Muffed Mars Meteorology Mission." On September 23, 1999, the celebrated Mars Climate Orbiter was supposed to slip into a stable orbit around Mars when it vanished. Rather than traveling around the planet as planned, the Orbiter went too low, entered the top of the Martian atmosphere, and burned up. Why? The scientists who were responsible for this high-tech mission had a major communication snafu. The team from NASA used metric measurements, but the Orbiter was programmed to take imperial units—feet and inches. The result: the loss of a satellite—a $125 million disaster!

Communication involves speaking so others can understand your message, writing clearly and well so others will comprehend what you have written, and truly listening. Success in communication at work is just part of what our children need. To be successful and happy in their interpersonal relationships, they have to talk to others in a respectful way. Name calling? Unacceptable. Sharing feelings in a genuine way? Absolutely.

In a global economy, we need these skills to collaborate, share information, and persuade others. This is true in any domain in our culture, in science, government, medicine, and the world of sports and entertainment. Zac Bissonnette, a business writer, facetiously titled one of his columns "Looking for a Job? Study Shakespeare."[6] Because employers lust after employees with good communication skills, Bissonnette suggested that college students take courses in "advanced composition" that require lots of writing. A course in public speaking could be most helpful because it teaches how to overcome your fears. Renee feels like she shrivels up when she has to speak to only 10 people around the conference table—not even a crowd. But being able to persuade her peers about the importance of doing pro bono work for an orphanage is too significant for her to gulp and swallow. Renee has to "find her voice" to share her good ideas. The public speaking course she picked up at her local university made all the difference for her. Now she can put in her two cents without ruining her suits' underarms. Renee is not the first to face down her speaking fear. In 1936, Dale Carnegie wrote *How to Win Friends and Influence People*, still a popular book in business communication.[7] According to Wikipedia, more than 8 million people have taken the Dale Carnegie courses.[8]

Communication no longer takes place only face-to-face or on the telephone. International boundaries are forded billions of times a day in cyberspace. Some of the blunders that American companies have made would be hilarious if they weren't so costly. According to the website Kwintessential, a company once printed the OK finger sign on each page of its spanking new expensive catalog distributed in Latin America. But because the OK finger sign is considered an obscene gesture in many Latin American countries, all the catalogs had to be reprinted.[9] In another communication blunder—again in Latin America—a new cooking oil was called something that meant "Jackass Oil" in Spanish. The company managers were shocked and appalled; imagine how many bottles would have to be recalled and relabeled.[10] Living in a global world means business as usual can be dangerous. Unless companies take the perspective of the country they are working in, they are likely to make gaffes such as showing a dog with a manly man in a cologne advertisement in Muslim countries, where dogs are considered unclean.

Being a good communicator, listener, or writer doesn't just happen. The 1940s comics Abbott and Costello were experts at conversations that went in circles. In their famous routine, "Who's on First?" they epitomize communications that fail. Speaking, listening, writing, and arguing persuasively are skills that have to be learned—in school, at home, and everywhere else families go. These abilities are honed in a predictable way through a sequence of levels. As with the other Cs, it all begins in the crib and gets revisited throughout the lifespan. And what babies do in the crib serves as the foundation for reaching higher levels.

LEVEL 1: RAW EMOTION

Crying. It is one of the first things new parents like Liz and Jordan notice. Their newborn baby Lulu cries . . . and cries . . . and cries. Crying gets attention; nature designed it well. Lulu's crying face screams, "LOOK AT ME!": her mouth is open wide, her eyes squeezed shut, and her tension is palpable as she shakes and stiffens. Lulu's parents would have to be brain-dead not to respond. Indeed, science has uncovered that this kind of communication is very effective. When Lulu cries, Liz and Jordan experience uncomfortable physiological changes such as increases in blood pressure and heart rate.[11]

The learning industry is right there to capitalize on parents' discomfort with their infants' crying. Some believe that there is sophisticated communication behind those gurgles and cries. Priscilla Dunstan has claimed that babies make five types of cries: "Neh!" means hungry, "eh" means "burp me!" "owh" means "I'm tired," "eairh" means "lower gas," and "heh" means "I'm uncomfortable!"[12] And because she appeared on Oprah, the learning industry is now offering the Dunstan Baby Language System. Lulu's parents are tempted. For only $39.95, they too can decipher Lulu's "language." But not so fast: Learning scientists tested the idea that people could distinguish between the meaning behind different kinds of cries and came up empty. We can tell something about the level of distress in a cry but not whether it means "poopy diaper" (a version of Dunstan's "I'm uncomfortable") or "feed me" (Dunstan's "neh!").

So why aren't we still crying? Over the course of the first year, the more Lulu is picked up and comforted, the less she will cry. Little by little, babies like Lulu become better communicators, expressing their emotions and desires in more sophisticated ways. Getting out of control, with ragged hiccup breaths, and crying so much that you can't stop is not an efficient means of telling folks what you want. Babies like Lulu who are comforted and learn to comfort themselves soon communicate in more mature ways. By about 12 months, before she can utter a single word, Lulu will communicate using what we call the *royal point*. In response to the little pointing finger, Lulu's parents rush to the fridge to retrieve the applesauce. Grunting and pointing get desired results faster than a primal scream.

When Lulu's parents rush to the fridge they are responding *contingently* to her nonverbal request, acting immediately after her point and trying to understand her meaning. Our research has shown that responding contingently in this way is the best way to help babies expand their ability to communicate.[13] We found that babies learn words better from people than from television; this by itself is a well-known finding. But we also found that it didn't matter whether the human teaching the word was sitting right next to the baby or on Skype. It turns out that those conversations with grandparents really work! When baby Ellie says, "Bimis," pointing to her pajamas, and Grandma Ann says, "Oh, you are wearing pajamas!" Ann is helping Ellie hear the sounds in *pajamas* pronounced correctly. Contingent communicative episodes build communication into the next level and beyond. What we as adults do rests on this foundation: When John talks about London and Cathy talks about the theater there, John knows that Cathy has heard him.

In school classrooms, children who are Level 1 communicators are often in trouble. These are the children who lack self-control, the children who lash out when angry and grab something when they want it. Not surprisingly, these children rarely become teachers' pets. There are tons of programs to train kids' communication and social skills. One of the first was *I Can Problem Solve*, created by Myrna

Shure, a professor at Drexel University in Philadelphia.[14] It has been used in schools to prevent violence and has won awards. Mark Greenberg, a professor at Pennsylvania State University, created another program called the PATHS Curriculum—Promoting Alternative Thinking Strategies.[15] His program, like Shure's, is based on science—not to mention common sense: Learning to express anger verbally is way more effective than slamming the kid who got to the swing first.

Level 1 communication yields to Level 2 when, after being told that she can't have another cupcake, Emerson says, "I am very angry" and stamps her foot, rather than taking sister Amy's cupcake or rolling on the floor screaming. Emerson's mom and dad have helped her come this far in managing her emotions by coaching her to direct her thoughts elsewhere ("Oh, but didn't you have a big ice cream cone at lunch?") or telling her to "use her words" when she was angry in the past. These warm and responsive interactions pave the way for better communication.

In their 2012 Job Outlook Survey, the National Association of Colleges and Employers found out how intertwined communication and collaboration skills are. The skill ranked highest on their survey is "ability to work in a team structure."[16] But collaboration can't occur without good communication. "Ability to verbally communicate with persons inside and outside the organization" is the second most important skill employers mention. Collaboration depends on it.

Sometimes communication entails writing too. The 2011 National Assessment of Educational Progress (NAEP) Writing Framework tells us, "Writing is a complex, multi-faceted, and purposeful act of communication."[17] Edmund was asked to take minutes at an important meeting. He forgets that he is writing for others who could not be present. No one who reads his minutes can understand what happened. Egocentric writing is like talking to oneself. Fully 21% of 12th graders in the United States do not reach this "basic" level of writing proficiency.

Even the captains of industry can return to Level 1 communication under stress. Meg Whitman, CEO of eBay is alleged to have verbally chewed out an employee and to have shoved her in the process.[18] It took a six-figure settlement to set that gaffe right. Going "roller derby" on an employee makes no sense. Although many work situations are high pressure, letting loose with an emotional tirade can, at worst, mean a pink slip. At best, it will take a long time to recover in the eyes of peers and supervisors.

Another amazing example of Level 1 communication in industry comes from eHow Money.[19] In 2001, at an unnamed medical software company, the CEO also lost his cool. By e-mail, he berated the entire staff for coming in late and leaving early. He even threatened revenge by taking away their benefits. In our tiny, interconnected world this kind of Level 1 communication can have wide consequences. One of the many recipients of this extravagantly furious e-mail gave the CEO a figurative punch by posting the e-mail on the Internet. The company sustained a massive drop in its stock price.

Good communication is about more than staying cool and expressing emotions in acceptable ways. Business leaders are desperate for workers with better communication skills, primarily speaking and writing. Our high school and college graduates may be able to do technical work on a computer, but can they communicate what they have found? Speaking and writing are becoming lost arts.

Listening skills matter just as much as good speaking and writing. We can be bad listeners because of our unconscious reactions. Sometimes gestures and facial expressions speak louder than words. Gary, a dean at a major university, would listen to a visiting scholar present his or her research and make faces that looked like Peewee Herman on steroids. Friendly colleagues had to tell him he was doing that. He was oblivious to the fact that his feelings were all over his face. Clearly, as with the engineers at NASA and the Mars

Orbiter, experience, age, and advanced degrees do not guarantee that an individual's communication has exceeded Level 1.

Finally, Level 1 characterizes people who are "hard of listening" (but not necessarily "hard of hearing"). Despite being a society for whom blogging, texting, and tweeting is irresistible, paradoxically we find that really listening is becoming harder and harder. Some of this is because people have difficulty putting away their devices. Laura's friends know that they will practically have to wrest her phone from her hands to have a conversation with her.

To borrow the title of a recent book, we are often "driven to distraction."[20] Sometimes the distraction comes at a terrible cost. A collision between a passenger train and a Union Pacific freight train in 2008 in California claimed the lives of 25 people. The train's engineer was texting and passed an absolute stop signal, moving right into the path of an oncoming freight train. Texting and cell phones make it harder for us to focus and to listen when our conversations take place in real time. Level 1 communication results.

We are truly driven to distraction. Ruth was sitting at the kitchen table with her husband Blair and their two twenty-something kids. Each person was on his or her own electronic device. Her son reflected, "Boy it must be hard to be a kid today—no one talks to you." Level 1 communication is like this: Everyone is on his or her own program. It's kind of like parallel play. Communication must get better than Level 1, which is analogous to posting what you had for breakfast on Facebook or just venting your emotions. At Level 2, at least the emotional element is more under control.

LEVEL 2: SHOW AND TELL

Pulp Fiction was the 1994 film in which Uma Thurman asked John Travolta, "Do you listen? Or do you wait to talk?" Travolta replied, "I wait to talk, but I'm trying to listen."[21] Level 2! It's just like when the teacher says, "Diana, it's your turn to show and tell. What did you bring to share with us today?" and little Diana, who has been sitting in her seat just waiting to bolt up and share her treasure (a wooden Chinese puzzle box that opens by a series of intricate moves), has barely been listening at all as Irving, Alejandro, and Schmuel have done their spiels. She can't wait to tell, and tell she does! Show-and-tell is really all about the show-er, not about the people watching and listening. It's better than Level 1 because at least Diana recognizes that there are others in the room. But she doesn't really care whether they are listening or whether they respond. She's just happy to talk! Don't we all know people like this who passed through first grade many moons ago? Social media is the new show-and-tell. There are approximately 845 million users of Facebook alone, not to mention Instagram, Pinterest, Twitter, and all the other sharing sites. They log on daily (guilty as charged). Little dialogue takes place on these sites; it's all about sharing pictures, events, and achievements.

Level 2 corresponds to the book reports we wrote when we were kids. Remember those? Philip writes one on the Harry Potter book. He has drawn a picture of Harry on the front cover. Then comes the meat of the project. But all Philip has provided is a recitation of events, without taking the reader's knowledge into consideration. First, Harry was a boy who lived with muggles. Then Harry gets a lot of mail telling him to go to Hogwart's school, and so on. Philip never explains that muggles are nonmagic people and that, unlike them, Harry is a wizard. Maybe Philip assumed that his audience had already read the book, but more likely, all Philip did was a brain dump with no evaluation (other than the obligatory, "I liked the book"). In college writing, this translates to papers that read like a laundry list—one point after the other, in no particular order, and with little synthesis. Sometimes these papers don't have a thesis and take the reader on "road trips" away from what should be the main point of the paper. The ability to write an A-level paper takes more than a regurgitation of the facts; it takes integration. In other words, how does the information fit together to tell a "story?"

Learning how to listen, how to work with others productively, and how to take a listener's or reader's perspective are among the most important things our children (and we as adults) need to know. There is even a well-known preschool curriculum that helps children cultivate these skills. "Tools of the mind," developed by psychologists Elena Bodrova and Deborah Leong, teaches kids who aren't lucky enough to get "listening lessons" at home.[22] Kids "read" to each other from storybooks using the pictures to tell their favorite tale. When it's Jonathan's turn to "read" he puts a drawing of a mouth on the table in front of him. Laurie holds a picture of an ear to remind her that she is not the speaker but the listener. Then it's Laurie's turn and they trade parts while Laurie selects her favorite storybook. Tools of the Mind, and other programs like it, overall are shown to be effective. Success in the Tools program does more than advance listening skills; it builds self-control and helps kids do better in reading and math.[23]

Because of the way teachers are pressed to drill children for tests, many classrooms in America function at Level 2—with the teacher doing the show-and-tell and the kids listening. As Jacqueline and Martin Brooks argue in their book, *Constructivist Classrooms*, the American classroom revolves around teacher talk instead of child activity.[24,25] One might call it the "font-of-wisdom" model. Teachers tell and expect children to repeat what they have "learned." A flow-chart of classroom communication would show most of the arrows pointing away from the teacher; few would point from the children to the teacher or between children. But why is this bad? After all, many of us went to schools like this.

School does not have to be show-and-tell. Kelly Fisher, who finished her PhD at Temple University, wanted to know the best way to communicate with 4-year-olds about what makes a triangle a triangle.[26] Would children learn the "secret of triangles" if she just told them or if she asked them to discover this information with her? Bethany at 4 is a chatty child and loves the individual attention Kelly gives her when they sit together. Kelly tells Bethany to pretend they are detectives and they even wear detective hats. Their job is to discover the secrets of the triangle (or whatever shape was the focus). What is it that makes a triangle a triangle? Kelly nudges Bethany to notice that triangles have sides and hints that maybe that's the secret. Bethany counts the sides, declaring, "Yup! Three sides!" Such satisfaction!

But the game differs for Bethany's friend Jennifer. Jennifer and Kelly are still detectives and still wear their hats, but Kelly discovers the secret ("Oh! It has three sides and three corners!") while Jennifer just passively watches her excitedly count angles and sides. Jennifer is in the "just-tell-'em" ("didactic teaching") group. In Bethany's "guided play" group, the *kids* count the sides and corners and then *they* discover the secret together.

But why play this game with kids at all? They know so much less than we do. Why not just tell them the properties of triangles? Telling seems so much more efficient and direct. Here's what happened. Bethany's guided playgroup learned much more than the just-tell-'em group Jennifer was in. At the test at the end, only those kids who had been in the guided playgroup knew that weird fat triangles or tall skinny triangles were triangles. The didactic just-tell-'em group who sat and watched Kelly discover the triangle's secret never fully understood what makes a triangle a triangle. Sometimes just-tell-'em backfires.

But could kids figure out what makes a triangle a triangle on their own? Peter is in the free play group, and he is given sticks to make up the shapes. It turns out that without any support from adults, children don't learn about shapes at all. Teachers have to scaffold their students' learning by inviting them to participate and not just telling them the information.

Learning in a passive Level 2 way may allow kids to pass the tests, but that's about all. Present them with an unusual triangle and they fall right off the rails. Although many of our schools use "scripted learning," keeping teachers from asking kids questions and following up, parents can ask kids questions at home and invite discussion. One of us played a game with our kids called Make an Argument: Tell your siblings and me which movie you want to see and why and defend your answer. Now although this sounds pedestrian, it really helped the kids learn to say what they wanted in respectful ways and to think creatively.

Ever hear of the flipped classroom?[27] It is based on the discovery that active learning is much more effective in high school and college than sitting in class and listening to lectures. In the flipped classroom, students listen to lectures at home and do what used to be homework problems together in class. Rather than enforcing student passivity as in the "font-of-wisdom" model, everyone gets to talk in class and operate on the material. This puts the responsibility for learning squarely on the shoulders of the students. It changes a passive sit-and-listen environment to a creative and dynamic class in which student participation is the norm and not the exception. But flipped classrooms aren't limited to high school and college. Ms. Treacher wanted to offer her second graders a flipped classroom experience in social studies. She asked parents to watch a video at home with their kids about maps that introduced the vocabulary they needed—words like *north*, *south*, and *map key*. The next day, in teams of three, children made a map of the neighborhood right around their school. The class had a blast using all their new vocabulary words and communicating nonstop. Which kind of classroom would you rather be in: traditional or flipped?

Level 2 happens a surprising amount of time in the world of business and nonprofit organizations. Kind of like parallel play, meetings with Level 2 communication turn the conference room back into the sandbox. Picture Roberta and Kathy at a nominating committee meeting of a nonprofit board. We were there to help select the next president. As the conversation progressed, we discovered that the "powers that be" had already decided on the next president. Why were we there? Poor communication.

Level 2 listening and speaking is a huge advance over Level 1 but doesn't mean there is true understanding. Tawnya Brown went into the hospital in 2003 to have surgery: 18 inches of her colon was to be removed. Although she was only 31, she never made it home. She was given 6 pints of the wrong blood type. How could that have happened? According to the Joint Commission Guide to Improving Staff Communication, if medical errors were on the list of major causes of death in this country, they would log in at Number 5, ahead of accidents, diabetes, and Alzheimer's disease.[28] Medical errors like the one Ms. Brown experienced occurred in 66% of the events that caused patients' death or injury between 1995 and 2004. Errors in communication—between highly educated, articulate, and accomplished people—were responsible for mistakes such as giving the wrong medication and performing wrong-site surgeries. From failures at airport landings to industrial disasters like the 1984 gas leak in Bhopal, India, that killed over 25,000 people, to medical error, life is too short to settle for Level 2 communication.

When we are Level 2 listeners, as management guru Peter Drucker noted, "We hear largely what we expect to hear. The unexpected is usually not received at all."[29] Other business leaders have also commented on the importance of *really* listening. Peter Nulty, a member of the board of editors of *Fortune Magazine*, believes that listening is the most valuable skill leaders have and that it distinguishes the great leaders from the run-of-the-mill ones.[30] People in positions of authority—be it in business, academia, or nonprofit organizations—have to take the other's perspective to communicate effectively and rise above Level 2. Otherwise, they are just communicating in show-and-tell to further their own agenda.

Growing up, one of us had an expression we used when family members engaged in Level 2 listening: "It'll be a nice day tomorrow if it doesn't rain." We used this absurdly obvious statement to jolt people out of Level 2: "Wake up! You're not listening!" Electronic screens are likely increasing Level 2 listening.

LEVEL 3: DIALOGUE

"Every time we open our mouths to speak, we are taking a leap of faith—faith that what we want to say will be understood more or less by our listeners as we mean it" (p. 242).[31] In her book, *Talking From 9 to 5: Men and Women at Work*, Deborah Tannen offered many examples of conversations gone awry between men and women. But you don't have to look to inter-gender communication for snafus; plenty of them are made by folks of the same gender! Still, in Level 3, real communication is taking place—the "back and forth" of conversation, which Professor Jack Shonkoff called the "serve and return."[32]

Elliott hits the ball and John runs to where Elliott's ball will land to hit it back. Then Elliott has to anticipate where John will hit his next ball. He runs there to prepare to return it. The players are *responsive* to their opponent's behavior, and a Level 3 conversation works the same way. We produce a nugget to share and—taking a leap of faith—hope that our listener will hear what we have offered, build on it, and send it back to us with some new information added. Then we respond back.

We took Professor Shonkoff's lead, and as researchers who study language development, wondered just how important that serve and return really is for learning to talk. Research on how moms communicate with their 2-year-olds tells the tale. Our team found that the more back-and-forth, serve-and-return kind of talk between moms and kids, the better children's own language is 1 year later.[33] What we call *conversational duets* are crucial for learning to communicate; one just can't do good communication alone.

On YouTube we found a wonderful Level 3 conversation between kids barely out of diapers.[34] This is their first time conducting an independent phone call—as the proud papa tells us. The children were videotaped in their respective homes, so we see both sides of the conversation with cuts back and forth to each child. The weighty topic under discussion is a rendezvous at the park. The opening bid is an invitation by Mahri to Judah to meet at the park. They do remarkably well staying on topic and even in discussing whether the big or the little park was the one they meant. They also discuss whether they should walk or take the car. They slip out of Level 3 when they point for each other to the park out the window. Of course, because they are in different places, pointing out the window won't work. Where they fail—pointing out the window—offers us a chance to look at how good conversations work.

People who are good communicators take the perspective of their listener. Level 3 conversations require what psychologists call a *theory of mind*. Four-year-old Sarah sees a box of M&Ms in the kitchen. Excited, she opens the box only to discover that the box is filled with paper clips. Her mom chuckles and asks Sarah what her 6-year-old brother, Larry, will think when he sees the box. Mom is startled to hear Sarah say, "Paper clips." How could Larry see the closed box with M&Ms on the outside and think it contained paper clips? It is as if Sarah doesn't realize that Larry will be influenced the same way she was—by the way the box looks. After all, Larry doesn't have X-ray vision. But this "paper clips" answer implies that Sarah can't imagine that Larry might think differently than she does. Once she knows that paper clips are in the box, Larry must too! She's having a hard time reconciling that she can think one thing, but Larry can think something else. When kids no longer say "paper clips" but say "M&Ms," they have a theory of mind—just what they need to take the perspective of the listener.

Level 3 communication requires that, at a minimum, we take the mind-set (theory of mind) of our listener into account. Not surprisingly, children change the way they play with others when they become Level 3 communicators. Now they can go back and forth and actually exchange information—just like Mahri and Judah did, although perhaps with more advanced vocabulary and fancier sentences. Elio and Reed decide to play firemen, and Elio tells Reed, "I'll be the fire chief and you be the helper." Reed doesn't really like that, so he says, "OK, but then I get to be the fire chief." This is progress! They are now coming up with a joint plan (collaboration). When Elio agrees to let Reed be the chief, he is also showing that he can take the perspective of the other. He gets that Reed too wants the glory of chiefdom.

Not all children are equally good at taking the mind-set of another. Sometimes children use Internet communication as an excuse to say things that they would not say in person. When Jonna was playing Animal Jam, a National Geographic online game, things turned ugly. Her animal avatar, a leopard, announced that there would be free ice cream at the Leopard's Den in 10 minutes. Jonna sat back and watched as speech bubbles began to appear over other players' avatars: "Yippee! Ice cream!" One player, however, said, "Is it OK I eat your face?" As Jonna tried to process what that message might mean, another speech bubble appeared over the same player's wolf avatar: "U not pretty," followed in rapid succession by several other, now undeniably rude statements. Jonna took off her headphones and told her mother what the offending player had said to her. This led to a great conversation over dinner about how the offending player, cloaked in online anonymity, enjoyed getting away with mean talk. Mom and Jonna then went online together to figure out how to use the game's block and report system.

You might think that school really helps kids develop their ability to engage in Level 3, meaningful conversation, but you'd be wrong. Schools today are about filling children's heads with knowledge more than about encouraging conversation. Professor Gordon Wells, a prominent researcher at the University of California at Santa Cruz, reported that in conversations with adults at school, kids hardly talk.[35] Although this study is from 1998, the same is true today despite the fact that research in the learning sciences has found that kids learn more when they can contribute to the conversation.

A wonderful set of experiments by Frank Murray at the University of Delaware showed how important conversation between children can be.[36] These studies were based on what Piaget called *conservation*—recognizing that quantities don't change just because they look different. We all fought about this when we were kids—especially at snack time. Five-year-old twins Neil and Marissa were each given five M&Ms by their mom, Karen. Even though the children watched Karen count them out, the twins insisted that Neil had more because his landed in a *pile* whereas Marissa's were *spread out*. Karen was amazed that the kids didn't realize that how the M&Ms were laid out didn't matter in regard to how many there were. Murray's experiments paired kids together—like Neil and Marissa—who also got this problem wrong. He asked the kids to come up with joint answers to similar sorts of problems. When they were tested individually later, both children were able to solve the original conservation problems. What happened? An argument! And somehow having to justify their perspectives to each other made both kids advance in their understanding. In Level 3 we can learn from each other if we really hear what our conversational partner is saying. Level 3 listening is now a tool for learning.

Teachers and parents help their children achieve Level 3 when they prompt kids to step into the shoes of the other. 'How would you feel if Martin did that to you, Louisa?' makes a child think. Rather than just shutting down the offending behavior, teachers and parents are more likely to help kids get to Level 3 with this technique. Kids will be more sensitive to others over time as a result of answering questions like these. When we witness Larry innocently asking Philomena whether she had "put on some weight," we know that even adults can hone their Level 3 sensitivity.

What about writing? Learning scientists have found that a Level 3 paper goes beyond being a "laundry list." It does more than just describe a sequence of events; it goes beneath the surface investigating the motivation of the characters. In college, a Level 3 paper earns a *B* or *B*+ because the student tells a coherent "story," probing how the pieces fit together. At this level, the student can make an argument and even give an "elevator speech" about what the paper is about. The Level 2 writer just strings elements together without a clear thesis. According to the NAEP 2011 report, and parallel to Level 3, the writers in 12th grade can produce texts that are coherent and well-structured and that include logical connections at transition points. They also reveal a solid, although not impeccable, knowledge of the mechanics of writing (grammar, spelling, etc.).

LEVEL 4: TELL A JOINT STORY

Jason, Babette, and Paulina were playing make-believe—the focus: kings and queens. Hampton Court had nothing on these kids. Replete with crowns and coronets, robes and maces, they were bowing and curtsying and mostly taking turns speaking. The whole panoply was quite impressive. These kindergartners, at a private school in the southeast, were totally immersed in their play.

This is Level 4 communication, reflected in pretend play. It rises above Level 3—dialogue—not because of the costumes or the content but because the children are *building a story together.* Had we been a fly on the wall, we would have seen Jason excitedly telling Babette and Paulina that they should play kings and queens, telling them about a book his mommy read to him about kings and queens, and Babette saying they should play the story of the "The Princess and the Pea." Paulina didn't know that story but remembered from the celebration of the Jewish holiday Purim how Queen Esther was the hero. They agreed that Paulina would be queen and save the day. Jason would be king and Babette would be their baby. They would all help Paulina banish the (pretend) bad guys from the kingdom.

Cooperative play contains all the elements of successful communication. It reached a high level with this crowd who stayed in character for 45 minutes playing out their scenario and taking turns moving the plot forward (or back), all the while maintaining their king and queen theme. Looking at this make-believe scenario through a learning science lens, we can see deeper into what's really going on.

- Creative innovation is seen in the development of the story line the children build together.
- They rehearse the rules kings and queens live by. This is common in pretend play—kids practice for adulthood in this way.
- Content is being built too—Paulina and Babette use words such as *royal* and *evil,* which Jason hasn't heard. He gets the meaning from context just as they learn the word *immediately* from him.
- Staying in character builds confidence in their abilities (despite small setbacks as when "baby" Babette trips on a robe and falls).
- Staying in character a long time also builds their attention span.

This pretend play episode built through collaboration could not take place without communication. David Dickinson of Vanderbilt University found that the more kids engage in such pretend play sequences, the better their language is a year later.[37,38]

Listening at Level 4 involves really hearing the message being offered. Eugene O'Neill wrote *Strange Interlude*, a play in which the actors "break" the fourth wall by telling the audience what they really think. Mamie says, "I love you, Stanley," although in the next instant she tells the audience, "I'll settle for Stanley because Homer rejected me." (TV shows also do this, as in, for example, *House of Lies* and Kevin Spacey's character in *House of Cards*.) In real life, listening— real listening—means taking all you know about the speaker into account, using your theory of mind, and reading between the lines. This rises to Level 4.

At Level 4, communication through writing decreases the reader's need to guess the message. We crave Level 4 papers. These papers define their terms and lay out the issues they will treat. They use details and examples. They don't leave us wondering about what the paper was saying because it framed a coherent argument. At the college level, these papers earn the treasured *A*.

In the world of business, communication is radically changing. Take Google—a business founded on communication. Now a household word, its reach is legion, and we use it about 10 times a day to find, for example, the name of that restaurant on 4th Street, the definition of words such as *ambergris*, and sources in writing this book. Google is a model of the way corporations in future will work. In 2010, Google was nominated as the world's most attractive employer for newly minted students. Why is Google so popular? Google has a progressive style of in-house communication. The culture created at Google feeds into Level 4 communication in a whole new way. Encouraging internal blogging, for example, enables employees "to actively contribute to the operation of the organization—to express their opinions, ask questions and move the business forward, all the while helping to create and evolve their corporate culture."[39] As Eric Schmidt, Google's CEO wrote, "This allows management to stay in touch with what our knowledge workers are thinking and vice versa."[40] Without Level 4 communication and unbridled collaboration, the creative innovation Google needs to move ahead would be stifled. Business blogs now refer to the "Google effect" as other companies seek to emulate this style.

Sophisticated and streamlined communication abilities also catapulted Wal-Mart onto the international business stage. Wal-Mart uses what is called *just-in-time economy*, which eliminates the need to store inventory.[41] When a product is needed in a California store, the communication lines ring at the manufacturing plants in Asia that immediately make enough to restock that product. Hyper-efficient supply chains reduce storage and eliminate tying up capital in products that are not yet needed. Wal-Mart and many other companies find that clear and efficient communication is key to lower prices and increased product demands. The communication lines in this model are so efficient that Wal-Mart became a major change agent in the Katrina disaster that struck New Orleans in August of 2005. Wal-Mart used its well-oiled communications system to do what the government could not: deliver water and aid to the refugees of the disaster.

What principles are behind Level 4 communication that distinguish it from Level 3—just dialogue? Paul Grice, a British philosopher of language, developed a set of maxims to describe the best communication practices.[42] Violating them leads to annoying interactions at best and misunderstandings at worst. Although we never think about these maxims—just as we never think about language but use it all the time—they really do govern how we communicate with each other.

The *maxim of quantity* holds that one's contribution to the conversation should be as informative as possible but no more informative than necessary. Answering queries crisply and precisely works best. The guy on the old television show *Dragnet* had it down: "Just the facts, ma'am; only the facts." When Maureen told her listener about every pit stop she made on the road to Sheboygan, she violated the maxim of quantity. For some, this maxim does not come easy!

The maxim of quality is 'tell the truth.' Rumors are rife at Level 3, and in business and politics they can be deadly. Cass Sunstein's book, *On Rumors: How Falsehoods Spread, Why We Believe Them, What Can Be Done*, tells us that if it is rumored that a company is about to fail, selling off company stock can actually cause the company to tank.[43] In the age of the Internet, rumors multiply as fast as flies on a dead cat. A few years ago on April 1, your dear writers were fooled by a story that a private school in Manhattan was now requesting DNA samples from parents. This seemed quite plausible to us given that parents were already writing essays (yes, just like college applications) and forking over exorbitant application fees. We were fooled—just as intended, given the April 1 date—and almost included this rumor in our talks. As revealed in the movie *Nursery University* in which we played a cameo (but crucial) role, parents in Manhattan are willing to do virtually anything to get their kids into the "best" preschools.

The maxim of quality has its limits, however. Telling the truth is a fine rule to live by, except when telling the truth goes beyond what people need to hear. Most adults realize that their opinion needn't always be expressed. People who don't get this become legends in their own time—but not for the right reasons. Lauren, a department chair in a university, actually sought out her female colleague to tell her she had a "terrible haircut," which kind of makes you want to cringe. Suppressing truth telling is not kids' forte either, probably because they lack a theory of mind. Kids don't realize how their statements might make someone else feel. Richard brings his girlfriend, Christie, to visit his sister's family. Five-year-old Rebecca blurts out, "You have really big teeth!" Truth be told, Rebecca was right. But most adults would have refrained from sharing this "truth."

The *maxim of relation* holds that a conversational tidbit should be relevant to the topic at hand. Relevance is a challenge to children who may start explaining their drawing and end on how Nickie tripped the lady. Kids talk about what's on their minds; they often don't even realize that there is a topic!

Finally, there is the *maxim of manner*, or how a speaker says something. Ray bloviates. We all know the type. Carol hesitates to invite Ray to her dinner party. Ask him a simple yes or no question and you might be in for a 10-minute discourse on why the question can't be answered. The maxim of manner requires clarity and brevity— apparently a skill beyond the capability of some adults. As for kids, it's hard for a 4-year-old to be clear without a theory of mind because they don't take the listener's knowledge into consideration.

Level 4 communication depends on following these maxims— and knowing how and when to apply them. According to Daniel Enemark writing in the *Christian Science Monitor*, e-mail and other social media gets in the way of Level 4 communication.[44] Without tone of voice and facial expressions from our listener or our ability to convey these nonverbal signals, we miss a lot and can get into trouble breeding misunderstandings over our devices. Our smartphones are often too smart for their own good. Whole websites are devoted to the phenomenon of "autocorrect." As when Gail texts Bruce, "I don't feel like cooking. Can you bring home human beef?" when she meant *hunan* beef.

Where can kids learn the maxims of good communication? These are not explicitly taught. Communication takes practice. Level 3 communication—going back and forth—is the staging ground for Level 4 as children get experience in conveying their meaning and in listening to others' responses. When Mom tells Harry they can't go mini golfing on Saturday with a surreptitious wink, she is reminding Harry that it is Dad's birthday.

What might get in the way of our kids attaining Level 4? Having the TV on during dinner? People texting and writing e-mails? Although we all love our devices, dinner might be a good time to turn them off. If parents are texting and responding to e-mails, they will fail to pick up on the horrible faces 11-year-old Kennedy is making at 8-year-old Russ. This violates the maxim of manner even though it's nonverbal. When in the middle of a conversation about dinosaurs, Russ wants to talk about Lexi's trip to Annapolis, if parents are on their devices, who will suggest he wait until they finish their discussion of dinosaurs? Violating the maxim of relation and being asked to wait to make his contribution may help Russ become sensitive to the implicit rules of conversation. Parents on devices will also fail to suggest to Kennedy that it is not nice to tell Russ that his hair looks like a porcupine's butt. The maxim of quality has to be observed! And of course, parents will be setting an unfortunate example if they can't put their devices away for the duration of a family dinner.

Thirty-somethings play an interesting game. They pile their cell phones in the middle of the table when they go to a restaurant. Whoever can't resist and picks his or hers up first has to pay the bill. Families could try something similar but with different penalties. Level 4 does not come from the air; parents and teachers have to make an effort to observe the maxims themselves if they want kids to learn them.

One of the things that make it hardest for us to reach Level 4 is gauging what our listeners want and need. Level 4 communication requires deep understanding of our audience. Only then can we inform and illuminate minds. Teachers who support kids' pretend play—like the teacher of Babette, Jason, and Paulina—know that children make faster progress in understanding others' points of view when they take on roles in play. For older kids, taking on characters in theater productions has also been shown to increase children's theory of mind. With *virtual distance*[45]—working on screens is becoming increasingly pervasive in all professions—developing the theory of mind needed for good communication is essential to success. Jim Rohn, the late American entrepreneur, author, and motivational speaker said it well, "If you just communicate you can get by. But if you skillfully communicate, you can work miracles."[46]

TAKING ACTION

How do we know communication when we see it?

In Yourself

We've all been there: eating dinner with friends when we get that text or phone call. And we are ever vigilant of that e-device resting delicately in our purse or on vibrate upside down next to the mashed potatoes. The minute it lights up, it compulsively draws our attention away from our children's eyes and onto the device. If you've been on the other side of the table, you know how this kind of behavior is a conversation closer rather than a conversation opener. When, in the ancient past, dinner conversation centered on the day's activities, it made us all feel valued—like someone cared and wanted to communicate with us. What can we do to bring back that feeling and to use communication as the family glue? We can ask specific questions. Not "How was your day?" or "What did you do in school today?" but instead "How did your meeting go with Mr. Bruer?" or "Did you paint anything at school today? What colors did you use?" Maybe the kids will follow your lead and dinner will become a source of food for thought.

As we reflect on our own behaviors, we see that many opportunities for conversation pass us by unnoticed. Remember when people took the time to know their neighbors, talked to the man in front of them at the gas station, and interacted with strangers? We used to call that *community*, and part of that was built on the heels of communication (the same root word). Perhaps we could rekindle that spirit in ourselves to get the conversation going. As we do, it would serve us well to reflect on whether we are talkers or listeners. Do we know about what our friends are doing? Do we care? Do we so quickly skim our Facebook posts that we have only surface knowledge of others in our networks? Sometimes it feels as if we post just to accumulate "likes" not because we really want to listen to others and to hear about their adventures. Can we become better listeners—even virtually?

In a recent seminar, a group of 30 teachers pondered about where they fell on the four levels. With 30 first graders per class and no aide, they had no time to listen to the kids during the school day. They were lucky if they could quiet them down and maintain discipline as they moved through their scripted assignments. But how much time does it really take? In one of our exercises with a large group of teachers from Pennsylvania, we answered that question. Give a child just 20 seconds in your day and you can learn a lot about what happened on the playground, how Oliver felt about the Four-Square game, and how his little brother embarrassed him. That 20 seconds of saying "I care" can be a game changer for the child and for you—the model—who can demonstrate the power of communication.

In Your Child

Our children learn from us. Nowhere is this truer than in communication. If you want to know why a child is fixated on the tablet rather than on the world around him, look at the patterns of the adults in his world. A *Boston Globe* reporter once asked how we might explain the increase in child swearing. Our answer, "They say what they hear." It became headline news.[47]

Are we hearing our children so that they have a chance to go beyond the screaming and attention-getting of Level 1? Are we giving them the chance to do a show-and-tell about the things that are important to them? Only when we value them and give them the space to talk and share will they become better communicators. Again, the kind of questions we ask matter to whether the conversation will continue. Open-ended questions make a big difference. When we ask closed questions that have one right answer (e.g., "What is 1 + 4?"), the conversation is done in just one turn. But when we ask, for example, "Can you tell me about your best friend at school?" we are allowing our children conversational space. This makes for language—and self-control—that flourishes. Our colleague David Dickinson at Vanderbilt uses the unforgettable phrase "strive for five" to remind us to have five back and forth turns when we talk to our kids, to keep the conversation going. Kids learn so much from conversations with us!

Where do your kids stand? Are they the ones who yell until they get their way? Do they whine endlessly? There is a wide range, and even children of the same age can be in very different places on the communication continuum. Take this scene from fourth grade, when seemingly everyone in Peter's class had just seen the movie *Titanic*. Peter longed to have a discussion about the deeper meaning of the plot, but dialogues were just not the way in which the guys in his class responded. The best he could get was a positive emotional grunt from those who thought it was pretty good. Taking stock of our children's communication skills is an important first step in fostering real communication.

In the Places You Go

Is your child's classroom the silent type or one where the happy sounds of kids engaging with one another is the norm? What kinds of pictures are on the walls and what kinds of activities spur collaborative communication? When children are working together in that block corner, they are often talking and plotting and building and using rich vocabulary and learning to construct that joint project. This kind of exchange happens in recess and playtime—bygone characteristics of some schools—and around lunch tables.

At home too, we can rate the opportunities for communication. If our kids are among the 8-year-old-and-older children parked in front of a screen for 8 hours a day—this is what the Kaiser Foundation reported—they are not getting practice in communication skills.[48] If we limit the time they are fixated to digital candy and we offer real props—call them humans—communication can flourish. Debates and disagreements are important parts of the communication scene. If we create environments void of discord, our children will never learn how to be verbal negotiators.

How Do We Create Environments That Foster Communication?

In our homes, we created opportunities for conversation through the revered family meeting. Because the kids had limited television time, they were used to playing with one another and sometimes getting in each other's way. The latter case was always one that created some conflict. We could have just solved the problem by separating the kids, but instead, we offered a context in which the entire family (this was mandatory) came together to discuss the problem. The "victim" spoke first and even though the "culprit" was jumping out of his skin, he had to have the self-control to hear the other side. His turn would come. In this way, no one got hurt, everyone developed respect for the other, and communication became the vehicle for resolving disputes. The family meeting allowed children to move from whining to discussing.

Teaching manners sounds so last century. But unless we help kids learn that when we talk to people, we look them in the eye and stop playing with our [fill in the blank], they won't know that it is necessary. We all know kids who don't answer when you talk to them. Not acknowledging someone trying to talk to you is rude. If our kids are to communicate with more than their screens, we need to scaffold their appreciation of how communication works. We model these behaviors by engaging in them ourselves. We can also talk with our kids to encourage them to follow the conversational maxims we've described. So much of parenting is about using language to share our expectations. And it is not just telling but engaging kids so that they do ask why and how. Why is it important to, say, ask permission to open the refrigerator at someone else's house? How should I tell my friend Lou that I can't go to his party? After all, even kids who have a really good theory of mind have to learn what their culture expects of them.

The point is that we can create contexts and settings that shut down or open up opportunities for communication. Just as we planfully take a child from multiplication to division to fractions, we can be thoughtful about the kinds of experiences that enable children to move through the levels of communication to become welcome and respected contributors to Level 4 dialogues.

THE ROAD TO SUCCESS

Communication paves the way for the things we want for our children. Good communicators stand on the foundation of collaboration. It is through communication that we then master content in reading, math, science, and the arts. It is said that children first learn to read and then read to learn. In fact, without strong language and communication skills, even early reading tutorials will fall flat. Sounding out the word B-O-Y is of little use unless you know the word *boy* in the first place. We learn vocabulary by having conversations with others, conversations that are built on those open-ended questions and on dialogue. The parents who tell their children to "use your words" encourage the word growth that will undergird literacy. Those who tell children stories engender a love of narrative that will help them learn academic skills and maintain friendships. Language, words, and stories are the building blocks of communication. They are the bricks that allow children to share what is in their minds and to peer into other minds. The story of global success rests largely on our ability to communicate; both hard and soft skills are built on its back.

CHAPTER 7

TOPPLING THE KING
THAT IS CONTENT

Tell me and I forget. Teach me and I remember. Involve me
and I learn.

—Benjamin Franklin, as cited in G. S. Wood,
The Americanization of Benjamin Franklin

In early 2005, Florida's Governor Jeb Bush signed the law authorizing voluntary prekindergarten education for all 4-year-olds. He was among the first to ride what would be a tidal wave of change in the national attitude over early childhood. Just a few months later, we were invited by Florida's Early Learning Quality Initiative to speak at their meeting. This sounded like a perfect venue: science and palm trees. The sun-bronzed audience of teachers and policymakers were eager to hear the hottest new findings on the reading brain and exciting ways to bolster vocabulary. And they hoped to apply these findings directly in their newly formed classrooms.

While we were fielding questions from the audience after our talk, a young third-grade teacher raised her hand and asked, "Have you heard of the FCAT pledge?" With a quizzical look on our faces, we both answered, "Nope." She stood up, put her right hand over her heart, and chanted the words that all third graders rehearsed daily in their classrooms in preparation for the Florida Comprehensive Assessment Test, a high-stakes test designed for children to take every spring starting in third grade:[1]

I will do my best.
I will focus.

I will get a good night's sleep and eat a good breakfast.
I will not give up.
I will take my time.

Color us in serious shock. Here we were at a conference sharing and learning from others about playful and stimulating ways to open young minds to the love of learning, and meanwhile, third graders were daily reciting a pledge to keep the state's high-stakes test in the front of their mind, on par with or maybe even superseding their daily Pledge of Allegiance. Could it be that at the dawn of the new millennium achievement is judged solely by a grade on a test—even for our youngest kids?

To be clear, we're not against testing. As many have said before us, if the tests assess real learning, then testing is great—perhaps even a learning experience. To find out whether Ms. Chaz's class actually learned that Ponce de Leon's search for the Fountain of Youth was apocryphal, some type of assessment must occur. But when content is the sole focus of education, all the other Cs fall by the wayside. Collaboration and getting along with peers is not needed. Kids take tests as individuals. Communication is irrelevant. When all children do is fill in bubbles, why be concerned with communication? We seriously need to get our bearings back if we are to craft environments, in and out of school, that support happy, healthy, thinking, caring, and social children who become collaborative, creative, competent, and responsible citizens tomorrow. And content by itself is never enough. Executive function skills that help children control themselves so they can learn are essential for success in school—and in life!

We are in the era of big data, where information is ubiquitous and cheap. Think of big data as the four Vs:[2] *Volume*—with 7 billion people on the planet, fully 6 billion have cell phones, and that's just one kind of electronic device; *velocity*—it is projected that by 2016 there will be 18.9 billion network connections, just about 2.5 connections for every human on earth; *variety*—data come in many forms; and *veracity*—which of those reports can we trust? Students in 19th-century classrooms had to memorize all sorts of things—state capitals, poems, formulas, and so on. But now, by the time children commit the information to memory, it has changed. Some things are stable—the square root of 9, the date of the Norman conquest—but lots of what we knew 10 years ago is no longer reliable. MIT, for example, will not accept credit for advanced placement biology even if a student received a five out of five on the test. The Biology Department stated that the information is out of date by the time the exam is scored.

In the era of big data, variety is exploding. There are data from business transactions, health data from sensors (are you wearing a band on your wrist that charts your movements?), route maps created from GPS tracking, articles posted on Twitter, and so forth. We cannot stuff 100 or 1,000 times more information into our 7-year-olds. Yet current curricula emphasize getting one right answer to put on a test. In the Google generation, children have facts at their fingertips. We know 7-year-olds who can find the name of the tallest building in Qatar in a matter of seconds. Information is a few finger strokes away. Children across the economic spectrum are growing up with computers. As Plutarch wrote, "Education is not the filling of a pail, but the lighting of a fire."[3] Yet we are still pail fillers! And the pail is overflowing with content—and content of a specific kind—the kind you learn in school and mostly in reading and math. No one talks about understanding people when they talk about content. Prasanna comes from India; her customs and beliefs are different from Patty's down the block. But with the emphasis on reading and math, social studies goes out the window!

The watchword for the 21st-century workforce is *adaptability* or, as Google refers to it, *learning agility*. Those who cannot learn and relearn—those who have no learning strategies—will be doomed to low-level, low-paying positions that will ultimately be replaced by computers. Pity the poor toll takers who were replaced by E-ZPass or the photographers who suddenly find their market glutted with thousands of photos taken with smartphones. Yet in school we teach the facts rather than teaching children how to learn, how to evaluate information, and how to draw integrative and innovative conclusions. As Frank Smith wrote, "The time bomb in every classroom is that *students learn exactly what they are taught* [emphasis added]."[4] Limiting education to the content that changes daily dooms our children to obsolescence before they graduate from high school.

We are not saying that content is unimportant. Having content frees our minds to solve problems. Think about the multiplication tables. We automatically remember that $9 \times 6 = 54$ in what feels like a nanosecond. It's incredibly efficient. This skill lets us quickly compute how many of those $9 candles we want to buy for our garden party. Or take reading: We get meaning from words so automatically that we can't ignore signage even when we want to. Can you remember sitting on a bus or a train and being unable to stop yourself from reading the ads, even though you are trying to solve a problem? And when we can get away without laboriously sounding out words, we free up our minds to grapple with what the text means. We want our kids to be rapid readers. Struggling to sound out *candy* means that Irvin may miss the fact that the sentence is telling him it's free! Content is crucial.

But we must go beyond teaching what is known. If our children are to have learning agility, they must learn how to think creatively so that they can assemble old parts to serve new functions. They must have the mental flexibility to change course as they solve ill-defined problems (those without a known right answer). And they must be in environments that present them with those ill-defined problems along with the well-defined ones so that they can get people to reuse what they know. This will not happen by using bubble tests that have only one right answer, whose importance is magnified by daily recitation of the FCAT pledge. What we need is deeper thinking, not shallow learning.

Two Canadian psychologists, Craik and Lockhart, developed a way to think about the deeper kinds of learning that are required for modern day jobs. Their Levels of Processing model dates from 1972 but is still highly relevant today.[5] Their model is about what it means "to know." Just remembering where on the page we saw the new word *prodromal*, or that it was written in italics, or how the new word sounded but not much else is *shallow processing* or superficial learning; we didn't learn the meaning of the word. Remember studying for the SATs and committing 500 words to memory? Bet you couldn't use *syzygy* and *synergy* in a sentence now. Deeper learning happens when we actually learn the meaning of *prodromal* and can use it.[6] Those essay exams in high school and college were different from the bubble tests, though. They assessed what we really understood. They made us explain and link up facts we might have learned separately.

We need deep content, and not only because robots and computers are increasingly taking the jobs that can be routinized but also because even robots are starting to "think" more deeply. We are indeed in a brave new world when leading computer scientists meet at the Asilomar Conference Grounds in Monterey Bay, California, to worry about whether robots are becoming too smart for their own good—or our good. The researchers discussed "possible threats to human jobs, like self-driving cars, software-based personal assistants and service robots in the home."[7] We are achieving these goals as we write—Google's self-driving car is here! Robots are already working in fields such as experimental medical systems. Can you imagine? You press your nurse call button when you are in the hospital for minor surgery and a robot glides in asking, "How can I help you?" You say, "I'm thirsty," and the robot says, "Of course" and glides away to retrieve a full pitcher of water, spilling nary a drop. Lest you think this is just about mindless jobs, futurist Sherry Turkle reminded us that as we write, companies are developing social robots—robots with "soft skills" who can hold your hand, empathize, and make you feel better.[8] Unless our workforce—from the boardroom to the factory floor—is "among the best educated, flexible, most creative, and most innovative in the world,"[9] our children will lose their jobs to automation—even those jobs that involve sophisticated data processing. Those jobs can be easily outsourced to machines.

Somehow our culture got duped into thinking that content is the only C of value—parents, schools, and the learning industry overvalue it. It is time to ask how we can educate children in a way that promotes deep learning. We need to stretch the definition of content to include HOW to find the answers needed to solve the problem and HOW to put together the information and resources to make it possible.

Darwin had the right idea: "It is not the strongest of the species that survive, nor the most intelligent, but the one most responsive to change."[10] We ask two questions here: How do we learn content in the first place and what will it take to learn content in a deep way that allows us to use it in the world? Twenty-five years of research in the science of learning—starting with work on babies—offers us lots of insight about the processes we use to learn content.

LEVEL 1: EARLY LEARNING/SITUATION SPECIFIC

Babies' worlds were once thought to be a "blooming, buzzing confusion,"[11] with objects and people moving hither and yon in a great unfathomable kaleidoscope. Now we know that babies start learning content before they are born. They remember stories and songs they hear from their mother while still in the womb.[12] They might not understand the meaning, but they surely remember the melody. And their learning zooms once they are born. How do they come to know that Uncle Joe is fun and Uncle Bo is scary? How do they know that Mommy puts me in the high chair for lunch, makes my lunch, and then feeds me? And that "The Eensy Weensy Spider" always ends the same way? Babies learn about the world through what they see, what they hear and smell, what they touch, and what they taste—using all five senses—and by experimenting like little scientists with hands and mouths.

To help make sense of their complex world, babies grab onto routines and scout out repeating patterns. Babies are born pattern seekers. They find some of the patterns in their world by making *associations*, linking Uncle Joe to smiles and laughs and Uncle Bo to frowns and hesitations. They also calculate *statistics* about how often things occur together. This helps them notice predictable links between events—like their lunchtime routine. Scientists like Jenny Saffran from the University of Wisconsin found that infants as young as 8 months make sense of repeating events.[13] Lunch from the perspective of 8-month-old Lauren is filled with routines. First, Dad announces lunch. As a baby, I mostly hear, "Blah blah blah," my name, "Lauren," and maybe "lunch" because I hear it so often. Then Daddy picks me up, plops me into the high chair, puts on my bib, goes to the refrigerator, removes a jar, sits down in front of me, and brings that beautiful spoon filled with yellow gunk (fruit) my way. And this happens three times a day—or more, with snacks! These event segments seem to hang together. Babies even notice violations of the sequence by 9 months—like putting the spoon to a baby's ear—and they often find these violations hysterically funny.

Another way babies learn is by *imitation*. Andy Meltzoff rocked the scientific world by showing that newborn babies stick out their tongue when you do. "Babies are exquisitely careful people-watchers, and they're primed to learn from others."[14] You might have played this game with a baby: You say, "How big is [fill in the blank]? So big!" and then lift your arms. The baby learns to do this too, delighting herself and us. But how? She first has to figure out which body part we are moving. What she sees as she lifts her hands looks nothing like what she saw when you lifted yours. How does she make the connection? Amazingly, her brain lights up in the arm area—what are called *mirror neurons* respond. Then she lifts her own arms.

Back to baby Lauren at lunch: She takes these little bits of content, noting how they fit together (likely using statistics and association) and uses them as a platform to learn more. An example from early word learning tells this tale. Babies hear their own name a lot: "Lauren, do you want to nurse? Lauren is sooooooo cute." Our research has told us that our babies are doing this by 6 months of age before anyone thought they could learn sound patterns.[15] If they paid special attention to that familiar name, maybe they could use it as a wedge into the language system. Hearing "Lauren's bottle is empty," Lauren learns the word *bottle* even before she can talk. This a big deal because the more words Lauren recognizes, the more new words "pop out" for her, making them easier to learn.

For babies, much learning takes place through good old-fashioned play. What happens if I throw my spoon off the high chair? Does it go down? Does it go up? Babies explore everything and do little on-the-spot experiments. Some of the baby's most infuriating behaviors are born of experimentation about the world. They really are like little "scientists in the crib."[16] Learning for a baby is analogous to a wave gathering strength, rolling bigger and bigger, as the baby slowly accumulates content by these methods and others. Before we know it, we are looking at a walking, talking preschooler.

To be sure, this kind of learning is situation specific and often not very flexible. What children—and even adults who are learning at Level 1—do is store their bits of knowledge in separate bins. There is little understanding. For example, at Level 1, sometimes people do things they see others do but really don't know why. For years, Mandy cooked her Thanksgiving turkey in a paper bag. She had no idea why she did it, other than the fact that her mom did it that way. She never did that when she cooked a whole chicken. If she had understood why she used the paper bag (to keep that bird moist), she might have applied the bag or a similar method to all kinds of things she cooked in the oven, yielding moister results.

Babies are like that too. They start out—in a famous example from Piaget—using the word *cat* only for the cat they see walking below their balcony. Jean Piaget noticed his daughter did not use the word *cat* anywhere else—not when looking at pictures of cats, or even when she saw other real ones! Knowledge is not really flexible at Level 1 because there is only minimal comprehension of the meaning of what you have learned.

Level 1 is when routines really matter. When 20-month-old Alva's mom has to go out and can't read to Alva at bedtime, Alva protests mightily. In Alva's world, bedtime equals stories. Repetition and routines help children predict what will happen next. When lots of things happen in your world that you can't predict, knowing implicitly that you can count on something like a story at bedtime really matters.

Level 1 happens to all of us when we seek to master a new domain. Whether we are learning physics or knitting, novice learners look for predictability. "What comes next?" and "What do I need to know for the test?" are novice questions. Novices do not look across domains to tie things together. What we learn in physics is seen as totally separate from what we are learning in biology. How knowledge in physics accumulates is not seen as relating to how biologists learn about living things. Novice learners look to experts for guidance, watch them closely, and then imitate them.[17]

Yes, we even imitate as adults—as when we see a new style on our cool friend, and we buy those sunglasses with the thicker frames.

Level 1 can happen in college and beyond. Level 1 is cramming for a test. We passed with a *B* because we reviewed the entire semester's notes in only 6 hours (with a little help from NoDoz and coffee). But we would all admit that we might have failed that same exam if we took the same test a week later. Even though essay exams are usually designed to probe beyond Level 1, Level 1 essays are sometimes what students turn in. These are no pleasure to read. In Developmental Psychology—our métier—it is basically a regurgitation of the material, presented as unrelated pieces. First there was Darwin (he said this), then Piaget (he said that), and then Vygotsky—you get the idea: There is no attempt at integration or looking across these theorists.

Mistakes are just waiting to happen when the content is there, but people don't bother to consider its meaning. To take an example from the corporate world, a killer tornado in Alabama in 2011 was followed the next day by an advertising e-mail from a company named BackCountry.com. The e-mail's content read, "Mother Nature hates you. Deal with it." Of course, this advertisement was created prior to the tornado, but the person responsible for sending it out never considered how the e-mail might be received by those who'd just survived nature's runaway freight train—he was just doing his job. This was so egregious that the CEO had to immediately apologize.[18]

George Bush appointed Michael Brown to head the Federal Emergency Management Agency (FEMA) on the recommendation of Joe Allbaugh, a Bush friend and former campaign manager and himself the head of FEMA.[19] Brown had apparently been forced out as commissioner of the International Arabian Horse Association. Brown clearly lacked the content needed to carry out his new job. This might have gone undetected with Brown harmlessly pushing papers, but then Hurricane Katrina happened. The rest is history.

Level 1 means that you don't know much and what you do know is quite superficial. Level 1 means that you learn by making associations and inductions (That microwave makes a beep! Maybe all things that make beeps are microwaves!), calculating statistics on the everyday events that happen over and over again (remember baby Lauren's lunch sequence or baby Alva's bedtime story), and by imitating others: Daddy says, "Buh buh buh," and then 10-month-old Johan says it too—albeit with great effort—and they laugh uproariously together. Even adolescents and adults use these same Level 1 learning methods. We imitate, we calculate statistics, and we make associations. But if that's all we do, our learning will remain quite cursory. In fact, in demanding classes, we'd be lucky to pass.

LEVEL 2: WIDE BREADTH/SHALLOW UNDERSTANDING

We know more at Level 2. We sample from a wider buffet with more choices of topics than we knew at Level 1. Here, a preschooler may be able to recite factoids about a broad range of subjects: names of dinosaurs, types of animals, counting to 50, and even reading a few words such as their own name and *stop* on a stop sign. Watch Stella on YouTube to see the most adorable little girl talking about dinosaurs.[20] Although she may know lots about what they look like and their names, she has no idea that dinosaurs came before mammals, had babies, and made noises. Nor does Stella likely realize that they lived and inhabited the earth over 65 million years ago—let alone understanding what 65 million years might mean.[21]

Knowing more at Level 2 is just part of what has changed. Children have language now—and they can use it as a tool to learn lots by asking questions. Sometimes this is maddening, as when we get caught in the loop of the infinite "Why?" Kids can also make inferences now and figure out that if something is "alive," it must breathe and have babies. And in Level 2, knowledge is more explicit. We are more aware of what we know. This means that children notice when something isn't quite right, as this mother complains on a mothers' message board:

> My 3.5-year-old becomes agitated and upset when someone says something that is incorrect or says it incorrectly. He shouts at 2-year-olds to adults, "NO! It's not XXX, it's XXX!". . . . And now, some children are figuring out that this is a way to push his buttons and are doing it on purpose to get a reaction out of him.[22]

Children have a sense of what's "right" now, and some—such as this 3.5-year-old—seem to require all to comply. The idea that content is either right or wrong is also Level 2 thinking. This is the time when kids deny that a hammer is also a tool. For young children, it can only be one thing: a hammer.[23] They also sometimes rely on what they see more than anything else. When Sarah's mom comes to pick her up at day care, Sarah gets hysterical and refuses to leave with her. Why? Because her mom had a perm and looks different!

At Level 1, children ride on the surface of knowledge; at Level 2, although kids can still be fooled by how something looks, they can sometimes go beyond what they see. Five-year-old Derek views the world through a Level 2 lens. Ask him what something is—from a *friend* to an *island* to an *uncle*—and he is likely to tell us what it looks like.[24] "A friend is a little kid," "an island has palm trees," and an uncle is "a nice man with a pipe." In Level 2, when appearances often rule, children think that the man pumping gas at the filling station must be a woman because he has long hair—as one of our children once told us. At Level 2, kids know a lot of stuff, but they are not always connecting the dots. They are just beginning to make inferences, only sometimes overriding how things look.

Professors Susan Gelman and Ellen Markman showed 4-year-olds three pictures: a beautiful tropical fish with yellow and black markings, a shark, and a dolphin.[25] The shark looked amazingly like the dolphin and nothing like the tropical fish. But children were told that the shark and the tropical fish were both fish. Then kids were told that the tropical fish breathed underwater, whereas the dolphin breathed air. Now came the big question: How would kids think that the shark breathed—underwater or air? Children could say that the shark breathed air like the dolphin because they looked so much alike. Or they could say that the shark breathed underwater like the tropical fish because they were both called *fish*. Kids overwhelmingly said that the shark breathed underwater, like the tropical fish. Even at age 4, children didn't answer the question just by how these animals looked. Instead, adding the word *fish* helped the children make crucial connections and to infer that the shark and tropical fish must have deeper similarities, even though they looked different. Being in the same category, they probably both breathed underwater. In Level 2, children can use language to help them go deeper (like fish). If two things are called by the same name, they must share similarities you can't even see.

When children go beyond the surface, they can think using *analogies*. We don't mean those formal problems that appear on the SATs, as in black:white as dark:light. We mean thinking about something in their lives and reasoning about that in someone else's life. Hector's mom is a lawyer and wears business suits to work. His friend Romeo's mom is an athletic trainer and wears "play clothes" when she works. At Level 2, Hector denies that Romeo's mom works. The way things look matter more than anything else, so if she wears play clothes, she can't be working.[26,27,28] Hector makes the first part of the analogy in his mind: mom wears business garb—she works. But of course, he can't make the analogy fit for Romeo's mom! Romeo's mom can still work even without getting dressed up. People can wear

129

a variety of things to work. We will have to wait for Level 3 for Hector to go beyond what Romeo's mom wears to agree that she works.

Using analogy is a fundamental way to learn. It helps you figure out how things or even ideas are the same and what they share, even without being told. This is the power of analogies, and we use them all the time in the classroom. Teacher Dedre tells 5-year-old Marvin that clouds are like sponges. She thinks Marvin will get that sponges collect liquid and so do clouds. But instead, Marvin is thinking, "Oh they are both soft and fluffy."[29] Although kids and adults alike use analogy all the time to learn, people who think at content Level 2 focus on physical attributes, unless they're explicitly told otherwise, as in the shark–dolphin example. We have to wait for Level 3 for kids to focus on the *relations* that the objects share.

If I showed a bunch of adults and 5-year-olds the top picture in Figure 7.1 and asked for a description, both the adults and the kids would say, "A cat is chasing a mouse." So far, so good. Then imagine the adults and kids are divided into two groups. Both groups are shown the target picture in which a dog is now chasing the same cat.

In the *neutral* language condition, half the adults and 5-year-olds are asked (while pointing to the top cat), "Do you see this one? What goes with this one in the bottom picture?" The other, the *relational* language group, is asked (while also pointing to the cat), "Do you see this one that's chasing? What does this one go with in the other picture?" What would you pick in each condition? In the neutral language condition, everyone picks the cat in the target picture. But in the relational language condition, where we call attention to the fact that the cat is the chaser, adults always pick the dog—also a chaser. But the 5-year-olds still pick the cat. It is just the way Level 2 thinkers approach this task: They focus on how things look rather than on the chasing *relation*.

At Level 2, kids have a really hard time with metaphors too and for the same reason. After a family visit, Luanne asked her 4-year-old

FIGURE 7.1. Images Used to Test Language Development

Base – Cat chasing mouse.

Target – Dog chasing cat.

From "Relational Language Helps Children Reason Analogically," by D. Gentner, N. Simms, and S. Flusberg, 2009, *Proceedings of the 31st Annual Conference of the Cognitive Science Society*, p. 1055. Copyright 2009 by D. Gentner, N. Simms, and S. Flusberg. Reprinted with permission.

daughter, Jillian, "Isn't Aunt Mabel sweet?" She was startled when Jillian looked at her uncomprehendingly and asked, "Is she made out of chocolate?"[30] We cannot resist one other adorable example of pure Level 2 thinking. Many years ago, 4-year-old Joan befuddled her mom, Helen, as she stood up and found many different ways to fall to the ground. After four or five trials, Joan stood up with a questioning face and asked her mom, "Is this how you fall in love?"

How is Level 2 seen at school? Learning for the purpose of taking a high-stakes test imprisons our children at Level 2. Our kids know a little bit in math and a little bit in reading and a little bit in science, but they don't really understand much in any of these areas. Nor do they understand that topics like science and math might actually be related. This kind of superficial learning that is tightly locked to accountability on tests has four unfortunate consequences.

First, as Linda Darling-Hammond, an education professor at Stanford University, said, such an approach "wastes scarce resources on a complicated test score game that appears to be narrowing the curriculum, uprooting successful programs and pushing low-achieving students out of many schools."[31] Forget that fabulous unit that kids loved in art. There is no time for art when the teacher's very livelihood might depend on her charges' test scores. And what about those special education children who need extra support? Teachers and principals in some cases suggested to these children's parents that it would be OK if they were "sick" the day of testing— or maybe switched to a school that "better met their needs." Low test scores have dangerous consequences for teachers and children alike. In 2015, for example, Governor Cuomo of New York State approved a state budget that stated that 40% of a teacher's evaluation would be based on their classes' performance on state achievement tests.[32] The emphasis on high-stakes tests comes even when a group of top-level educational researchers concluded,

> There is broad agreement among statisticians, psychometricians, and economists that student test scores alone are not sufficiently reliable and valid indicators of teacher effectiveness to be used in high-stakes personnel decisions, even when the most sophisticated statistical applications such as value-added modeling are employed.[33]

Second, given the pressure from above, teachers are mostly teaching to the test. This means emphasizing narrowly construed learning across a set of subjects that are mastered through memorization. Memorization—although sometimes necessary—leads to shallow learning unless it is accompanied by authentic problems that are meaningful to kids. Rote memorization doesn't always allow kids to apply their knowledge in new situations. Level 2 knowledge impresses Aunt Minnie though, who loves hearing her 3-year-old nephew count up to 25 or 50. Does he know what 25 *means* or how it relates to 50? Probably not.

Third, the emphasis on content and testing makes kids miserable. The specters of stomachaches, tears, fear, and anxiety often accompany children on the school bus. What used to be a safe and fun place for many children becomes a place to dread. What about recess to run around and relax from the pressures of the classroom? Especially in low-income schools, there is little time to let kids play.[34]

Finally, high-stakes tests encourage cheating—and we don't mean by the students. The head of the Atlanta school system resigned in ignominy because she was encouraging her minions to alter kids' responses on their bubble answer sheets.[35]

The architects of these well-intended educational reforms— No Child Left Behind and the Common Core—were hoping for more. But children's learning, although broader than Level 1, still by and large reflects Level 2 truncated understanding. The emphasis on shallow learning across a range of subjects also hampers teachers. One teacher from Delaware complained that she had lost her autonomy in the classroom. Administrators in some schools give "being on the same page" a whole new meaning. "If an administrator enters your room and you are not on page 23 of the scripted guide, you'll be called on the carpet!" The teacher lamented that "sometimes the children look back at me and I can tell by their eyes that they don't get it. But I don't have the time to stop and explain;

I have to stay on script." You just have to get through the day's material.

In her celebrated book, *Tested*, Linda Perlstein echoed this Delaware teacher's comments when she wrote about an elementary school in Annapolis, Maryland.[36] Perlstein described a curriculum leader who observed classes for how close they stuck to the approved lesson plan. This leader was concerned that classrooms at each grade level didn't have the same number of vocabulary words displayed and that they weren't all the same size. This is so Level 2!

Is it any wonder that students claim that school is boring and that anxiety, especially around the time of the high-stakes tests, is rampant? Is there any wonder that a $20 billion-dollar tutoring industry has arisen, with 22% of its revenue coming from our youngest children between 3 and 5 years of age?[37] Parents we've talked to are assuming that if their children do poorly on these standardized tests, there will be no hope for their future.

Most tests ask children to spit out rehearsed facts or apply memorized mathematical formulas to a new set of numbers. But research from learning science tells us that memorization is not an optimal learning strategy. Children can memorize mechanically, repeating material with little attention to its meaning.[38] A wonderful example is this version of the Pledge of Allegiance produced by a real child: "I pledge allegiance to the frog of the United States of America and to the wee public for witches hands one Asian, under God, in the vestibule with little tea and just rice for all." Memorization by itself does not foster analysis or retention and teaches students to be inert swallowers rather than critical analyzers. Yet critical thinking—the next C we review—is essential for learning success.[39,40]

At this shallow level of content knowledge, children know lots of things but in a limited and fragmented way. A little knowledge can be dangerous when you have shallow understanding. On a fantastic website called "I Used to Believe," adults share things they used to think. Sara wrote,

> When my sister and I were little, my dad told us the cows on the hills were "hill cows" and that two of their legs were shorter than the other two so if they stood on a flat ground they'd fall over.[41]

Someone who called herself "Operator Lady" wrote, "I used to believe that if you played with the phone without permission the operator would come through the phone holes and stab you in the ear."[42] At Level 2, when knowledge is shallow and pretty limited and when you focus on how things look, you can believe all sorts of impossible things.

Focusing on how things look today—and *only* today—is a problem in government, in education, and in business. Why invest in repairing our infrastructure when that bridge looks good?[43] In education, focusing on the surface suggests that the sooner we teach children in a formal way, the better. This has led whole school systems to make kindergarten the new first grade. Yet learning science tells us that kids need time to explore and set the foundation for school learning. As Nancy Carlsson-Paige, a professor emerita of education at Lesley University in Cambridge, Massachusetts, put it, this trend represents a "profound misunderstanding of how children learn. I've seen it many, many times in many, many classrooms—kids being told to sit at a table and just copy letters. They don't know what they're doing. It's heartbreaking."[44]

Not probing how your company is doing, even when things are going well, is the equivalent of Level 2. Having a CEO who is unwilling to continually question and question everything leads to stagnation and ultimately failure. Take the case of Blackberry maker Research in Motion. Blackberry was doing well when they were totally blindsided by the appearance of the iPhone and the Google

Android. The two co-CEOs appeared clueless about the tablet and smartphone markets and took no responsibility for the company's precipitous fall. When CEOs stop challenging the status quo and allow themselves to be seduced by success, this leads to nowhere fast. Blackberry is back, but it went through a bad time when they appeared to drive themselves off a cliff.

Then there was Polaroid, the company that made it possible for us to capture Jeff and Suzy's engagement and the baby's first steps instantly. Even though Polaroid invented their own digital camera, they just kept doing what they did. Polaroid ignored the wave of new digital technology that would ultimately make their product obsolete. While others were snapping shots they could instantly modify and upload to their computers, the only pictures Polaroid was taking was of management's sad faces. Bankruptcy and dissolution happened in 2001 because Polaroid was operating at Level 2: Things looked good, so why not stick to the status quo? Companies have to continually question where they are going and why, just like sharks have to keep moving to breathe, or they too, might die.

And in the science realm, even sophisticated paleontologists can be fooled by how things look. A Chinese farmer created a bird-like creature in what looked like a fossil. With its apparent plumage, it looked like a cross between a dinosaur and a bird and was hailed by the venerable National Geographic Society as a missing link showing that birds evolved from dinosaurs. But "Piltdown chicken" was a hoax.[45]

LEVEL 3: MAKING CONNECTIONS

A big shift happens in thinking at Level 3. Now 10-year-old Tonya can figuratively spread her wings and take her learning to new places while 5-year-old Deborah is still stuck at Level 2. Annette Karmiloff-Smith, a well-known British developmental psychologist, showed this important shift with a clever drawing study.⁴⁶ She asked both Tonya and Deborah to draw a house. Both drew happily away until Annette made a strange request: "Draw a house that doesn't exist." She wanted to see how flexible these children's thinking was; she was testing learning agility. Could they use what they knew about houses in a new way? Could they draw a house with genuinely new features, moving away from what they typically did?

Five-year-old Deborah vigorously attacked the task and quite enjoyed herself. But her "house that doesn't exist" looked very much like what she drew the first time, except that she added more windows and omitted her door. Deborah, still at Level 2, couldn't think outside the box—or the house in this case. But 10-year-old Tonya changed the *shape* of the house to be a combination of triangles. She put windows only on the topmost triangle and omitted doors, leaving what looked like tent flaps. Tonya had no trouble conceiving of a house that doesn't exist, whereas Deborah just kept drawing essentially the same design. Flexibility lives: Tonya and other Level 3 thinkers can use their mental representation of what a house is to go beyond it.

EXECUTIVE FUNCTION, SELF-REGULATION, AND LEARNING-TO-LEARN SKILLS

Low-level *executive function skills* are part of the reason Deborah couldn't switch gears to draw a house that doesn't exist. Deborah did not yet have the brain development needed to inhibit an old response (to draw a house) and then shift to a new one (a house that doesn't exist). These two qualities of mind—being able to stop from doing the same thing over and over again and thinking of how to do something new—are crucial for thinking flexibility. As a recent report on the development of executive function stated,

> Being able to focus, hold, and work with information in mind, filter distractions, and switch gears is like having an air traffic control system at a busy airport to manage the arrivals and departures of dozens of planes on multiple runways. In the brain, this air traffic control mechanism is called executive function.[47]

Remember when you were a kid and you kept doing the same problem in math getting the wrong answer? You were unable to switch gears. Even as adults we can get caught in loops. Sometimes we can't abandon talking and thinking about a disturbing event that happened to us weeks before.

Executive function, sometimes also called *self-regulation*, is crucial for being able to learn in school. Picture Emily who has trouble paying attention to Mr. Ramp and is squirming and wiggling in her seat. She's noticed a blue jay sitting on a nearby tree branch and has spent most of her time looking out the window and not listening to the book Mr. Ramp is reading to the class. Emily also speaks out of turn many times and Mr. Ramp has to ask her to give other children a chance to talk. Later in the day, when her teacher asked all the students to help clean up after art class, Emily put away some of the painting supplies but then quickly moved on to play with a puzzle and never finished cleaning the rest of her work station. When Mr. Ramp asked Emily to stop playing with the puzzle, she immediately started crying and fell to the floor in frustration. Emily's story is one that many kindergarten teachers (and parents) can certainly relate to. In fact, the number one concern that kindergarten teachers like Mr. Ramp report is "difficulty following directions," indicating that about half of their class or more struggle with this problem.[48]

But why should we care about executive function skills? Preschoolers' self-regulation is linked to their early literacy, vocabulary, and math skills and helps them transition to a more structured and formal schooling environment once they reach kindergarten.[49]

Children who have good self-regulation skills in preschool are more likely to do better in reading and math achievement in elementary school.[50] In fact, these skills may be even more important than measures of general intelligence.[51] Teaching children how to regulate their own behaviors may be even more important than teaching academic skills. Emily would improve if she had the opportunity to engage in some of the training programs available.[52] Executive function skills can be taught. The learning industry doesn't talk much about executive functions skills, but learning scientists have shown repeatedly that children who can't focus and pay attention can't learn nearly as well as those who can. Learning-to-learn skills should be present at Level 3, although some children are still challenged. The kernels of these skills are seen in preschool.

By age 10, the switching gears part of executive function skills becomes easier too. This lets children extend their knowledge to new situations. In Level 3, children shift their attention to *relations*—to the connections things share and not just how they look. Language undoubtedly helps, as the prior studies we talked about showed. Derek, now 9 years old and in Level 3, when asked those same questions he was asked in Level 2, responds as we might: "A *friend* is a kid you play with," "An *island* has water around it," and "An *uncle* is my mom's brother." He's not totally at Level 3; kinship relationships are hard! But now Derek understands that palm trees are not the sine qua non of islands. Maybe some islands don't even have them. Now Derek gets that *island* means something about the relationship between land and water.

In our cat and dog example on analogy, the same kids who are now 2 years older at age 7 mostly pick the "chaser" in the target picture (the dog) in the relational language condition because they focus on the relationship between the two characters in the top picture. Language helps them to do that. At Level 3, children can apply what they have learned to real-world situations. Eighth-grade

Talia uses her math knowledge to calculate how much paint she needs to cover her bedroom walls. It would be wonderful if most schools used "authentic" problems like this that kids really wanted solutions to.

In fact, the arts fuel the learning of content—and executive function skills. Speaking of paint, the arts are being pushed out of many schools. When content is king, the arts are the first to go. Yet, the arts spur children to understand material at a higher level— Level 3—because they ask children to *extend* what they know and to make connections in a new domain. The arts prompt kids to get to deeper Craik and Lockhart levels of understanding. That rap sixth grader Tyrone wrote speaks volumes about how he uses language to create rhythm and rhyme. It also gives Ms. Klein a real glimpse into what he sees going on in his "hood." Talk about content: This is language and literacy and social studies all in one.

Drama invites kids to look for analogies between the characters and the situations in the play and the people and situations children face in real life. Now that is deep learning. Drama increases children's empathy for others because it requires the actor to step into someone else's shoes.[53] Play a homeless person, and you'll never look at one the same way again. There are even schools—like Public School 94 in New York City—that use drama with children on the autism spectrum. This school claims that putting on plays brings these children to heretofore-unseen levels of competence.

A recent report by neuroscientists and psychologists called *Learning, Arts, and the Brain* suggested that children of all socioeconomic strata can move to Level 3 thinking through the arts.[54] Drawing and painting, dance, music, and drama enhance children's capacities for learning information deeply. Creating a drawing of a scene from a story and explaining it to your teacher is a powerful way to increase your comprehension. Want to help children appreciate the difficulty of settling our country? Put on a play about the hardships our ancestors endured. Building their own houses, finding their own food (what? no supermarkets?), making their own clothes (no Kids' Gap?), all help children see how difficult the pioneers had it.

The study of the arts, in all of its forms, presents far-reaching, Level 3 learning opportunities for children. This is why STEM— science, technology, engineering, and mathematics—is becoming STEAM, with A for arts. When American technology companies had to go overseas to fill their positions, a great hue and cry was heard. Why aren't we training enough people to fill these highly technical jobs? STEM education became the watchword, just as if the Russians had landed another Sputnik. However, the new emphasis on STEM often had the unanticipated outcome of pushing out English, social studies, and the arts. Governor Rick Scott of Florida proposed cutting funding for liberal arts education and degrees that don't offer a good return on investment.[55] Tell that to the fifth graders who were lucky enough to have a storytelling artist visit their school. The children were so transfixed they forgot to blink as he spoke. He brought language and history and the power of storytelling to life. Those kids took more books out of the public library the next day than they did the whole semester. The arts offer students an opportunity to move to Level 3 by encouraging and nurturing deep understanding of content. Part of this comes from the exercise of their executive function skills. Those fifth graders in Florida were deeply absorbed in that storyteller's tale—you could have heard a pin drop.

The great irony is that learning science has known for years how good learning happens. The four keys to learning that promotes Levels 3 and 4 can be encapsulated in a tweet: Active, engaged, meaningful, and socially interactive.[56,57,58] These are the means to facilitate deep, Craik and Lockhart kind of learning that moves beyond Levels 1 and 2.

The *active* mastery of content means doing something with the material. Listening to a teacher lecture takes less mental effort than working on a group project. Putting on a play, writing a joint paper, and writing a persuasive essay on giving to charity are all examples of how children can learn actively. This is not the direction many—though not all—of our schools are taking; couch-potato learning occupies much of the school day. How much more exciting would school be if kids could ask and answer their own questions?

Children are often fascinated by fire—that's why we hide the matches. Tapping into their fascination invites deep learning. If kids want to learn about fire, they could visit the fire company and interview the firefighters. They could plan out questions to ask the firefighters in advance and record what the firefighters say for later transcription. They could read about flame retardants and discover how they are everywhere and a possible threat to kids' health. They could learn more science through studying how fire extinguishers work. They could use their imaginations to write and illustrate who "discovered" fire. Friends' Central School in Philadelphia took this approach around the concept of flight. The teachers pick a different theme every year. When the learning activities are designed to spill naturally across different disciplines, learning becomes organic and exciting for children.

The activities we described for learning about fire breed *engaged* learning too. Kids' motivation is high to learn about a topic they are really interested in. Engagement is seen at every turn—when they interview the firefighters and when the teacher demonstrates a fire extinguisher. Engaged learning capitalizes on children's interests. But children don't always start out interested in something. Ms. Yaler's inner-city sixth graders didn't know how cool it would be to learn about fruit—some of them weren't even sure what a fruit was. Is a cucumber a fruit? It's sweet. Is a tomato? But when Ms. Yaler visited various ethnic markets around the city and bought fruits from all over the world that the children had never seen, they were very excited to taste them and learn more. Good teachers know how to build interests that kids didn't know they have.

Making learning meaningful is about linking it to our lives. Years of research has taught us that tying new learning to what we already know makes the learning "stick." Sticky, flexible learning is what we are after. Why learn about immigrants? When children are asked to interview immigrants they know, the whole idea of moving to a new land becomes real. Language barriers? Isolation? Finding housing and a job? Children are much more likely to understand these things if they know someone who faced these problems. Immigration can mean something.

The same is true for adults. Take opioids—no, don't *take* them, consider an experiment designed to see how physicians would most effectively learn about the rules for prescribing them. One group of docs was just told what the rules were and then asked a week later to recall them.[59,60] Not only could they not remember what they had learned but they also actually made up some new rules. Another group was given the same information in a narrative about a fictitious patient. This group remembered the rules really well. Making learning meaningful works much better than teaching abstractions. "Hooking" opioid rules to a specific patient makes the rules easier to remember.

Deeper learning happens through *social interaction*. We don't mean when Raymond and Carol just sit together; we mean when they jointly construct what they need to learn. Learning scientists have known this for a long time: People learn best from other people. Pair up a good student (Raymond) and a poor student (Carol). After working with Carol on different kinds of rocks, Raymond does not slide backward but understands even more about metamorphic rocks from having to teach Carol. Carol feels freer with Raymond to say that she doesn't quite get how sedimentary rocks formed than she does by asking her question in front of the whole class.

A recent news story about how social interaction feeds learning comes from Eric Mazur, a physics professor at Harvard. Mazur

143

began to question the lecture model so widely used in physics classrooms. He came upon the work of David Hestenes, a physicist at Arizona State University, who developed a test to assess the conceptual understanding of physics among the students in his lecture classes. One of the test questions was the following:

> Two balls are the same size but one weighs twice as much as the other. The balls are dropped from the top of a two-story building at the same instant of time. The time it takes the lighter ball to reach the ground will be . . .[61]

The answer, based on Newton's second law of motion, is that both balls will reach the ground at the same time. This is a fundamental concept in physics. Yet, most of the students—even those who got As in the class—got it wrong. The same test has now been given to tens of thousands of students around the world, and the results are shocking. Traditional, passive, lecture-based physics classes produce little or no change in most students' fundamental understanding of how the physical world works. According to Hestenes, "Students have to be active in developing their knowledge. They can't passively assimilate it."[62] Mazur changed this passive lecture-based learning to creating small groups that worked together on problems in class. Learning skyrocketed.[63] We know how to promote deep learning that sticks. The learning sciences offer much for raising learning to Level 3 and beyond.

LEVEL 4: EXPERTISE

Level 3 is a big advance because children now see new connections between things they know and can extend their learning in new directions. They can use what they know in an increasingly flexible way. At Level 4, we gain expertise in an area—whether it is running that luncheonette, coaching that team, or driving that taxi—and that frees us to think about how to improve and modify what we know.

"Can we talk?" as the late Joan Rivers used to say to huge audiences as if they were among her best friends. Let's talk about Malcolm Gladwell, the prolific writer who had all four of his books on *The New York Times* bestseller list. In *Outliers*, he wrote about the work of psychologist Anders Eriksson who proposed the 10,000-hour rule: To become an expert in something, 10,000 hours of work are required. Even Gladwell, on his own career path, claims to have followed the 10,000-hour rule. He said that although he was a basket case at the beginning, he felt like an expert at the end; it took 10 years—10,000 hours of practice—to become an expert in something.[64] Whether you are Malcolm Gladwell or Skippy Weldon, the boy down the street who excels in tennis, an expert does not just emerge, no matter how much natural talent someone has. To quote Gladwell again: "Achievement is talent plus preparation," and the amount of preparation is extensive. Although the number of hours of practice varies depending on the field, Gladwell has now said, no surgeon ever just walked into an operating room for the first time to remove an appendix, and the Beatles' White Album could not have been written by teenagers. Hard work, perseverance, practice, grit and failure (we'll talk about confidence later), perspiration, and talent too make experts, but not as much as hard work.

What does it take to be an expert comedian like Joan Rivers or an expert writer like Malcolm Gladwell or an expert tennis player like Skippy Weldon? The PISA test given to 14-year-olds around the world helps us understand what an expert can do that children at earlier levels can't. Students who score really well can *link up* the ideas they learned in algebra with ideas they learned in trigonometry. They can identify when *constraints* operate on problem solution (I can't use this strategy in this kind of problem), and they can *flexibly translate* between solution types. They can even *apply insights* they develop on the spot to forge new relationships to help themselves. Being in Level 4 means that you can go beyond extension of what you know (Level 3) to envision new ways to do things (Level 4).

There is actually a whole field in the science of learning that distinguishes experts from novices. Even children can be experts. Micky Chi, at Arizona State University, studied children who were experts in chess.[65] In her studies, adults could remember more numbers than kids could (so-called digit span subtest on the IQ test), showing that they had a bigger memory capacity. This is not a surprise. But children who were chess experts could remember more chess positions than adults. Show champion children pieces arranged on chess boards, and they are much better than adults 2 and 3 times their age at remembering what was where. Experts—and people operating at Level 4 in any area—are better at solving problems in their area (e.g., getting out of "check"), noticing and seeing features novices don't (that pawn can be part of my strategy), analyzing the problem more deeply, and operating really quickly because they remember more in their area (that move saved me before).[66]

Another homespun example is golf. Golf is frustrating because it takes years to build up proficiency. When approaching a hole on a fairway on a new course, experts with deep understanding can apply their knowledge and principles to new situations.[67] Should Lois attempt to hit her ball over the creek that runs through the middle of the fairway, risking its loss if she can't make the shot? What club should she use? Will the wind help or hinder her attempt? Even the fact that the golfer is considering all these variables is huge. Lois is not just plowing ahead—as duffers at prior levels might do—but is also thinking about the best course of action. Nor is she throwing up her hands (or clubs) thinking the task impossible. Experts are like that. They work at solving problems, applying what they know. Then they evaluate their actions and think about what they might have done differently. Level 1 or 2 novice golfers don't even ask the questions of themselves that Lois did; they just watch as their shot takes a nosedive into the creek. The Level 3 golfer might change clubs but might not consider all the relevant factors. She doesn't yet have enough of a big picture of the variables that matter and finds it hard to hold them in mind and weight their values simultaneously. Lois can do that. At Level 4, she might win the club tournament.

When Lois approaches a similar hole later—with a sand trap dividing the fairway—she makes a connection between this hole and the one five holes before, even though there is no creek. The expert sees the "deep structure" of the problem and recognizes that this is another situation where a barrier must be forded, even though on the surface the holes are very different. In fact, the expert has such deep knowledge that she can teach her thought process to a novice friend, reframing it at a lower level to help her friend understand.[68]

This is why we want our children taught by experts at Level 4. Experts can explain and demonstrate and come up with multiple examples. Novices can only do what is in the curriculum guide. Experts, like Mr. Cochran, realize that in that fractions problem, eighth-grader Marcy thinks 1/15 is bigger than 1/4 because the denominator is bigger. Mr. Cochran zeroes right in on what Marcy missed in the fourth grade when fractions were introduced. Mr. Cochran will address the problem immediately and help Marcy reach higher levels of knowing.[69,70] Or take Ms. Olson and how she helps Sam grasp the need for multiplication. He knows some of the times tables, but they have no meaning for him. She tells him she wants to give him some stickers for helping others in the classroom, but first he will have to tell her how many stickers she is offering him. She lays out eight sheets of stickers with six stickers on each sheet.

When he starts counting she asks him what else he might do that would be so much faster? First he tries to count faster but then he realizes—like a light bulb went on in his head—"I can multiply!" and from then on he is eager to learn his tables.

There are so many ways we can help children, college students, even ourselves reach Levels 3 and 4. We can look for the meaning too, and go beyond the surface, as when we study tablets to decide which one is best for our needs instead of buying the one that comes in the pretty case.

Levels 3 and 4 are important in the world of commerce too. Baristas at Starbucks have to speak in certain ways to the public and learn how to use a computerized cash register. Sales people—whatever the field—must learn the names and properties of hundreds of products (e.g., a "tall latte mocha with skinny milk") and represent them accurately and with enthusiasm. Event planners must be both big-picture and detail oriented to make tons of decisions lest that wedding or bar mitzvah becomes a disaster. Scientists spend years in graduate school learning their trade (e.g., developmental psychology) by working with mentors who guide them and critique their work. To reach Level 4, those developmental psychologists must then move on to create their own sense of their field. Although content is different for each career, it is indispensable and essential.

But content is not static. Any business that is not moving forward and examining and reexamining their strategy is vulnerable. To reach Level 4 in accumulating content about the customer, the company must always be sniffing out their customers' unfulfilled needs. Apple Inc. is a model in this area.[71] Their researchers go into chat rooms to see comments, complaints, and concerns. Who knows that the tablet was not born of Julia chatting with Sydney about how amazing it would be to have a computer you put in your purse? Apple's drive for content allows them to take a big bite out of the computer market.

Another Level 4 example is Corning, the company that makes those wonderful unbreakable dishes that even your 3-year-old can't smash. Corning recognizes the link between new business opportunities, new technology, and examining their products in a cultural and historical light. They have a yearly conference at which experts from academia and industry present. Corning keeps forging ahead—and backward—by considering where they have been and where they are going. The 54th Annual Seminar on Glass in October of 2015 featured their exhibit entitled, *America's Favorite Dish: Celebrating a Century of Pyrex*. Who knows what ideas their designers, marketers, and engineers will get from hearing talks about "Food is Love," architecture, and gender roles around food.

Learning new content is a lifelong project, regardless of the career path one takes. Jiddu Krishnamurti, the Indian philosopher, put it best:

> There is no end to education. It is not that you read a book, pass an examination, and finish with education. The whole of life, from the moment you are born to the moment you die, is a process of learning.[72]

Perhaps we need a new FCAT pledge for lifelong learning. Put your right hand on your heart and say,

> I will go beyond the facts and learn deep concepts.
> I will learn "how to learn" because information is exploding.
> I will get a good night's sleep and eat a good breakfast. (Still important!)
> I will not give up but collaborate with others to increase my understanding.
> I will look for how to apply what I have learned.

This new pledge should keep you learning and enjoying it. Expand your content!

TAKING ACTION

The key is to remember that content does not only come from the learning children do in school. They can learn lots of things outside school—through conversations with you at the pharmacy and in the supermarket and even from traveling with you on a train or a bus. There are teachable moments everywhere that can deepen your children's understanding of the world and encourage them to ask questions. Children who are having fun learning outside of school are more likely to want to learn in school too. Children only spend 20% of their time in school, so we can enrich their lives mightily by example and by the actions we take with them.

In Yourself

There is no question that content matters to you. The fact that you are reading this book means that you want to learn. Motivation is key, and you have it. Where would you rank yourself on the grid for content? Everyone has expertise in something, so give yourself some credit. But maybe you only have it in areas that are of specific interest to you. Are you more narrow in the content area than you might wish? Does your mind go blank when your partner starts talking about that new project at work? Are you open to going new places and learning new things? We know that you cannot be an expert in everything. No one can. But there are times when we all need to stretch to learn new information. After all, this is what school asks our children to do all the time.

Asking your partner good questions about that new project will not only show that you are listening (i.e., communication) but will also genuinely increase your interest the next time you discuss a related subject. Taking advantage of a vacation day to go to that Impressionist exhibit you've been dying to see at your local museum will make you feel good. And take your children! Ask them to tell you what they see in those paintings without figures or what is happening in those paintings that show scenes. If you open yourself up to learning new things, your child will want to be like you!

For those things that you are good in, have you tried to help others learn what you know? This is really how to hone the expertise you have—explain it to others who want to know. This will also come in handy with your children. Are you an expert baker? Help your children learn your skill by engaging them and offering them tasks to do as you work together. Do you know a foreign language? Help your children learn how to say things that only they will know—kind of like a secret language.

Answering children's questions in an honest and forthright way and modeling enthusiasm about how you learn is a wonderful gift to them. All children eventually ask questions you cannot answer, including the proverbial "Why is the sky blue?" Have some fun with this—ask your children what color the sky should be. Why? Then you can model how to find the answer on the Internet or in the local library. We all want our children to become life-long learners—like we are. Show them how you do it.

In Your Child

A friend of ours recently called one of us and said that her son was required to read aloud 15 minutes each night to a parent and it was just about killing them. Why? Because the parents were busy (on their devices, perhaps) and viewed this as a giant pain as opposed to an opportunity to share a fun activity. Of course, the child followed their lead and had to be coaxed to comply. Just by deciding to take a different approach, to get into the story and discuss the characters and how it linked up to the child's life, reading became a fun time. The parents were surprised themselves at how much fun they had.

Remember that the four pillars fueling learning that we described as active, engaged, meaningful, and socially interactive are not academic abstractions but real ways to help kids more deeply understand what they are learning. How can we link up the content in school to what Jesse likes? We can take Jesse to visit a colonial site when his class studies the pilgrims. Or we can visit a farm or a petting zoo when they focus on where food comes from. Local universities and colleges often have museums for things kids really like. The University of Delaware has a small rocks and minerals museum given by a donor. When our children were little, they loved going there. Many agricultural schools have entomology departments where children can see creepy-crawlies for free.

One of us liked nothing more than doing her "homework" along with her children and providing them with little healthy treats as they worked—oranges or apples or hot chocolate. She did not isolate her children in their room and tell them not to come out until they finished. When they were young, she encouraged them to work alongside her and share the excitement of what they were learning. Content can be inspiring! And if you create circumstances that help children focus, you are helping them hone their learning-to-learn or executive function skills.

In the Places You Go

Don't forget the park! So much at the neighborhood park can be fun and can fuel learning. In the fall, you can pick up beautiful leaves to paste onto paper or to trace at home. In the spring, you can keep returning to see how those flowers are getting ready to bloom. There are so many wonderful opportunities for learning all around us. As the old saying goes, the best things in life are free.

Even if your child's school does not engage in many art projects, you could do that with the content your child is learning.

Watercolor paints can be used to represent the scene your child just read in their new book. When children are doing their homework together, you can ask them to act out a scene from it! There are many ways to incorporate dances, write songs, and so forth, for things that children are required to learn. And if you get involved, you are modeling how much fun it is to learn. Getting involved in your child's education takes on a whole new meaning when you support your child and make learning fun.

Parents and caregivers can help children develop their artistic side through after-school programs or classes or summer camps if they are so inclined. Many children are eager to participate in a theater camp, whereas others who are a bit shyer might enjoy art camp. Fueling your children's imagination through the arts is a great way to enrich their thinking and build their executive function skills too. Ever watch children participate in a drum circle, each equipped with their own instrument and following a beat? They need to concentrate hard and filter out distractions. They are completely engaged and involved, building their attention span and ability to focus. Research has shown that these kinds of musical activities expand children's executive function skills, helping them cultivate the learning-to-learn skills they need.

How Do We Create Environments That Foster Content?

The easy answer is to turn off the television and make sure that children are not glued to screens. But even some screen time isn't bad—it all depends on the content the screens show. In computer games such as *Sim City* children plan what they want in their city, and some video games sharpen children's hand–eye coordination. We are not Luddites. We recognize that older children especially can learn from screens.

What really matters in helping children love learning is taking their interests seriously. Following their interests is bound to

153

build engagement because the topic is already meaningful to them. Is your child fascinated by spiders? As a child, one of us read every book she could find on spiders. If you are seeing dollars signs, think again. The public library is a fantastic place for families. When our children were little and all the way through grade school before they could go themselves, we went every week and took out books. Imagine the power children feel when they get to pick their own books. We loved those books as much as they did and read them over and over until the next time we went to the library.

We also took our children to arts performances. Again, we bet you are seeing dollar signs. But there are local orchestras, singing groups and dance groups that enjoy performing for audiences. Kids generally love the arts and it can spur interests that they will want to read about or draw pictures of. One of us took our child to see the show *42nd Street* in New York, and we tap danced together all that night!

Don't forget children's museums for spurring your child's love of learning. These are the last bastions of playful learning in America and they fuel children's imaginations at the same time. Centered as they are on what children find interesting and compelling, children's museums offer content, social interaction, physical activity (we still love climbing in the web at Port Discovery in Baltimore), and opportunities to learn without sitting in a seat and conforming to the pace of other children. Furthermore, many museums have days that are free; watch for those! Research by Catherine Haden and her colleagues has shown that talking about what you have seen after you come home builds your children's memory.[73,74]

But you can spur your children's memory even after a visit to the laundromat! Those large overbearing machines and the noise and money to put in the slots are all fodder for children who have never been to one. Tell Mommy or Daddy what it was like there: Was it a quiet place or a noisy place? Tell Mom (or Dad) about its special smell and how you liked it. Tell Mom (or Dad) about the new friend you made while we were waiting! Any place you go becomes an adventure to learn from if you are a child—especially if you have a parent who talks with you about what you are noticing and follows up with good answers to your questions.

THE ROAD TO SUCCESS

Although content should not be king, it is definitely important for children to learn content. But it is also important for them to learn how to learn and how to be life-long learners like their parents. If your children see you loving to learn, most of the time they will too. If your children believe that you take their questions seriously and try to get them answers or help them find answers, they will learn to do that for themselves. And if we recognize that content is everywhere—not just confined inside school walls—we will enrich our lives and our children's lives. The road to success is paved with experiences you share with your children. And these experiences don't have to be expensive or taxing. Children thrive when we spend time with them so find those teachable moments all around you and help your children ask questions and probe for more!

CHAPTER 8

CRITICAL THINKING:
WHAT COUNTS AS EVIDENCE?

It is the mark of an educated mind to be able to entertain a thought without accepting it.
— Aristotle, *Nicomachean Ethics*

Picture us crashed in the back seat of a limo, having just given an address on early learning in Long Island to 350 people while sharing one mike. By the time we got to 20th Street in Chelsea, we were ready for a nap. Instead, we made every attempt to spruce up. We grabbed a quick shot of caffeine and entered an old brownstone that had missed out on renovation. Trekking up the creaky stairs, we found Marc Simon, who was working on an entertaining documentary that has since come out called *Nursery University*.[1]

Marc asked us, "How do highly educated well-off parents get stuck believing that if their kids don't go to a specific set of fancy New York preschools, they will never get into a good college?" The phenomenon is well known. Manhattan boasts consultants who actually make their living by being paid to critique application essays parents write about their 5-year-olds. These parents think that they have to get their progeny into New York City's private Dalton School (yearly tuition: $42,960) to start their children's journey to [fill-in-the-blank]. The documentary *Nursery University* is an exposé of this problem. It shows how families deal with the preschool admissions process and the outcome.

Nursery University documented how even folks who have lots of choices worry about the wrong things when it comes to their kids.

But *Nursery University* is about all of us and our society. It's about how all parents came to think that stuffing a lot of information into the heads of children was the ticket to success. In fact, this cultural mantra has been repeated so often that virtually everyone believes it. It goes something like this: If you want your child to get into college, you better make sure she is ready for kindergarten, and to be ready for kindergarten, you have to ensure that she goes to a high-quality preschool that will drill her on letters and math so that she can be starting phonics by age 4, reading books by age 5, and counting dolphins on laminated cards to show her burgeoning math scores in preschool. Author Frank Bruni called it the "college admissions mania" and suggested that the phenomenon starts as early as kindergarten. In his book, *Where You Go Is Not Who You'll Be*, Bruni argued that the elite private school that leads to the elite college is not what matters for children's (or parents') lives.[2] We made a similar case based on the science of learning in our book, *Einstein Never Used Flash Cards: How Children Really Learn and Why They Need to Play More and Memorize Less*: Preschoolers don't need computer science or a weekly French class to get into a good college. In fact, a serious case can be made that to help our children become happy, healthy, thinking, caring, and social children who become collaborative, creative, competent and responsible citizens tomorrow we need to focus on their academic, social, and physical development. Children have more than a head.

Nursery University revealed how in the most extreme case, in Manhattan—where many extreme trends begin—the rush to find a good school is a pilgrimage that begins at a child's birth. But this kind of thinking is all about cramming children's heads with content—a black hole in critical thinking that affects people from New York to Minnesota to Oregon—no one is immune. Knowing to question and ask for evidence is pretty important for keeping us out of trouble.

Critical thinking also has another component that is a crucial skill in our democratic society. Without critical thinking, we would just blindly accept whatever we heard without questioning. Making informed choices demands that we question—not just repeat—what we have learned. The 2008 U.S. election for president made this blatantly obvious. "Obama is not a citizen of the United States": There were politicians like Donald Trump and pundits that kept repeating this tale even though it was patently false. That Sarah Palin wanted Alaska to secede from the United States was another ridiculous claim. Critical thinkers took these assertions with a big grain of salt. Voting should be an exercise in our critical judgment, an exercise in which we make rational and informed decisions.

Critical thinking is also essential because of the information explosion we face in this world of big data. Unless we learn how to organize and select from among the many choices that confront us when we go online to buy a new washing machine, we are likely to overpay for fewer features that we value. Psychologist Diane Halpern put it best in an article published almost 20 years ago but that is still quite current in its message:

> People now have an incredible wealth of information available, quite literally at their fingertips, via the Internet and other remote services with only a few minutes of search time on the computer. *The problem has become knowing what to do with the deluge of data* [emphasis added]. The information has to be selected, interpreted, digested, evaluated, learned, and applied or it is of no more use on a computer screen than it is on a library shelf.[3]

She wrote these words only 6 years after the first text message was sent and the same year that Google became a company—Halpern didn't know what was coming! In the years since, as we're writing this book, the amount of available information has doubled five times.

The choice is a simple one: Either we learn how to navigate the tidal wave of content and information coming at us or we drown in the deluge. Either we learn what questions to ask when we are offered deals that look too good to be true or we pay out our hard-earned cash for the promises echoed in *Nursery University.* Critical thinking is the learning science answer to navigating the big data surrounding us. But how do we learn to engage in critical thinking? And what do we mean by this phrase anyway?

Critical thinking is evidenced when we take a *skeptical stance.* Harry Truman came from the Show-Me State of Missouri. Missouri's U.S. Congressman, Willard Duncan Vandiver, who served in the United States House of Representatives said in a speech in 1899, "I come from a state that raises corn and cotton and cockleburs and Democrats, and frothy eloquence neither convinces nor satisfies me. I am from Missouri. You have got to show me."[4] When we say "Really?" to the claim our friend Laurie just made that babies can learn to read, we are essentially saying, "Show me." When we doubt this and then look up "baby reading" on our smartphones, we are engaging in critical thinking. When we take that skeptical stance and we ask probing questions about what it really takes to get a good education, we are much less likely to fall prey to half-truths and distortions.

Calls to teach critical thinking have echoed through the halls of education. Beyer suggested that to meet these calls, we have to embrace a simple definition: Critical thinking is using "reasoned judgment."[5] And teaching critical thinking will require that children learn how to analyze, synthesize, and evaluate information that comes from all sorts of places—from "observation, experience, reflection, reasoning, or communication."[6]

Shouldn't we arm our kids with the realization that not all information is equal or vetted or evaluated, let alone true? The Internet is loaded with junk. That's why urban legend websites exist: to debunk weird rumors that spread like wildfire. How about that Facebook hoax that Oprah Winfrey committed suicide? How about alligators in the sewers under New York City? Unfortunately, students don't get much help these days in questioning information that seems outlandish; to the contrary, when kids are taught "facts" and discouraged from questioning, they are likely to think that anything an adult tells them must be true. But kids need to become skeptics; critical thinkers are open-minded and consider different points of view. Critical thinkers use evidence. They will even be open to changing their position when they learn new things.

However, critical thinking is not universally encouraged. When the Texas Republican party crafted their 2012 platform, they included this paragraph:

> Knowledge-Based Education—We oppose the teaching of Higher Order Thinking Skills . . . which focus on behavior modification and have the purpose of challenging the student's fixed beliefs and undermining parental authority.[7]

Of course, this is not what all Republicans—or Democrats, for that matter—think. However, failing to challenge students' "fixed beliefs" could be a big problem. Kids believe all sorts of things (and we don't just mean Santa Claus and the tooth fairy). Learning about the world means letting go of childish beliefs and understanding what really causes food to digest (not little men in the stomach) or cars to go (not horses inside the engine) or people to be mean (witches don't really exist). It seems that we should want to encourage critical thinking in our children. Without it, we doom our children to accepting whatever we or another authority says, with no tools for evaluating their claims.

LEVEL 1: SEEING IS BELIEVING

We do not start out as critical thinkers. You have to know something (i.e., content) to be able to evaluate new information. Infants and toddlers are just learning about their world, and it's pretty complicated.

But even after 1 year on earth, infants are making judgments about which actions make sense and which don't. At 14 months, Olga is just starting to walk and talk. In the Gergely baby lab at the Hungarian Academy of Sciences, she meets a friendly graduate student holding a blanket around herself with both hands as if she is sitting on a bucket of ice.[8] The woman says hello to Olga and then bends her head, using it like a switch to turn on a big round light on the table with her forehead. A "headlight"! Or is it? A week later when Olga comes back to the lab she is seated in front of the light. What does she do? Does she use her forehead to turn on the light like the lady did the previous week? Or does she use her little hands? If she uses her forehead, she is blindly imitating. But if she uses her hands, she is evaluating what she saw. It is as if she is saying, "That lady only used her head because her hands were tied up holding the blanket." Eighty percent of babies used their hands. They judged the situation critically and didn't just blindly imitate. There are kernels of critical and rational thinking even in infancy.

At Level 1, children mostly start out believing what they see and what they are told, despite the stunning demonstration to the contrary described earlier. Babies also have some sensitivity to when someone is a trustworthy purveyor of information. Diana, a charming 14-month-old with giant eyes, is introduced to two new friendly ladies as she sits in her high chair. The first lady looks into a bucket and oohs and ahs. She shows the baby a toy in the bucket. Then Diana sees the second lady look into a different bucket. She oohs and ahs too, but when she shows Diana the interior of the bucket, it's empty. Why, Diana might be thinking, would the second lady ooh and ah over an empty bucket? Then the first lady looks behind a screen and Diana cranes her neck to see too but can't. When the second lady looks behind a different screen, Diana doesn't even bother trying. Who can trust the behavior of the lady who oohs and ahs over empty buckets? This is the beginning of taking the source of information into account. Once they are a bit older, say 3 years old, children will take the personality of the informant into consideration, not trusting a mean puppet but trusting a nice one. Who wants to listen to a meanie?

Seeing is believing. Imagine 4-year-old Noah is shown a cat. Noah pets the cat and is in feline love. Then the sociable researcher puts a dog mask on the cat. It covers the cat's whole face. "Is the animal still a cat or is it now a dog?" Noah is asked. "Oh," Noah says with great authority, "It got to be a dog!" Fooled by appearances! It's almost hard to believe. Show Sage a sheet of gray transparent plastic. When put in front of a white plastic egg, it makes the egg look like a rock. "It's a rock," Sage says. And she will now agree that it is a rock and will be heavy to pick up. Voila! Remove the plastic, and it's an egg again.[9]

Children under age 4 are likely to see and believe, hence the name of this first level. In some ways, this makes sense. After all, you are a little kid and what do you know? Children eventually come to appreciate that things are not always as they appear, but this takes time and experience. Children at this level may be scared out of their wits at the scene in *The Wizard of Oz* when the Wicked Witch shrivels into goo when water hits her flesh. The world is a pretty scary place if everything is real. One of us remembers worrying that the roaring MGM lion would leap off the screen at the beginning of movies. Her parents' chuckles and reassurances that it wasn't real made no difference, and she was still left quaking and covering her head with her coat. One of us also remembers 2-year-old Adam who refused to go out for recess anytime the leaves were rustling in the wind. It took us 3 months to find out that he was scared that the Wicked Witch of the West would show up at his school on his playground when the wind blew.

There is a whole organization based on the premise that kids are easy to influence because they believe most of what they see. The nonprofit Campaign for a Commercial-Free Childhood, founded by former Harvard professor Dr. Susan Linn, was designed "to end the exploitive practice of marketing to children and promote a modern childhood shaped by what's best for kids, not corporate profits."[10] If children were critical thinkers and recognized that commercials presented biased or misleading information, we might have fewer kids in supermarket aisles begging for sugary cereals.[11]

If I think the world is flat, you know I have a false belief. That's because you have a theory of mind (ToM), as we described earlier in the book. ToM is crucial for critical thinking.[12] For example, at Stanford University, John Flavell and his colleagues told 3-year-olds about Robin, a little girl who liked to put her feet on the dinner table. Immediately after they were told about Robin, the researchers asked the children, "Does Robin think it's OK to put her feet on the dinner table?" Amazingly, most children disagreed with this question and said no way. If they couldn't put their feet on the table, they thought that Robin couldn't either![13] Deanna Kuhn, a psychologist at Columbia University, called these kids *realists* because they find it hard to imagine that others can hold different beliefs than they do.[14]

At the next level, Level 2, children know that they can think differently than their friend or mother does. ToM is happening right now for this very situation: Although we, the writers, think that you are absorbed in this book, we have to recognize that you may be thinking about taking the laundry out of the dryer or about your next business deal that has to close by 5 this evening.

In the world of commerce, Level 1 plays out as "that's-not-my-job" mentality. People who use this phrase don't get that they are part of a team. They also don't get that they should either figure out how to help the customer or ask around until they find the right person who can help the customer. Does "that's not my job" mean "I don't have time" or "it's beneath my dignity?" Whatever it means, as Laura Stack, a business writer, says, it's "the lamest excuse in business today."[15] Thankfully, some department stores and other businesses that pride themselves on service make it their policy never to say this to customers, even if the request is outside the salesperson's bailiwick. The flip side of "that's not my job" is "I was just following orders." This is another limited, Level 1 response. But juries sometimes buy it. In the wake of the Enron scandal in 2005, Theodore C. Sihpol III, a broker with the Bank of America, was indicted and tried for doing illegal after-hours trades. His defense? Just following orders. The jury acquitted him of all 29 counts.

LEVEL 2: TRUTHS DIFFER

At Level 2, people recognize that there are multiple points of view. Some say Columbus discovered America; some say it was Amerigo Vespucci. Some say the Native Americans were already there, so neither Columbus nor Vespucci should receive the honor. At Level 2, we recognize differences in opinion and simply pick one. We make black or white judgments without evaluating the evidence. But Level 2 is progress: children can now recognize that truths differ for different people. Liz's daddy told her that if you swallow a watermelon seed, you can grow a watermelon in your tummy. She proudly shares this information with her friend Gaby. But Gaby knows different: If you swallow a watermelon seed, you can have a baby! At Level 2, Liz and Gaby think a statement can only be true or false and they will continue to fight about this.

Children can now engage in some critical thinking because they can compare what they have heard with what they see in the world.[16] Authority (i.e., big people) is still greatly respected, so Liz is likely to believe her dad, who is a doctor. But given that she never met anyone who said they had a watermelon in their belly, she is starting to wonder. Children, like Liz, begin with a bias toward accepting information—especially from adults—as true. But starting at around age 4, kids also begin to weigh an individual's *level of expertise* to decide what is true. So overhearing Liz and Gaby arguing, we might hear Liz say that because her daddy is a doctor and knows all there is to know about the body, Liz's dad must be right.

Critical thinking starts with questioning. We don't want our children to "question everything" as the old '60s expression went. Sometimes we just need them to listen. We don't want them to ask us four times why they can't touch the hot stove or go up on the roof or cross the street alone. But they can question why we added flour to the soup or whether there is another way to mix the brownies (e.g., "Can I use a fork instead of a spoon?"). Great scientists and most children see the world as a laboratory and are not afraid to ask about many interesting things they see there. Why does the mountain look like it has layers, like a cake? What happened to make it that way? Do red apples from the supermarket grow on the same trees as green apples? Do they taste the same? Questions like these are a way for children to start realizing what they know and don't know. Once they become aware of their own limitations, they are perhaps more likely to recognize others' limitations too. Critical thinking means being skeptical—not just about what you think but also about what your friends and parents think too.

By age 4 or 5, children know that other minds exist. Interestingly, this is just what many children with autism lack, although there is big variation. Along with Julia Parish-Morris, Beth Hennon, and Helen Tager-Flusberg, we found that autistic children who can infer what another person is thinking do much better at learning new words.[17] When you name an object in the environment for your child (e.g., the big round clock), it might be on an opposite wall from where you are. Toddlers who can figure out what you are focused on will be more likely to learn the word *clock* than those who don't even try. So developing a ToM is important for critical thinking and is also useful for learning from others.

Critical thinking involves questioning one's own thoughts and feelings. Good teachers help kids do this. One of us watched a kindergarten teacher ask her charges, "What day is it?" One child said "Monday," and the teacher countered with, "How do you know?" "Because," the child responded, "yesterday was still the weekend and we come back the first day and that's Monday." Questioning children about the source of their knowledge implicitly teaches them that parroting is not enough. We need to know *how* we know something.[18]

Families are all different. Some make jokes and puns a lot. Families who use humor are setting children up for understanding that people don't always say and do what they mean. Why might this be important? One psychologist, Meredith Gattis at Cardiff University in Britain, described how she created a faux near-tragedy for her 4-year-old daughter, Ella.[19] Meredith acted as if she were going to drop an empty egg carton as she moved across the kitchen to her refrigerator. Ella had seen Meredith put the eggs into the refrigerator but was willing to suspend belief when mom jostled the carton around, steadied it, and made as if to trip before she put it in the trash can. Ella laughed hysterically. This got Gattis thinking: Why was that scenario so funny to Ella? Gattis realized that Ella had to see her mom's behavior as different from the norm—as when you try to write with the pencil's eraser instead of its point—and understand that her mom was doing this on purpose. Recognizing that people can do something wrong intentionally to fool around requires that Ella has a ToM. So when Dad calls his boot a cupcake or pretends to put a slice of pizza on his head, children often find this hilarious. Humor implicitly teaches kids that others can think and do wrong things on purpose. Gattis said, "That's an easy entry into duality—the idea that an action can mean more than one thing—a very difficult concept for young children," but it is probably aided by having silly parents.[20]

Deanna Kuhn referred to people in Level 2 as *absolutists*—either a "fact" is true or not true.[21] Level 2 people think reality is obvious—it's pretty much what you can see. Level 2 people compare the fact and the world. Global warming doesn't have much chance in the worldview of these thinkers because its effects aren't obvious. You can't see it, only what it causes. It doesn't match their everyday experience. It's hard to take a long view and grant that there are forces we cannot see that might be playing havoc with the climate if you are an absolutist.

Level 2 thinking can affect the likelihood that you will be depressed. The term *metacognition* captures the way we think about thinking. For example, if Saul tends to frame events in his life negatively, he might ruminate or obsess about that slight he received at the pharmacy from Kenny. If Saul could be guided to examine how he frames things in a negative way, if he could be guided to critique his way of thinking, he might get out of the loop anxious and depressed people often find themselves in. There are therapy treatments based on this idea. Even children can be encouraged to consider the negative things they tell themselves when they think. Controlling these negative thoughts has been shown to reduce anxiety and depression.[22]

Critical thinking is touted as a skill the private sector in our country really values. Need help in learning how to do it? There are courses and workshops and seminars all over the web offering to train people in business to think critically. David Garvin of the Harvard Business School said, "I think there's a feeling that people need to sharpen their thinking skills, whether it's questioning assumptions, or looking at problems from multiple points of view."[23] But at Level 2, "questioning assumptions" is tough if you believe that reality is staring you in the face and that everything is going just swell. In Level 2, no advance planning is needed. Take British Petroleum (BP).[24] When one of their oil platforms blew up in 2010 and millions of gallons of oil flowed into the Gulf of Mexico, BP was not prepared. They had not considered the possibility that a disaster of this nature could happen and had no prearranged plan for how to deal with it. A failure of critical thinking cost them roughly $12.5 billion.

We sure hope that Neil Gabler was exaggerating when he wrote in *The New York Times* that critical thinking has yielded to blind conviction, stuck at Level 2:

> It is no secret, especially here in America, that we live in a post-Enlightenment age in which rationality, science, evidence, logical argument and debate have lost the battle in many sectors, and perhaps even in society generally, to superstition, faith, opinion and orthodoxy.[25]

LEVEL 3: OPINIONS

We have all heard the phrase "They say . . ." preceding some advice or talk about a new drug or a way to get your kid into Yale. Don't you always wonder who "they" are? Level 3 thinkers are happy to stop at "they say" for two reasons. First, "they say" acknowledges that people think differently. Second, because "they say" sets a low bar for evidence, it gets the speaker off the hook: "I don't have any evidence for this, but someone does." Opinion is often good enough to satisfy the "they sayers." Although we all do this at times, people can get into a lot of trouble relying on only opinion.

Business blunders abound at this level.[26] Take the razor sold in Qatar called the *Tiz*. In Iran, where the company was located, the brand name *Tiz* meant *sharp* and had good customer acceptance. The problem was that no one in the Iranian company checked what *Tiz* meant in Qatar, where it was slang for *buttocks*. You need not go to the Middle East to find such cases. In 2002, the sports manufacturer Umbro in Britain put out a type of new sneaker. Unfortunately, they called the new model *Zyklon*. Sound familiar? Zyklon B was the name of the gas the Nazis used to murder millions of Jews. One wonders how these gaffes could happen, but they happen all the time. They happen because no one thinks to dig around to see whether these ideas will work. They are just accepted.

At Level 3, opinion, people recognize that there are other points of view but still rely too heavily on their own personal reality. They can even understand that reality is not so clear and that others can experience different realities.[27] Diane Halpern, the critical thinking psychologist whose work we mentioned earlier, recalled an editorial in *USA Today*.[28] It was about a vast study one of us was involved in on the effects of day care on young children. The findings were that quality day care was not harmful to children. Numerous studies by now have reached the same conclusion. But the author of that editorial preached to readers to trust their instincts. Not in the sense of "Trust your instincts while you're evaluating day care for your child," but the writer said readers should trust what they already believed about the negative effects of day care and to ignore what the research found. This is Level 3 critical thinking: The column acknowledged that there are differing opinions but then raised personal belief to the same level as the evidence captured in a large-scale scientific study. At Level 3, opinion rules. Evidence? What's that?

There are glimmers of critical thinking that involve analysis even in young children. The great psychologist Jean Piaget is renowned for offering beautiful examples of children's thinking by watching their behavior, in this case, his daughter Jacqueline's. At age 20 months, she approached a door that she wished to close, but she was carrying some grass in each hand. She put down the grass by the threshold, preparing to close the door. But then she stopped and looked at the grass and the door, realizing that if she closed the door the grass would blow away. She then moved the grass away from the door's movement and then closed it. She had obviously planned and thought carefully about the event before acting.[29] There you have "visible" thinking.

Jacqueline didn't just act. She thought about it and envisioned a problem, showing that a kernel of critical thinking was at work.

Larry went to visit his precocious 3.5-year-old grandson, Beau, who lived about an hour away. There was nothing unusual in that, except that Larry didn't usually come during the week. Beau asked him, "How come you are here, Pop Pop?" Larry: "I came to see you." Beau: "No really, why are you here?" Beau wasn't buying it. Larry was deviating from his pattern, so there must be another reason. This is critical thinking too. Beau is no longer accepting what grownups tell him hook, line, and sinker.

Critical thinking involves considering "*Who* says *what* to *whom*?"[30] Do we know enough about the *who*? Kids, starting at about age 4, can recognize that some people know more than others. Need to get your bike fixed? Take it to a bike shop and not to the shoemaker.[31,32] Adults often evaluate the source of information too, but at this level, we can still fall for self-proclaimed authorities. Some among us might remember "Joe the Plumber" during the 2008 presidential election campaign. Although he was not a plumber but aspired to own a plumbing business, he was dubbed "Joe the Plumber." His real name was Samuel Wurzelbacher, and he asked Obama a question about whether his taxes would increase under an Obama administration. McCain and Palin started to take him to rallies and claim that taxes would increase under Obama. Although Joe was neither named Joe nor was he a plumber, we all unquestioningly believed him.

Evaluating the *what*, the information itself, may depend on how relevant the information is to us. If we are interested in the theater, for example, we may more closely evaluate the claims in that online review of a new play than someone who is not a theater buff. Kids know less than adults and are likely to be more uncertain about the *what*, especially if the informant has made errors in the past. When Aunt Rose tells 7-year-old Sophie that Hanukah (whose dates are based on a lunar calendar) and Thanksgiving are happening on the same day, Sophie dismisses this claim as preposterous. She remembers when Aunt Rose told her that crossing your eyes makes you permanently cross-eyed. Mom had to straighten Aunt Rose out about that.

Being stuck at Level 3 can lead to bad outcomes—for every aspect of our lives. As Candice Mills, Professor at the University of Texas wrote,

> Believing in inaccurate or unsubstantiated claims can lead to a whole host of consequences, from educational (i.e., missing questions on a test due to treating Wikipedia as a reliable source) to interpersonal (i.e., getting in an argument with a classmate due to a rumor), to health-related (i.e., making medical decisions based on trusting a questionable Internet source), and beyond.[33]

Now that's downright scary. A failure to appreciate the difference between opinion and science can lead people who have oral cancer to engage in cunnilingus instead of getting treatment. We are not kidding. Michael Douglas, the actor, claimed that cunnilingus causes and then cures oral cancer.[34] Fortunately, that was not all the "medical" assistance he sought.

A prime example of a lack of critical thinking in adults on medical matters can have dire consequences for children's lives. Some people continue to claim—incorrectly—that vaccines cause autism. Take Polly Tommey of London, who has a child with autism spectrum disorder (ASD). She is an actress (not a scientist) who calls herself a "world authority on autism" and publishes *The Autism Files* (http://www.autismfile.com/). A sample issue includes topics such as how and why vaccines and autism are the vilest things the human race has faced. We wonder whether she would rather have had smallpox or polio. Despite the fact that the Centers for Disease Control and Prevention and many other outlets have reported that "no links have been found between any vaccine ingredients and ASD,"[35] there are still many individuals who believe that vaccines cause autism. What failing to vaccinate children does cause is preventable diseases, such as measles, that can kill children. "Unvaccinated individuals make up the bulk of cases—75 percent"[36] of the 132 cases of measles recently seen in San Francisco. The absence of critical thinking by adults has a direct impact on public health.

Children who can consistently think at Level 3 tend to be middle school age. These are the kids Professor Diana Kuhn called *multiplists* because they realize that authors express their opinions rather than facts. Although many historians say that slavery was one of the main reasons for the civil war, others argue that it was more about economics than slavery per se. Multiplists can appreciate these differences—different people can hold legitimately different ideas. It won't be until Level 4 that individuals Kuhn calls *evaluatists*—true critical thinkers—will appear. That will be when kids realize that although everyone can hold different beliefs, there are actually standards of evidence that can be used to put them to the test. Although people can have their own views, not all are equally correct.[37]

The key to engaging in critical thinking is to question and not just accept the first "answer" that comes along. Understanding is enriched by asking questions about why things are done the way they are. We all admire those people who question the status quo, the ones who ask why can't we talk to each other from far away (this led to the telephone) or why can't we fly like a bird. You get the drift.

How do students get there? Critical thinking can be taught. Of course, asking questions is just one part of critical thinking. We also need to find opportunities to have children consider the evidence. This starts when they are little. Help them put themselves in someone else's shoes: "Why do you think I don't want you to hit your brother?" Not only will this encourage questioning and critical thinking but it will also model your thinking processes in your selection of punishments. Children will understand why doing [fill in the blank] is not acceptable but neither is punishing using physical force. Steve is an active boy—to put it mildly. But little on-the-spot discussions with his mom about rules have led to more advanced critical thinking skills and better behavior—a double bonus!

Children's questions and challenges to parents multiply fourfold during adolescence. Nothing is safe from the critical scrutiny of adolescents who can now imagine different realities. This sometimes-annoying quality can also be harnessed by asking them to actively think about alternatives with you: "How else could we have laid out the living room?" Good luck with Level 3 and your adolescents. Welcome this new questioning state; it means progress in your children's thinking.

At school at Level 3 we can encourage students to share opinions and to debate. Now children can be helped to recognize an argument (e.g., "But what does the chapter say about why the civil war started?"), brainstorm ideas (e.g., "How can we get people to give more to charity?"), and read to support an opinion (e.g., "Can you find even a shred of evidence for your claim that vaccines cause autism?").[38] The web is full of ideas to promote critical thinking in the classroom by, for example, offering students a provocative prompt and asking them to find evidence to support both sides. A high school debate question "Students should be allowed to go out on school nights" would certainly generate some heat.[39]

Although Level 3 critical thinking means that people are aware of alternative points of view and that they can see all sides, they're still not home free. At Level 4 we come to appreciate that some answers are better than others. Some issues can be decided on by looking for evidence. We can go beyond mere opinion.

LEVEL 4: EVIDENCE OR "MASTERING THE INTRICACIES OF DOUBT"[40]

The famous Harvard biologist E. O. Wilson said, "We are drowning in information, while starving for wisdom. The world henceforth will be run by synthesizers, *people who put together the right information at the right time, think critically about it, and make important choices wisely* [emphasis added]."[41] A National Academy of Sciences book called, *Education for Life and Work*, reported that there is widespread agreement on the importance of critical thinking (or the closely allied skill of problem solving).[42] It appeared in virtually all descriptions of 21st-century skills. Not everyone will reach Level 4, but with the nature of occupational requirements rapidly changing and robots entering all sectors of society, those who do reach Level 4 will have a serious advantage over people stuck at earlier levels.

Critical thinking did not just pop up on people's radar. It has been prized for a long time. What is changing, though, are the demands of the workplace. Now there is a premium on critical thinking. Blue-collar jobs that did not require critical thinking are going the way of tollbooths manned by humans. Only one fifth of all jobs in 2009 in the United States were blue collar. Think about your own work environment. Middle-level jobs such as file clerks and secretaries are also disappearing as the file cabinets are being carted away. At one of our universities there used to be one secretary for about four faculty members. Now that ratio has jumped to one secretary for 24 faculty members. Demand is growing for expert thinking, whereas low-level jobs that can't be computerized (e.g., service jobs such as health care aides and security guards) also continue to grow. With the middle dropping out, either the kids of the future will head for the top where critical thinking is essential or for the bottom where they will be considered relatively unskilled.

Howard Gardner, who has thought long and hard about what it means to be intelligent, thinks that there are five minds needed for the future. One of these is the *synthesizing mind*. In his words, "The ability to knit together information from disparate sources into a coherent whole is vital today."[43] It "involves selecting crucial information from the copious amounts available" (p. 155) and then using it for the current task. Increasing the number of ingredients in a recipe won't yield a great soufflé; knowing how to select and combine the ingredients is essential. Of course, just as Chef Jacques will not derive new recipes from ingredients without some study and experience, Gardner says that people need to acquire a "disciplined mind" to think within their domain, be it business or medicine or engineering, and so forth. And more and more of what we do requires knowledge of more than one area. Chef Jacques keeps up in chemistry and agriculture.

Interdisciplinary study is becoming the norm as lines between knowledge domains continue to blur. In medicine, for instance, the mind is more and more recognized as a source of variability in people's physical well-being. In education, teachers, administrators, and policy makers have to be aware of how food insecurity and other poverty-related issues can lead to anxiety in children, overloading the areas of the brain that deal with executive function.[44]

Level 4 is where people, as Candice Mills wrote, "master the intricacies of doubt."[45] We do the best we can to gather information to solve a problem. But we recognize the information itself isn't perfect. Linda Darling-Hammond is a professor at Stanford University who wants all our schools to *teach for understanding*.[46] What does that mean? Although memorization is part of what kids have to do, if they don't understand, their knowledge will be "a mile wide and an inch deep"—Level 2—making the analysis and synthesis called for at Level 4 hard to achieve. In her 2008 book, *Powerful Learning*, Darling-Hammond quoted from two letters that appeared side-by-side in *The New York Times*, one from a European student and one from an American. The European student attended high school in Europe and then college in an American university. He said that whereas American students are "bombarded with facts and figures that they were forced to memorize, . . . European students are taught the same subjects, but instead of memorizing them, they are forced to understand them." He also claimed that "critical thinking, analysis, . . . research techniques" were taught in high school in Europe but only appeared here in college.[47] Interestingly, the American student concurred, "The main reason we rank at the low end in education is that we are primarily taught to memorize text until we reach 10th or 11th grade." Only in 11th grade was this student asked "to think logically to solve problems." The student asked plaintively,

> If we do not know how to analyze a problem, how are we ever going to compete in the real world? The problems we are going to face are not all going to be written down in the textbook with the answers in the back."[48]

Importantly, we don't have to wait until high school to invite our children to engage in critical thinking. Ms. Kooby had her third-grade class read about how parks are designed. She could have stopped there and quizzed them on what they had read. What is the name of the person that designs the park? What climate is this park made for? and so forth. She could have done that but she didn't because she wanted the children to be more active and engaged and more critical of what they had read.

She divided them into small groups of three and asked them to think about what they thought the park they read about was missing. She encouraged them to think big—what would make a park really great? She really got their creative juices going. She asked them to write down what they wanted and to draw each new element.[49] After they worked for a while, she asked them to all share what they thought and drew in the following context. She told them that they had to decide—as a class—what three new things they would want to add to the park. They had to make a case and to argue for what they wanted and why, and all the ideas would be listed on the board. The class would vote at the end for which three new elements to include. Can you just see the children's excitement as they discussed and struggled together and critiqued each other's suggestions? This is using critical thinking in a context children know something about. A permanent ice cream truck that gave away free ice cream? A park bench that played music? Why is the former a good idea but not the latter? Argue for what you want!

Researchers like Deanna Kuhn are still struggling to understand what propels the kind of thinking used at Level 4. Does going to school do it? Does it happen with age? Are folks in different disciplines better at it than others? Another question has moral overtones. Do adults see evaluatist thinking as worthwhile? It is, after all, somewhat in conflict with societal values of tolerance and acceptance. "Live and let live" and "to each his own" may work against developing evaluatist thinking. But "it is a deceptively simple step down a slippery slope from the belief that everyone has a right to his or her opinion to the belief that all opinions are equally right."[50] Thinking at that level—Level 3—is what makes some in our society demand that intelligent design be taught alongside evolutionary theory or that everyone is entitled to their opinion on climate change.

At Level 4, evaluatists make choices between positions based on the evidence. They read diverse sources to try to assemble a position on an issue, a synthesis. A friend of ours needed a hip replacement. She questioned her doctor about what was the best material to use for her new hip. When he responded that there was only stainless steel, she went on the web and found a variety of implant materials.

One wonders whether her doctor knew about other materials. In this case, her skepticism may have saved her much grief, especially after she learned that a stainless steel implant would have been a real problem if she had a metal sensitivity.

Psychologist Diane Halpern argued that there are several components to teaching critical thinking skills.[51] The first is dispositional or attitudinal. This is parallel to assuming a critical stance. Remember the old "question authority"? Even people in positions of power don't know everything. This is why our friend googled what hip replacements were made of. We can imagine that even an expert might not be up on the latest information—for a variety of benign reasons. This is what happens if you have a critical stance; Google becomes your go-to.

Second, there are ways to teach critical thinking skills—as Robert Sternberg has argued.[52] Helping students become critical of what they hear, like the commercials on TV, is one way to approach this. Listening recently to a pitch from a dating website, we were astonished to hear that the site in question was first in marriages, first in marital satisfaction, and that individuals who used this site were more likely to marry. "First" compared with what? No comparison group was offered. Were people who used this site more likely to marry than individuals who did not use dating websites at all or more likely to marry than priests and nuns?

Other ways to heighten critical thinking are to help students find and evaluate arguments in written or oral communication and to generate hypotheses based on the premises. If that dating website is "first in marriages," students might hypothesize that other dating websites should report proportionally fewer marriages. Drawing diagrams, criticizing premises, thinking about the additional information required all help students to generate more critical solutions to problems.

In business, given the information explosion, critical thinking is central to success. Elizabeth Edersheim wrote that it seems logical that all the information available at one's fingertips would make managing a company easier.[53] To the contrary, all the clients Edersheim consults with struggle mightily to figure out which of the vast amount of information available will be useful and how. Level 4 knowledge workers who can evaluate and synthesize this information can name their price!

When we think about the explosion of information, it is not surprising that so many people are duped by advertising from nursery schools that promise to help your children learn computer science. After all, we all want our kids to succeed. But the chances that our kids will get that job at Google because they attended The Genius Nursery are slim indeed. Perhaps we need to escape from the illusion that content is king and recognize that those who will succeed will be the synthesizers and navigators in an expansive sea of content. Even critical thinking will be limiting, however, if we do not know how to put information together in new ways to solve problems that no one has ever seen before. And that skill requires that we leap to the next C, *creative innovation.*

TAKING ACTION

How do we know critical thinking when we see it?

In Yourself

Do you consider yourself a gullible person? We are all at Level 1 sometimes—it partially depends on the domain. Frank tells his psychology class that he has two clay balls that weigh exactly the same; he shows this on a balance. He then asks the class to watch while he flattens one into a pancake. He asks the class whether they will still weigh the same amount or whether one will be heavier than the other. They look at him like he is from Mars. Of course, they will weigh the same. This is Piaget's classic conservation task, and adults are generally pros at it whereas children below about age 6 fail because they get fooled by how things look. But even big smart adults can be fooled. He then rolls the pancake into a ball again and tells his class that he is going to shoot one of the clay balls through with gamma rays. Will they still weigh the same? His class is stumped because, they tell him, they don't know much about the effects of gamma rays. In circumstances like these, we might be gullible too. But once we know something about the domain, we know we can ask questions and take a critical stance.

Sometimes we don't want to take a critical stance—as when we need to have a medical procedure. Sylvia brought Jason along with her to the doctor to be her advocate and ask the hard, critical questions because she was too upset contemplating the surgery to do it for herself. But in other domains, Sylvia pushes and probes.

Do you find yourself saying "they say . . ." a lot? This might suggest that Level 3 is your home now. Asking questions is not always easy. But when the stakes are high, being at Level 4 and asking for the evidence might be a crucial step in making a decision.

In making an argument in writing, Brendan saves up his critique of the literature he reviewed to the end of the paper. He writes, "I find these experiments to be poorly done" and then writes nothing more. But this is not enough. If we are to reach Level 4, Brendan must give a reason why he thinks the research missed the boat—what did they do wrong? Being critical of his own thinking and writing will make Brendan's performance shine. Knowing how to craft a good argument—where it succeeds and where it falters—is something he needs to learn. But he doesn't see that yet.

We can all improve our critical thinking skills. We can all seek answers to the questions that face us on a daily basis. The Internet allows us all to do this with a touch of our fingertips. Asking numerous questions about the terms of that warranty could be the difference between buying that new car or holding on to your old one.

In Your Child

Playing games, telling funny stories, reading books, asking why—these are all ways to spur your child's critical thinking skills. Games fuel critical thinking because they make children aware of rules and when they are violated. But first they need to learn the rules. We have all been present when our children are arguing over who goes first, why that move didn't count, and myriad other disagreements. Disagreeing is not bad though and fuels the development of critical thinking. If we instill the ability to disagree with others but in a respectful way (no hitting, no shouting), we can watch our children solve these problems with their siblings and peers (most of the time). Learning to negotiate is part of communication too, and learning how to be critical is an important skill for children to learn.

Storytelling is a lost art. But a good storyteller is a pleasure to listen to. Parents and caregivers can tell their own stories. Our children loved to hear what we did when we were their age. And they always have a million questions. Questioning is necessary to learn about the world and to develop a critical stance. Notice too, that this costs us nothing and helps build the bond between us and our children and grandchildren.

Reading books is a great place to use critical thinking. When the story takes a surprising turn, children often ask questions such as "Did that really happen? How come they didn't fall off the cliff? Why did they . . . ?"—you see where this is going. Books create an alternative reality and although it's fun to get lost inside it, it's also fun to ask "What if?" What if you were a princess and found it boring? Would you throw away your crown? Thinking up alternative endings for stories builds creativity, communication, and critical thinking. It communicates to children that things didn't have to be that way; there are equally plausible alternatives.

Our children often asked us questions about why people acted the way they did in real life. "Why did Bobby call Carol a bad name?" Children are greatly motivated (aren't we all?) to understand what makes people tick. It removes some of the unpredictability from their social relationships if they can figure out *why* others act in surprising ways. These are great opportunities for discussion if we don't shut them down by saying, "Because he's a bad boy." We can ask children to think about what would make Bobby do that. How did he feel when he did that? Was it a nice way to treat Carol? Were there other things Bobby could have done instead? These are all ways in which we can engage our children's critical thinking skills and jointly work through puzzlement with them. They do not have to just accept the status quo, and they need to understand that not all people who get angry use bad names or take advantage of others. We have to encourage children to question and realize things could be otherwise.

If you are feeling really ambitious, you can even invent new games to build critical thinking while you are on family vacations. One of us did just that with her three sons. One year, the children were all challenged to find evidence of whether King Arthur existed. We traveled to and fro across the British countryside looking for Arthur's tomb, any evidence of Guinevere's existence, or even whether there might have been a castle at Camelot. Another year, in Israel, we wrote statements on index cards as we traversed the country. The kids' job was to tell us whether the statement was true or false and to supply evidence for their choices. To make it even more challenging, we offered points for cheap evidence (1 point for asking a guide when you are taking a tour) or expensive evidence (3 points if you noted that the architecture of the building bricks matched a particular period of

time). All the boys tried for more points and kept themselves occu-
pied on the bus as we moved from one town to another. These kinds
of games can be played anywhere, and they not only teach the kids
some history but also help them become better critical thinkers. And
they don't have to take place in foreign countries. They can happen
in your city or town.

In the Places You Go

Opportunities for engaging in critical thinking are everywhere.
Samantha was in a class where the teacher would brook no dissent
and even discouraged questions. Controlling teachers and parents
tend to shut down children's questioning. Short of changing her class,
what can we do to foster Samantha's critical thinking? Art class might
help. In art, we have something in mind that we struggle to represent
accurately. It makes us think when we find ourselves not meeting our
mark. And it makes us ask, "What can I do to make this better?"
And what exactly does "better" mean—just a better rendition or a
rendition that is infused with perspective? Drama is another venue
for critical thinking. Children in plays have to understand the character's motivation: Why did Rina jump into her car and ride away so
quickly? Situations like this will promote discussion and there may
well be disagreement.

Almost any place you go with your children gives you an opportunity to ask why and to stretch their thinking. Why do they think the
current situation prevails? When you go to the neighborhood pool the
weekend after Labor Day, you discover that it is closed. When your
kids ask why, you can turn the question back on them: Why do *you*
think the pool is closed? Or when Phyllis stopped at a red light and
Margaret asked, "Why do we need lights?" you are doing your child
a favor when you ask them to think about what function traffic lights

serve. Small everyday conversations like these are golden opportunities to invite your children to think and question, all prerequisites to becoming critical thinkers.

How Do We Create Environments That Foster Critical Thinking?

The first thing we think of is respect. If children are treated with respect, if their questions are taken seriously, they will feel safe to question and to move beyond the information that they see. Even when as young as 2 or 3 years old, children need to be respected for their interests and queries. Sensitive and responsive parenting or parenting that takes children's perspectives into account and responds to them in ways that they can understand is key. Taking the time to do this will pay you back tenfold because your children will know they can count on your wisdom and coaching to help them. And of course, you are nurturing their critical thinking at the same time.

THE ROAD TO SUCCESS

Who are the inventors, entrepreneurs, scientists, and engineers who make breakthroughs? They are us. They are our children. They are the people who engage in critical thinking to see the problems others don't. These are the people we call visionaries or futurists who notice the trends even before the rest of us realize we are in the midst of them. Some of the people are found at Amazon, a company that brings critical thinking to a new level. Among owner Jeff Bezos's principles is "disagree and commit."[54] In his view, many workplaces overvalue harmony. Giving blunt, even painful, feedback to coworkers is to be valued if the products and ideas that emerge are to be stellar. Why couldn't Amazon deliver packages more quickly?

An operations executive named Stephenie Landry figured out a way to make deliveries happen in minutes for urban customers. Within a little over 3 months, Ms. Landry was in Brooklyn directing Prime Now, a service for people who place Amazon orders and need their treasured Elsa doll or toaster ASAP.

Our next chapter talks about the creative innovation needed to solve problems discovered through critical thinking. But no problem can be solved unless it is perceived. Critical thinking makes that possible.

CHAPTER 9

CREATIVE INNOVATION: REARRANGING THE OLD TO MAKE THE NEW

*There is a fountain of youth: It is your mind, your talents, the cre-
ativity you bring to your life and the lives of the people you love.
When you learn to tap this source, you have truly defeated age.*
—Sophia Loren

How many different uses can you think of for a paper cup? You
can use it for drinking and for watering your plants, as a paper-clip
holder, and . . . what else? Take a moment to consider what ideas
you can generate.

In 2010, the cover of *Newsweek* heralded a new international
malady: the creativity crisis. Creativity surfaces as essential in every
review of 21st-century skills. From the *Harvard Educational Review*
to the *Business News Daily*, American educators, industrialists, and
entrepreneurs know that prosperity rests at the edge of creative discovery. Unless our workforce unleashes more creative innovation, our
children will lose their jobs to offshoring or to automation. As John
Seely Brown, a corporate visionary said, "I create; therefore I am."[1]

Our children are woefully unprepared for the growing demand
for creative thinking among top employers.[2] Indeed, Kyung Hee Kim,
who teaches at the College of William and Mary in Virginia, looked
at 300,000 scores on the classic Torrance Test of Creative Thinking.[3]
Scores increased until 1990 and then started to trend downward over
the last 2 decades. On this test, people of all ages are invited to complete a picture by adding lines and shapes to a minimal design they've
never seen before. Since 1990, people have had lower scores than
they had in the past. That is, they are not creating as many original

and unique designs than they were before. Nor are they thinking of as many novel uses for a cup. How many uses can you think of, and how many are uniquely different from those your friend can generate? Who cares about cups and designs? We do, because these downward-trending findings mean that we are adapting less well to our rapidly changing environment. When your child asks for a new toy, can you figure out how to use silver foil and toilet paper rolls to make one? Imagine your car is stuck on the ice. Can you think to put a board under the back wheels to give it traction? And these are just the day-to-day problems we face. How will society meet the challenges of climate change and poverty without creativity?

Is creativity different from intelligence or just being smart? Although being smart never hurts, creativity is not the same as intelligence: We all know people who are geniuses but who panic when a road is closed or can't think how to use the leftovers to make a new dish. We need to be strong critical thinkers or we will not be intelligent thinkers, but even that will not be enough if we cannot create new solutions from old parts—if we fail to become master tinkerers.

Articles like Kim's in the scientific literature and in the popular press put a spotlight on creativity. Sophia Loren, according to our opening quotation, thinks creativity is a way to maintain one's relevance and youthfulness. But what is it? Survey the field and you'll find dozens of terms used to try to capture the sentiment behind creativity. There's "divergent thinking," "creative potential," "creative cognition," "insight," and "originality" used as overlapping and loose synonyms. J. P. Guilford defined *creativity* as the ability to produce a number of different responses to new problems—like the earlier cup example. In his own words, Guilford described *divergent thinking* (and hence *creativity*) as the "generation of information from given information, where emphasis is upon variety and quantity of output."[4] To unpack this, we can ask *how many* examples you generated for the paper cup problem, how many *kinds* of examples (e.g., containers vs. props), and how *original* your responses were (e.g., did anyone consider earrings?). Tasks like this became the pillars on which the study of modern creativity research stands. A creative person is one who can generate many responses (i.e., fluency) of many different kinds (i.e., variety), many of which are unusual or clever (i.e., original).

Sir Ken Robinson, a British creativity expert who wrote a book with a great title, *Out of Our Minds: Learning to Be Creative*, said that there are three misconceptions about what it means to be creative.[5] First, many think that creativity is only for "special people" and that not everybody can be creative. Believing this myth puts creativity beyond the reach of us mere mortals.[6] Richard Florida argued that fully 38.3 million Americans, or 30% of all workers, are in the ever-emerging "creative class" where they are depended on to engage in complex, high-level problem solving.[7]

Our economy is moving from traditional industries to an economy where individual and collective creative contributions matter more and more. Fortunately, "virtually everyone has the ability to make creative contributions in various fields of knowledge. Creativity is not an either-or-trait."[8] We are all under the big tent of creativity!

Speaking of the arts, this is what Robinson called the second misconception about creativity: Not only is creativity for "special people" (Myth 1) but it is also about "special activities"—like the arts (Myth 2). Of course, the arts thrive on creativity. But Robinson's point is that creativity is needed everywhere, influencing everything we do. To relegate creativity to that painter who creates trompe l'oeil images that look like cardboard but are really made of fiberglass (Ivin Ballen) or to that choreographer who designed the dances for *West Side Story* (Jerome Robbins) or to the team that wrote the score for *A Christmas Story* (Pasek and Paul) is to fail to recognize how creative innovation is needed everywhere and practiced by everyone to some degree. It is just easier to see it immediately in the arts. But don't be fooled: Creativity was behind the printing press that created this book and even the ideas we share here from other minds and our own.

In Italy, they really get the idea that creativity is everywhere. There, tucked away in a small town between Bologna and Milan, we find Reggio Emilia, a town devoted to a well-known early childhood curriculum that has captured the imagination of the world, inspired by teacher and visionary Loris Malaguzzi. Children (and adults) might be asked to have a conversation with a tree—you heard us right—a tree. Does this sound a bit bizarre? Children have no problems interpreting this idea, and they are even better than we are at using their imaginations to draw, sing, and talk to the trees in a language the Reggio team calls the "hundred languages" of learning through creative imagination. At a recent conference in Italy, you should have seen the projects that our friends generated after they got over the mini shock that they were going to learn about trees by literally getting to know them. When given the time to think about those beautiful, everyday, normal props that are waiting for us outside our window you can see them in a whole new way. One of our colleagues got a business call during our tree exploration and even had the courage to tell his mate, "Sorry I cannot deal with this now. I am talking to a tree."

Another lesson plan in the Reggio demonstration school invites the children to play with lights and shadows as they use their imagination to figure out just where those shadows come from and how they might make a shadow longer or shorter. When is the last time you picked up a flashlight, aimed the beam at the wall, and played with light? Remember those hand silhouettes we used to create on our bedroom walls and the stories we used to make up about how our two "animals" were talking together? It's time to dispel that second myth that creativity is bestowed on special people who work in special mediums.

Finally, the third myth about creativity: Robinson thinks that when we use the word *creativity*, people have an image of a single individual running in circles (or with scissors) wearing a court jester's hat and screaming wildly. Maybe some creative individuals are like that, but 99% are not. Because creativity takes education, skill, imagination, and discipline, people who are creative do not have to have Albert Einstein's hair or wear Madonna's bustiers. Look in the mirror and see a creative person: Creative people look just like us. Mark Runco, the man who literally wrote the book on creativity said, "Everyone has the potential to be creative, but not everyone fulfills that potential."9

HOW DOES CREATIVITY DEVELOP?

Can creativity be taught? And what makes it safe for us to start drawing outside the lines? How can we help our kids to become the inventors, entrepreneurs, and big thinkers of tomorrow? How do we abandon what psychologists call *functional fixedness*, a fancy way of saying that we can't imagine, for example, how else to use a hammer other than as a nail knocker? A hammer can also be a doorstop or a paperweight or [fill in the blank]. Being creative involves thinking outside the box. Remember the nine-dot problem? This may be where the phrase "outside the box" comes from. Imagine nine dots lined up in a "square" of three equally spaced rows, three in a row (see Figure 9.1). The exercise is to connect all the dots using no more than four straight lines and without lifting your pen off the page. The only way to succeed is to literally go outside the box subtly created by the three rows of dots. Most of us become flustered trying this problem because we implicitly assume that we have to stay within the square box. Once we are shown that there is another way to think about this—voila: success!

How important is it to free ourselves from coloring only within the lines or from inside the box? Professor Allan Snyder, director

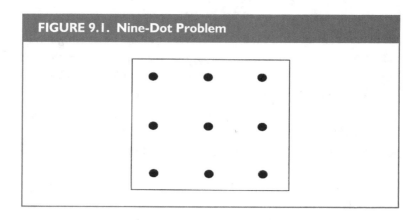

FIGURE 9.1. Nine-Dot Problem

of the Center for the Mind at the University of Sydney, suggested that this is a key feature of what he calls the *champion mind-set*. Champions in any domain (he has studied athletes and political leaders from around the world) are not content with the status quo. They stretch their thinking in ways that take multiple perspectives. With global warming, poverty, and antibiotics running out, we sure need thinkers across domains who can free themselves from the obvious "what is" to conceptualize the "what might be." Who would have thought we could have invented limbs that work like real ones, give hearing to completely deaf babies using cochlear implants, or even go the moon as an average citizen (we hear tickets are available)?

Success in the new world order demands that we nurture business environments and schools that value creative innovation and critical thinking. To borrow an analogy, Apple Inc. developed its own signature products—the iPod, Apple 2E, and many others—and celebrated their mission when they used the ad campaign "Think Different" in 1997.[10] Quick pictures of iconic faces that changed the world, such as Albert Einstein's, John Lennon's, and Ted Turner's, implicitly classed Apple with the best and the brightest in but 1 minute.

The campaign was tremendously successful. They also made posters with these faces and used the following quotation to capture what creative innovators often face:

> Here's to the crazy ones. The misfits. The rebels. The trouble-makers. The round pegs in the square holes. The ones who see things differently. They're not fond of rules. And they have no respect for the status quo. You can quote them, disagree with them, glorify them, or vilify them . . . you can't ignore them. Because they change things. They push the human race forward.[11]

How can we educate our kids to support creative thinking? The science of psychology gives us hints at how creativity develops and how it can be nurtured.

LEVEL 1: EXPERIMENTATION

What use of color and line! This artist was exceptional. He was born in 1954 and was handed a pencil and a card when he was 2. By the age of 4, he had made 400 drawings and paintings. True, none was an image that could be given a name, but they were colorful and kind of interesting. He even appeared on British television. Who was this popular and sought-after artist? His name was Congo. He was a chimpanzee. Congo is a great example of Level 1 experimentation because his specialty was mucking around and investigating the materials he was offered. Of course we could be wrong and Congo might have been trying to create the next Mona Lisa, which is unlikely: Congo was into exploration.

Explorers and discoverers "play" with elements *devoid of a grand plan*. In the same way, we can peek in on 3-year-old Elena who, given her first block set, begins to explore how the pieces fit together. She is working hard and ignoring everything taking place around her—she's in a zone! As she experiments, she's figuring out what these little blocks can do. "Which ones work together and which don't? How high can I make a block tower before they all fall?" As Sandra Russ, an expert on play and creativity wrote, "Play is creativity . . . the child is making something out of nothing."[12] When children play, they follow no rules; they only follow their own creative inspiration. Level 1 creativity captures our "novel and meaningful interpretations of experiences, actions, and events"[13]—like when Elena goes through her novel machinations.

At Level 1, children are uninhibited by conventions because they don't know many. They are still learning how the world works. Kids typically wear shoes to school; this is a convention. Some kids—especially when it's hot—will try to challenge that and have to be told what the convention is. Many things that adults take for granted as the norm are not the norm for children. Before children get the message that they are to color within the lines (a convention), they can play freely with all kinds of ideas. This is exactly what we learned from the Reggio Emilia form of education. If we let the children know that they can create, that they can experiment, then we begin to develop a mind-set that is creative and artistic from its inception.

A recent study by Professors Elena Hoicka and Jessica Butcher of the University of Sheffield in England showed that parents play a huge role in fostering creative development or in hindering it.[14] In their research, parents of 16- to 20-month-olds pretended that a toy duck was a hat or that a block was a galloping horse. Children quickly followed suit and learned to tell the difference in mere pretending (e.g., "I am the king") and in joking (e.g., "Let's call a duck a *hat*"). They were given permission to be more creative and to imagine more possibilities.

Adults empower children to play, but their strict supervision can also get in the way of creative expression. In fact, children who come from large families test higher for creative potential, likely because they have more frequent opportunities for play and maybe less constant adult monitoring. Parents who support kids' independence tend to have children who are more creative than those who don't.

But don't assume that Level 1 is only for kids. Adults who create new things or ideas also often start out messing around and experimenting. Research tells us that if there is too much evaluation of new ideas rather than letting them flow freely, or if a physical model is fashioned too early in the process, it shuts down the creative process. For example, in product development, a quick and dirty prototype is often created.[15] In the car industry, producing a prototype too early shifts people's attention to improving features of the prototype, taking them away from the problem the new product was meant to address in the first place. Perhaps this is why recent research has suggested that kids learn best when their fantastical approach is invited.[16]

In the corporate world, creativity and innovation were assigned in the past to the *skunkworks*—a small group of individuals, usually from different disciplines, who were tasked with coming up with new ideas. But this is Level 1 for today's world. Howard Gardner, the psychologist and author, has argued that the divide-and-conquer strategy of isolating creativity to a small group within a company no longer works: "If creativity does not infiltrate the DNA of an organization, it is unlikely to be passed on to the next generation that joins the company."[17] The 3M Company is a great example. They reward anyone who comes up with a good idea, knowing that creativity is a chancy undertaking that must be fostered.

Having environments in which it is safe for creativity to emerge also means encouraging effort. We should applaud drafts, not just final products, and we should encourage the hard work that creativity involves. Companies like Google, IDEO, and Apple get it. Employees are encouraged to tinker. By making it clear that it's OK to play, they create an environment that welcomes innovation. The crayon drawings of little kids may, at first glance, seem no more than random scribbles. On closer examination, however, a 4-year-old's drawing of his family is an act of symbolic representation that is rich in intent even if you can't find fingers, let alone hands. Our inability to see the wonder in the drafts has fostered a creativity killer. School walls around the country are papered with cutouts of preformed apples that were placed on preformed trees. These products have little to do with real creativity.

Nor is creativity about digesting the creative products others have produced, as in some computer games. Creative innovation can be found in the most mundane places. When a child has nothing to do and must fill the time, creativity can emerge. It can be right there in a file drawer or a kitchen cupboard or in those shiny new markers lying on the table. And it can sure be found on the web. The web has turned us all into explorers who look for information on one thing and wind up learning other unexpected tidbits. Programs like GarageBand, for example, can make anyone into a composer and musician. And wonderful programs like Professor Mitch Resnick's Scratch (https://scratch.mit.edu) make anyone into a creative programmer and storyteller. Scratch now has 7 million followers in the 8 to 16 crowd in over 150 countries around the world, and members of the Scratch community can even share their creations at yearly conferences.

LEVEL 2: MEANS–END

At Level 1, experimentation, we encountered Elena learning about her blocks and how they fit together by examining their parts and trying out ways to join them. We also met the knowledge workers in the auto industry brainstorming at a meeting, throwing out gobs of ideas to try and identify and ultimately overcome problems with current car designs.

At Level 2, we see *means–end* creative innovation. Elena is now making a house, using her creative impulses toward a particular goal. And watch Arnie: Instead of spilling paints and getting lost in the process of discovery, 3½-year-old Arnie now uses what he has learned through exploration to design a product with a purpose. Arnie wants to paint a boat today, but tomorrow his artistic purpose is the creation of a monster. Perhaps his boat will be transformed into the monster. Another child may use finger paints to create a landscape or a portrait of his mother and can actually talk about why he made it. Children at Level 2 intentionally engage in creative production for extended periods of time, directing it toward a goal they can identify. We can think of Level 2 as using the same means (i.e., materials) to create diverse ends and also as using different means (e.g., blocks, paint, clay) to create the same end: that hairy scary monster.

Interestingly, when kids are invited to creatively discover how something works, they do better than when they are told what to do. Elizabeth Bonawitz and her colleagues showed preschoolers a really cool-looking toy. It had tubes and pipes, mirrors and boards; pulling one pipe caused a squeak and looking in another revealed your reflection. Amy, the graduate student on the project, told kids different things when she showed each of them the toy. Amy told the kids in the instructed group, "Look at my toy! I'm going to show you how my toy works!" Then she demonstrated one of the uses of the toy by pulling the yellow tube out of the purple tube to make a squeak. She told a different bunch of kids (call them the naïve group), "I just found this toy!" As she pulled out the toy from under the table, she acted as though she pulled the yellow tube out of the purple tube by accident. When it squeaked she said, "Huh? Did you see that?" feigning surprise. Then each child was left alone with the toy. Which children would discover more of the things the toy could do? The children in the instructed group just kept doing the same thing Amy showed them over and over. They discovered few other things the toy could do. But the kids in the naïve condition kept exploring and figuring out more ways to use the toy.[18]

Thus, although teaching is really an efficient way to tell kids about how the toy works, it also dampens exploration and discovery. Why should this be so? Apparently, if a knowledgeable adult tells you something, it must mean that that adult knows how the toy works. Why bother looking for more functions? Allowing children to have an experimental, creative experience improves outcomes in a Level 2 means–end task. Findings like these prompted Professor Alison Gopnik and her colleagues to speculate that little folks are even better at figuring out gadgets than college students.[19] If using new programs on the computer is evidence, then we know that this must be true. Our kids are much quicker than we are at figuring out and using each new "feature" that is introduced in the digital landscape.

Level 2 children are already finding novel combinations in creative ways. Four-year-old Renah, for example, dubbed herself a "mushroom princess." Level 2 creativity is designed to capture our "everyday activities, such as those creative actions in which the non-expert may participate each day."[20] Renah's mother is a mycologist who specializes in the study of mushrooms; princess is a role Renah enjoys playing. Bringing these ideas together will surely get Renah's mom's attention!

In school, children allowed to explore potential solutions to problems are likely to be more creative than those taught the right answer and given step-by-step instructions.[21] We can see this same tension when children play with construction toys. The boxes that give set instructions on how to build a palace or a train station are likely to thwart creativity in a way that loose blocks do not.

The same is true for another type of problem solving: Applying what you have learned to new instances, or *transfer*. Transfer is the holy grail of education. What good is it to teach a child something she or he can only get right on the same kind of problems and in the same classroom setting? Educators want children to take their knowledge out to the world to use it productively to help them solve new challenges. Take fractions, for example. In the fourth grade, kids are taught how to add fractions like 3/5 + 7/9. Our national tests tell us that many kids can't do similar problems outside of their math classrooms. What good is it to know how to add fractions if you can't do those problems in real life? Fractions are relevant to how you divide the bill in a restaurant and to measuring the amount of space that new chair will take up in your living room. Transfer happens best when we go beyond Level 2 learning.

Our Level 2 schools are often moving in the wrong direction for the 21st century, when innovation is more essential than ever, given pressing national and international problems and rising economies everywhere else. On December 10, 2006, *Time Magazine* put the crisis in perspective when Claudia Wallis wrote,

> There's a dark little joke exchanged by educators with a dissident streak: Rip Van Winkle awakens in the 21st century after a hundred-year snooze and is, of course, utterly bewildered by what he sees. Men and women dash about, talking to small metal devices pinned to their ears. Young people sit at home on sofas, moving miniature athletes around on electronic screens. Older folk defy death and disability with metronomes in their chests and with hips made of metal and plastic. Airports, hospitals, shopping malls—every place Rip goes just baffles him. But when he finally walks into a schoolroom, the old man knows exactly where he is. "This is a school," he declares. "We used to have these back in 1906. Only now the blackboards are green."[22]

Kids sitting in rows with flat faces, head in hands, trying to pay attention? Silent classrooms with the teacher at the front imparting pearls of wisdom? That's what we look like more and more—a return to the past. Americans want educational reform. Guess who else does? China. But here is a great irony: China wants to encourage creativity just as we are returning to 19th-century educational methods and encouraging memorization. In fact, Betty Preus, a professor of education at The College of Saint Scholastica in Minnesota, quoted a visiting professor from China as saying, "It is interesting that something we learn from you is just what you want to change."[23] China wants to become more learner centered. They also want to deemphasize rote learning because they recognize they are creating passive, unmotivated students who are interested only in passing the tests. This sounds painfully familiar. We might need to coin an expression parallel to the one used in China, *gaofen dineng*, which literally means "high scores but low ability."[24]

Making it safe to create means encouraging creativity—and not stomping on it—when it emerges. As we build our playrooms and look at our schools we must ask ourselves: Are these places that encourage creativity? The answer is an unqualified yes! Take Rigamajig (http://www.rigamajig.com), an invention by Cas Holman that encourages kids to make moving structures out of big, beautiful wooden pieces that interconnect. A short look at her demonstration video tells the story of what children can do if given the tools, the safe space, and the time to explore. They organically turn into engineers. A project by Kaboom and well-known architect David Rockwell makes the same point with their cleverly designed Imagination Playground (http://www.imaginationplayground.com). To be honest, Cas had her hand in Imagination Playground, too. Here they reasoned that if given the parts and space and time to reimagine their own playgrounds, children could assemble the pieces and invent their own worlds. And invent they do. Taking a peek at the video demonstration illustrates the possibilities that can bring creativity to life. Kids get the means and develop a joint vision of what can be. Finally, a trip to The Tinkering Studio in San Francisco's Exploratorium (http://tinkering.exploratorium.edu/) is a feast of how children can build new items out of old parts. The "junk" lying around the house and the museum becomes fodder for new inventions that take us all to a higher level of creative thinking. The Tinkering Studio, under the direction of Karen Wilkinson, even has webinars where folks can join in the fun even if they are not in the Bay area.

Of course, nurturing creative thinking demands that we take a break from the usual hustle and bustle of our lives and that we make space for playing and thinking. Sometimes it seems as if we are constantly rushing to get our children to the next sports event, language lesson, or art class. These activities are generally controlled by adults rather than by the children. Although our children are surely enriched by joining the neighborhood soccer team, overcontrolling our budding athletic stars comes at the expense of fostering creative thinkers. According to Matthew Robinson, a soccer coach who trains children who are potential Olympics stars, American players are known for being mechanical and showing little creativity on the field (M. Robinson, personal communication, October 1, 2013). They can learn the strategies they are taught, but they have trouble adapting when the game does not unfold as planned. They stand flat-footed on the field. Because children cannot be taught every soccer contingency, just as they cannot be taught how to solve every problem they face, they have to be taught in a way that nurtures their deep understanding and creative juices. Without those pick-up games of bygone eras, adults run the athletic show, robbing kids of the opportunity to approach their soccer challenges in novel ways. How do children invent new plays? What makes it possible for soccer players to move beyond their training on the basics to wow the crowd? Level 3, voice, is where these creative instincts come together.

LEVEL 3: VOICE

Creativity is hard work. As Robert Weisberg, an expert on creativity at Temple University argued, something does not come from nothing.[25] Creativity, in his view, is more an incremental process than a giant *aha!* experience. To reach the higher levels of creativity, a child or adult has to master skill and technique and typically know something about the domain. Getting to Level 3 doesn't happen overnight.

How, for example, does one become a Level 3 chef?[26] Michael starts out at Level 1. He likes to cook, and he experiments most of the time because he wasn't taught and doesn't want to bother reading recipes. Sometimes Michael's dishes come out surprisingly well, and sometimes he just sucks it up (not literally) and eats yogurt for dinner instead. But once he learns the difference between how cumin, coriander, and curry taste and how broiling and roasting work, he enters Level 2: He can now put together new combinations of ingredients to create unusual and tasty meals most of the time. There are fewer failures now as his experimentation phase has paid off! Now Michael is enjoying cooking so much that he takes a few courses. He even goes to France for a week to pick up a course at Le Cordon Bleu—a world-renowned cooking school. In the kitchen, he moves to Level 3, competently executing cuisine a mother would be proud of. His friends beg for invitations to his abode to be his guinea pig as he develops new dishes on the basis of what he has learned. Without cooking school or reading recipe books extensively, it is unlikely that Michael would have moved to Level 3. Although Michael might not ever reach Level 4 and attain the level of James Beard or Marie-Antoine Carême, he is certainly operating at a high level. Kaufman and Beghetto call this the level of professional creativity that misses changing the field but still shows ingenuity and uniqueness.[27] If graduate school in psychology doesn't work out for him, he might have a future as a chef!

Kathy, who was a music major and composer throughout college, never really understood why in college she was asked to "compose like Bach or Beethoven," which she humbly admits was quite impossible. But why was she even given such a charge? This was because unless she learned the techniques of the masters, she would never be able to adapt those techniques and find her own voice. Kathy went on to create albums of children's music.

Elio is an expert on animals—all animals—and knows tons of things about them. Echidnas bear live young. Emus lay astonishingly large eggs. He has little replica models of more animals than we have books in our collections. He is always trying to learn more. Although Elio cannot read yet at age 6, he has sufficient depth in his understanding of animals to come up with a theory of how they wound up in different places on the planet. He told his mom one day that animals travel around to find the best food. When they find the food they like best, they stay there and populate the area. She was astounded. Was he right? Not necessarily. Was he amazingly creative? You bet!

At Level 3, folks know a bunch about the area in which they work. They have "prepared minds," so when they see an opportunity for a better mousetrap, using their critical thinking they can seize it and bring that niggling idea to fruition. Post-it notes, for example, were invented by accident by Dr. Spencer Silver working at 3M. He had to convince his bosses that a glue that didn't stick too tightly or mar a surface was worth pursuing. He envisioned uses for it that his supervisors did not. He was lucky; his invention actually saw the light of day—as the surface of our laptops, crowded with Post-its, attests. But not all novel inventions (or entrepreneurial schemes) will get to emerge. Cornell professor Robert Sternberg pointed out that creativity depends on practical skills too.[28] To create a prototype of that new mousetrap, to bring it to the attention of the right mousetrap makers, and to ultimately brand and market it requires additional skills beyond the creativity to invent the design.

Scientists with PhDs who know lots about their specialty can be at Level 3 too. We know colleagues who specialize in, to use a homely idiom, "turning the crank" a quarter of a revolution for each new study they conduct. Are they competent? Sure! Are they creative? Yes, but not as creative as other scientists who ask probing questions and even invent whole new "cranks"! These scientists are probably at Level 4—their work is novel, creative, and influences others in the field. This kind of work usually has staying power and is valuable in the long run. It is an advance over the research that continues to show pretty much the same thing with each tiny turn of the crank. Society decides which turns are big and which are small. The development of the computer was a big crank from what existed before. Designing a better seat belt saved thousands of lives. And consider that you are likely reading a book printed on paper, which was invented in ancient China during the Han Dynasty (206 BCE–220 CE) but was first made of materials such as papyrus, parchment, and palm leaves. We profit from the fact that the crank was turned to use cheaper materials like wood and rags.

Moving beyond convention, at Level 3 we incorporate our own personal expression. The novelist comes up with a new form that is an important variation on what others have written. The systems analyst develops her own software to help chart continuous improvement in a furniture business. And 10-year-old Jon, equipped with an erector set, eventually becomes an "architect" designing an airport for which there is no existing model. No more re-creating the Ferris wheel on the box; Jon can now move beyond the model. Once people understand their tools and have considerable knowledge of their field, they can develop their own means of creative expression.

Creative innovation can be taught, as Robert Sternberg argued, when we offer children the opportunity to change endings and dream up totally new ways to do things.[29] Why can't grandma, after all a runner of marathons, outrace that wolf? Why can't we have houses that are round? At these last two levels of creative innovation, we know lots of content, have done our share of critical thinking, and know in our bones that better solutions are possible.

The fact that we can train creativity is a good thing, appropriate for this era. As Sir Ken Robinson cogently argued, "We're living in times of massive unpredictability."[30] The pace of innovation is accelerating—just as the amount of information we produce is exploding out of all proportion. Two MIT business professors have written a short but powerful book called *Race Against the Machine*.[31] Without problem-solving abilities and creativity, our jobs will go the way of the tollbooth collectors. This is because digital technologies are transforming the world of work. As technology accelerates and as more and more tasks are done by machines, there will be a "great restructuring" of the workforce that will make it difficult for our children to find jobs, unless we concentrate on increasing their capacity to create and innovate. The authors of the book call themselves "digital optimists," but without changing our schools to encourage creative thinking, it's hard to imagine how "ordinary" kids will find employment. Organizations like the Partnership for 21st Century Skills agree; they write that "repetitive, predictable tasks are readily automated." If a task can be designed for a computer or given to a robot, humans will no longer be needed. All workers will have to be able to solve "complex, multidisciplinary, open-ended problems." After all, they continue, "The challenges workers face don't come in a multiple-choice format and typically don't have a single right answer."[32]

LEVEL 4: VISION

Gordon and Susan went on a bike trip to Mississippi only to discover that they had left Gordon's medications at home. What to do? They called their daughter, who, of course, sent the pills to them using FedEx. Frederick Smith essentially invented the concept of FedEx in an economics term paper at Yale. The paper did not get an *A* because it seemed to propose an impossible idea. Setting up a company like FedEx would require a ton of capital and changing a lot of government regulations. In fact, all who heard the idea predicted it would fail. You know what happened.

In the mid-19th century, childbed fever was a serious problem. Having a baby meant taking your life in your hands. In one clinic of the Vienna General Hospital in Austria in 1842, as much as 15% of new mothers died from childbed fever (formally called *puerperal fever*). Dr. Ignaz Semmelweis, the resident obstetrician, worked hard to figure out why this clinic had a much higher rate of childbed fever than a second clinic in the same hospital. Even before the germ theory of disease was invented, he noticed that when physicians washed their hands they seriously reduced the rate of infection and death in new mothers. The medical community rejected his ideas flat out.

Some of our readers are old enough to remember how documents were copied in the "dark ages" of the last century. At Cornell, where one of us went to graduate school, we referred to these chemical-smelling copies as "purple perils" or "dittos." Mimeograph machines were not fast enough for Chester Carlson, an engineer and law student who, in 1938, invented the Xerox process. He had a hard time getting people to take his new invention seriously. It took him 8 years to get any traction with an investor. IBM and the U.S. Army Signal Corps turned him down flat. Now we are on the verge of having 3-D printers at every port. Just this year, one pharmaceutical company suggested that 3-D printers might radically transform their business. Rather than shipping pills, they will just send sheets of flat compressed medicine that can be printed in any size or quantity at the host medical facility.

These seemingly disparate examples have three important things in common. The first is a great irony: The best ideas are often initially rejected—and rejected outright because truly innovative ideas take people outside their comfort zone and seem wacky—whether in the arts (e.g., many publishers rejected *Harry Potter*) or science (e.g., ulcers are not caused by stress!) or engineering (e.g., Atari and Hewlett-Packard rejected Steven Wozniak's personal computer pitch).

The second thing these examples have in common is that they all represent what we call Level 4 creativity: Vision. Each of these inventors set out to solve a particular problem—from the invention of a reliable overnight mail delivery system to the creation of a fast way to copy documents. Without recognizing that there was a problem to solve (i.e., critical thinking), these inventions would never have come into being. When these inventors examined the status quo, they realized they could do better. They saw the shortcomings in how things were done and were not willing to continue in that vein.

Finally, these breakthrough examples have something else in common: preparation. Individuals who succeed at this level need background and usually some education in their area to comprehend the shortcomings in current solutions and envision better ones. In his book, *Outliers*, Malcolm Gladwell used the term the "10,000-hour rule," based on the work of psychologist Anders Eriksson, claiming that the key to success amounted to at least 10,000 hours of practice. Penicillin's discovery by Alexander Fleming is a great example of this. Fleming was already searching for a wonder drug and came back from a vacation to start over by washing all his petri dishes. He noticed that one of the dishes had white mold growing in it (nothing unusual there, as we all know from that moldy bread on our counter). But this mold had somehow killed the *Staphylococcus aureus* that had been growing in that dish. Eureka! Another scientist might not have noticed; Fleming had put in the hours!

But wait a minute! Are we saying that only the Rowlings, the Carlsons, and the Wozniaks of the world can reach Level 4, or what some researchers call "big-C" creativity?[33] Are we saying that only adults with advanced degrees can reach the highest level of creative innovation? We are all capable of creativity. We all have our Einstein moments, moments when we rise above the status quo, look above the fray, and envision a totally new solution. Sometimes it's just two kids putting their heads together. Two Canadian teenagers sent a LEGO man into space using video cameras and some equipment they bought on Craigslist. They spent every Saturday for 4 months on their project. Collaboration undoubtedly fueled their creative breakthroughs. The Internet is full of examples of children inventing useful things for society. For example, Pamela Sica, at the age of 14, won the Weekly Reader National Invention Contest with a push-button device that elevated a car floor to facilitate loading and removing cargo.[34] But for the cost of hiring a patent attorney, she would have patented her invention.

Even masters still find room for growth. Eighty-five-year-old Jiro Ono is known as one of the finest sushi makers in the world, putting together excellent ingredients with the most creative and festive displays. In the documentary *Jiro Dreams of Sushi*, this man, who has won three Michelin awards for his work, is shown still striving to be even better at what he does.[35] Famous jazz pianist Peter Nero still practices his instrument for 6 hours a day!

Level 4 can be reached by communities, too. New York's park in the sky, the High Line, cuts through the meatpacking district on the west side of New York City. Built in the 1930s, the New York Central Railroad used to run on these elevated train tracks. When the High Line stopped running trains in the 1980s, it was overrun with grass and trees. In 1999, two men, Joshua David and Robert Hammond, rallied the neighborhood to preserve the High Line and turn it into a public park for pedestrian use only, an elevated greenway. Fifty million dollars later and the High Line is a monument to collaboration and the creative use of space in a crowded city.[36] Its success is so amazing that urban mayors, like Mayor Rahm Emanuel of Chicago, have said that the High Line is "a symbol and catalyst" for neighborhood gentrification.[37]

Wearing a T-shirt, blazer, and sneakers, Tim Brown, one of the founders of IDEO, gave a TED Talk in which he described the "serious play" that leads to the design breakthroughs IDEO is known for globally. To illustrate why "rules for creativity" are instituted at IDEO, he first told audience members that they had 30 seconds to draw a picture of the person next to them. Try this and see what happens. Adults' responses are predictable: They laugh, get embarrassed, and even apologize to their neighbor for making them look like the Frankenstein monster or his bride. Brown pointed out that kids don't have this reaction at all; they love their little masterpieces. Adults live in fear of the judgment of others. Armed with that insight, Brown and his cofounder, Kelly, promulgated IDEO creativity "rules" to try and return adults to the playfulness of their childhoods. Slogans such as "Defer judgment" and "Go for quantity [when generating ideas]!" help adults regain their lost freedom to avoid self-censoring and just let the ideas flow.[38]

Another rule is to create a low-resolution physical prototype of an idea quickly so it can be manipulated and more readily envisioned. The halls of IDEO resemble a preschool, equipped with colored paper, crayons, and scissors, whereas most corporate environments have the sterile look of a hospital corridor. From a primitive prototype that used a roll-on deodorant came the idea for the computer mouse. IDEO even uses role-play—just like the pretend play scenarios children cook up—to help them to design better services. IDEO recognizes that just as kids put on the garb of firefighters to figure out what that means, their designers have to put on the role of the patient or consumer or user of a service to make it better. If you are a hairy male, could you imagine the pain of having your chest hair waxed? Someone on IDEO's staff did this to understand what it was like to live with chronic pain. As he said,

> In this environment, to be successful, you need to be a good *communicator* [emphasis added], an advocate for yourself and your ideas, a consensus builder, an intimate *collaborator* [emphasis added], and someone who truly believes that the best quality work comes from building on the ideas of others and not from the individual.[39]

Creative thinking depends on communication and collaboration, but there is still more to it. One of the most interesting things about creative people is that they don't give up. Without confidence and a willingness to try and fail and try again, most of the inventors, entrepreneurs, scientists, or anyone who has made a difference in our culture could not have made creative breakthroughs. It's reminiscent of the Thomas Edison line "I have not failed. I've just found 10,000 ways that won't work."[40] Building a better mousetrap can take years. Why is it that the toddlers who fall down every third step keep pulling themselves up to get to that red plastic shopping cart? How do we develop the perseverance Liza shows when she keeps drawing that rainbow until she gets it just right? Creative innovation demands *confidence*, the last C, which we talk about next.

TAKING ACTION

A recent book by Kobi Yamada called *What Do You Do With an Idea?* introduces us to a "brilliant" idea and to the child who tries to bring it into the world.[41] With the grit and perseverance to stick with it even in the face of adversity and with growing confidence that his idea is worthy enough to pursue, he breathes life into his vision and watches the idea take flight. We have already seen that creativity lives all around us, in the trees, in our shadows, and in our vibrant imaginations. But so often we don't give it the space to move about freely or to explore its boundaries. The fundamental challenge of this chapter is to ask whether we are ready to jump-start creativity for our children or whether we prefer business as usual with handcuffs restraining their creative imagination. We can reverse the downward trend that Kim has shown us, but to do so, we might just have to imagine a few more uses for paper cups and 3-D printers.

In Yourself

As a first step, we have to look inward and ask whether we give ourselves permission to be creative in our jobs and in our homes. Being creative means taking risks and trying out some things that are destined to fail. We can start by making a new recipe for dinner that mixes spices we have never mixed before. It is possible that you will be eating out that night, but I bet the kids will applaud the effort. One of us still remembers her mother's purple soup. Good? No. Memorable? You bet, and the pizza dinner that followed was delicious.

When was the last time that you dabbled in art—painting or drawing or music or photography? Everyone can be a photographer today—we just whip out our cell phones. When we are willing to be creative ourselves, we model that for our children. We are often so afraid that we are not good enough that we don't even try. Who cares if our attempt at drawing that apple looks more like unidentifiable squiggles on a page?

Let me assure you that our group of 12 folks at the Reggio Emilia Centre Foundation felt pretty silly when the instructor invited us to talk to that tree. What were we supposed to do with this instruction? Seriously, we are not going to talk to a tree, are we? If we all did it and it felt safe enough to try, then why not give it a whirl? The ideas that emerged from this activity were simply inspired. One woman— a leading activist and educator from South Africa—worried that the tree might not have enough water, so she made a beautiful clay bucket for the tree and watered it. Another told a story about her mother who took care of trees when she was young. She used the tree experience to bring forth emotional connections. The point is, we have to leave the humdrum that comes with routine and regulation, schedule and expectation, to give ourselves the chance to be creative. When we do, we open new possibilities for ourselves and let our children know that divergent thinking is a plus.

In Your Child

Could we all take 15 minutes out of each day and let our kids invent? What might we do with that old broken vacuum cleaner or the box that housed the new dishwasher? Might they build a taxi with paper plates as headlights? Could they tell a new story that came from a fort built from sofa cushions? Do our children get the opportunity to string together toilet paper rolls, to use finger paint, or just to scribble drafts of family portraits that are proudly displayed on the refrigerator door? Most of us don't build creativity into our lives, and then we wonder why our children write traditional five-paragraph essays or do art projects that amount to putting precut apples on precut trees. We tend to buy construction toys that ask the child to assemble parts rather than buying the loose parts, and we tend to stick to instructions or to the stories in the book rather than generating new ones.

But now that we know this, we can give creativity a little breathing room. One of us (the one with three sons) used to play a wonderful game each morning before going to school. I hated getting up early (I still do), and my sons loved bouncing into the room fully awake and ready to go at 7 a.m. I needed time! So we played "Imagination is . . . ," and it kept everyone enchanted while I opened my eyes and struggled into some semblance of a waking state: "Imagination is when you're lying in bed. You close your eyes and open them. You're somewhere else instead. Where are we?" The boys would all chime in with their most imaginative offerings. We went to forests in Germany, to the bottom of the big blue ocean, on safari in Africa, and even to their favorite store at the mall. In each place, we created a story and any one of the three boys was allowed to break rank and force us to change location by simply saying, "Imagination is . . ." and continuing the saying.

When our kids were school age and we traveled, one of us had them make journals, full of receipts and tickets and souvenirs and pictures they drew and stories they told. Creativity doesn't take place only at home: Hotel and motel rooms and while visiting friends work just as well! We wrote entries in the journals too. They are remarkably fun to look at now that the kids are grown up.

When children know that they are allowed to be creative, they surprise us with their genius. Can we serve breakfast and turn the moment into a Broadway show? We did that often. The shows were pretty terrible, and we would never want to share them with an audience, but we were all singing and dancing as the eggs cooked on the stove.

If we want creative thinkers, we have to nurture creativity in our children and model it for our children. Those parents in the Hoicka and Butcher study did just that.[42] They made blocks into horses, and we can add many more: bananas as telephones, cups as eyeglasses. Our children will probably be even better at this game than we are. They sure were when asked to talk to the tree!

As our children grow their creative expertise, we can challenge them to not only learn the basics but also to hypothesize about what could be different. Are there different ways to kick a soccer ball, different strategies for getting a goal? Can you mix musical styles to create a new sound? Can we create new paint colors by mixing what we have?

In the Places You Go

The backyard or the front stoop are wonderful settings in which to watch creativity grow. What can we make with tree bark? Can we collect leaves and make a collage? How do you paint with water? And what happens to that beautifully painted concrete water art when the sun shines its warm rays? Can you find the shadows? Can you make shadows grow and shrink? How about sidewalk chalk as an experiment in color and form? All of this is right at your doorstep.

Inside creativity is also at your fingertips. Pots and pans become drums, bottles become wind instruments, and the house is abuzz as a makeshift orchestra. Put on a show about your favorite story. In just 15 minutes a day your children will probably use less screen time and develop more creative playtime. The neighborhood children are likely to join in as well as your place becomes destination creativity. Have you ever tried brushing your teeth in a whole new way? Outside the home too look for opportunities to do something new and to use everyday tools in new ways or to reshape activities and routines.

How Do We Create Environments That Foster Creativity?

There are many ways to make your lives more creative. The first is to have space and time to nurture creative thinking and to applaud it, even if it does not always reap what you expect. That drawing of the family dog might not look anything like Fido, but it still deserves a treasured place on the refrigerator. Our children's musical compositions might not quite sound like they are ready for Beyoncé, but who cares—if your child has created a tune, enjoy it. One of us had a son who wanted to study jazz violin. It is really difficult to find anyone who can teach jazz violin (it is not your common jazz band instrument), and the violin is a tough instrument to play. As one of us is fond of saying, "I never knew there were so many notes between C and C-sharp." But compose he did, and we, the audience, applauded.

Seeing creativity is also key to fostering it. Art museums, school art exhibits, community center art exhibits—all show that real people draw and express themselves visually. If they see it, they can do it, or at least try it.

Music and drama also abound, from school performances to professional offerings. If you get involved—even in games of charades—your child will too.

Save your junk! Keep that paper towel roll, those dead flowers, those old clothes that you would never ever be seen in—think costume drawer. All are invitations to creativity.

Look carefully for good apps that spark creativity—not the apps that tell a child exactly what to do but those that invite active, engaged, meaningful, and socially interactive creative play. There are wonderful painting programs, tinkering shops, and musical composition studios that extend the boundaries of what children can do. When used within your set time limits, the vast bank of digital offerings can be a boon.

Finally, we cannot leave this section without drawing attention yet again to Mitch Resnik's Scratch community at MIT. Mitch's lab is known as the Lifelong Kindergarten; a virtual tour of what he does is simply inspiring. He is the same man who inspired LEGO to add the motor to the blocks so that our creations can move.[43] When your children are old enough, these open-source, but protected and well-monitored, spaces are oases for creative expression and learning. Also, look out for Maker Faires in your area so that you can witness for yourself the growing community of innovators who are using discarded pieces to solve real-world problems.

THE ROAD TO SUCCESS

In the global economy, creative thinkers are the kings and queens. These flexible innovators quickly assemble what they know to build a future of possibilities. To date, we have not done enough to help our children move deftly into the unknown. We have not reinforced the use of imagination but instead have often designated it as an accessory to learning rather than as the heart of learning and success. Kim's findings from the Torrance data on diminishing creativity illustrate this crisis. But we can reverse this trend. Creativity is malleable. With strong home, school, and community settings that celebrate creative expression, we can help all children exercise their creative muscles. We simply have to make the space, offer the models, and let their creative engines roar.

As we move to the last of the Cs, we must reckon with one more fact. Divergent thinkers will travel a road that is less well-travelled. We must prepare children with the content and critical thinking they will need to create, but even that will not be enough. They must have the confidence and persistence to press forward even in the face of potential failure. Creative thinkers are discoverers, pattern seekers, path makers, and entrepreneurs. And they often don't take no for an answer!

CHAPTER 10

CONFIDENCE: DARE TO FAIL

Failures are finger posts on the road to achievement.

—C. S. Lewis

We first met Norman Vaughan when we traveled to Alaska to watch the start of the Iditarod, the 1,000-mile trek across the frozen Alaskan tundra. An energetic 92-year-old who had a long scruffy beard, deep wrinkles, and a twinkle in his eyes, he was a caricature of the great American explorer. In 1928, Vaughan was the chief musher for Admiral Byrd on the first expedition to Antarctica. In 1973, he was at the starting gate for the first Iditarod, which celebrates a 1925 serum run that brought needed medicine to the young children of Nome. And at age 89 he climbed the summit of the mountain in Antarctica that bears his name. An Alaskan icon, Vaughan had been off the Iditarod trail for 5 years but joined his comrades at the opening banquet to meet old friends and share his new book, *My Life of Adventure*.[1] He inscribed our copy with, "Dream Big. Dare to Fail." Vaughan was able to boldly go where others feared to tread because he had the knowledge of how to survive and he had the confidence and persistence to explore and discover.

Confidence has two components. The first is the willingness to try. One of our favorite quotations captures it: "You miss 100% of the shots you don't take."[2] Without confidence, people cannot accept new challenges and stretch beyond their comfort zones. The second aspect of confidence is persistence. Angela Duckworth, a professor at the University of Pennsylvania, calls this *grit*—having the passion and perseverance, the stamina, to hold onto your long term goals.[3] Confidence or grit allows inventors to continue working out the kinks in their ideas and keep experimenting with intermediate versions of the final product. It enables students to push for understanding when at first they are flummoxed by what they are reading. The difference between students who succeed and those who do not may be the confidence to persevere. How many times did you as a child hear the old proverb, "If at first you don't succeed, try and try again"? William E. Hickson, a British educational writer, is credited for popularizing the proverb in the middle of the 19th century.[4] The full proverb reads, "Tis a lesson you should heed: Try, try, try again. If at first you don't succeed, Try, try, try again." Its message is the theme of this chapter. How do we get our kids to try and then to try and try again in our present climate when failure is anathema (think high-stakes standardized tests) and where awards are given for the most trivial achievements in our celebratory culture (think kids' sport teams: all kids get trophies whether they win or not).[5]

If we are to prepare our children to be explorers on the frontier of ideas, we must encourage them to experiment, think, ask questions, and yes, fail, so that they can learn from their failures and try again. Our failures give us a way to compare what works and what does not. Even tennis is like that. When you have played long enough, you will have tried many ways to hold the racket and many different shots. If all you cared about was winning (which is equivalent to getting the one right answer), you would never try to hit the ball with spin or shift your grip on the racket ever so slightly. But if you dare to try new things, you may sometimes fail; but your mini, everyday experiments will ultimately lead to a better game of tennis. In life, in industry, and in the laboratory, greatness arises when we try different options to see what happens and sometimes fail. When we have confidence, we make corrections and change directions on the basis of those outcomes. We don't pack up our racket (business plan, test tubes) and go home.

Lessons about learning from failure abound; and failure is not just for kids. Who among us has not heard about the many publishers who rejected J. K. Rowling's *Harry Potter and the Sorcerer's Stone?* Rowling is laughing all the way to the bank. The 2011 Nobel Prize for chemistry was awarded to Daniel Shechtman, a 70-year-old Israeli scientist who discovered that crystals appeared in a novel form no one had previously envisioned. He recorded the initial observation in his notebook on April 8, 1982. Picture the young Shechtman entering a colleague's lab to tell him about what he had seen. His fellow scientist waved him off saying, "Come on Danny, I have better things to do." Shechtman, however, remained undaunted. He had confidence in what he was seeing and spent the rest of his career demonstrating that there indeed was another type of crystal formation. He received the Nobel Prize for his discovery—and for the confidence and grit he had to persevere.

We have to think about failure as an opportunity rather than as a defeat. Children can build a sense of their own power if we let them get that bad mark on a test and then improve on the next one, experience that failed attempt at creating a sculpture in art class, or fall occasionally in their play. How many skinned knees did we have growing up? Lots.

The process of gaining the confidence to try and to persevere passes through a number of levels. It begins with the child (or adult) who barrels on with false confidence (as a kid you thought you could do absolutely anything) and moves on to comparing your accomplishments with others. Starting to understand what you excel at, you give up field hockey and move to volleyball. Dampening the sense of "I can do anything" is good, else children would forever think they could leap from tall buildings. At the next level, we take calculated risks, often supported by a safety net. Think of the novice skier who is determined to learn but knows he has to start out on the bunny slope if he ever hopes to become good enough to ski the black diamond trails. Now compare that person with the professional who literally soars through the icy air landing hundreds of feet away. That expert has hit a few trees and swallowed a lot of snow. Those bumps and bruises paved the way toward Olympic Gold (or just an impressive run at Aspen).

Perseverance or confidence is not just for kids. The lesson of learning from failure is beautifully illustrated in business by the example of the introduction of "New Coke" in 1985.[6] Coca-Cola engaged in market research and internal decision making to prepare for the anticipated announcement. Customers wanted a sweeter formula, and Coca-Cola was ready to abandon their old recipe for a new one. The switch would cost millions, but the company felt this would help them regain market share lost to Pepsi. Contrary to what research had indicated, once "New Coke" was unveiled, it was not well received. Many scrambled to find coveted bottles of the original formula. This failure, however, did not spell doom for Coca-Cola. The company acknowledged the mistake and reintroduced the old formula, capturing an even larger share of the market than they had prior to the switch. Abject failure led to ultimate success. Coke didn't just "barrel on"; they owned their failure and retreated, only to be rewarded with more market share. They also did not fire the folks who failed, providing a model for other employees who came to understand the power of trying. Clearly, new ideas—even if they didn't work out— were prized.

LEVEL 1: BARREL ON!

Eleven-month-old Lucy will not sit down. When she is awake, all she wants to do is have her fingers held and walk and climb everywhere. Where would we be as a species if we did not have the determination to walk, as manifested in this baby? Walking does not happen overnight; it takes time and much effort. This tendency to barrel on makes Lucy's parents occasionally crazy, but it is essential if Lucy is to learn the skills required of humans. This is the advantage to this type of rudimentary confidence. Barreling on may be evolutionarily adaptive for kids. David Bjorklund of Florida Atlantic University argued that youth is not wasted on the young.[7] The long childhood humans have helps us forge ahead to master all we need to know to survive. Cognitive immaturity and the persistence that accompanies it may well be a "deferred adaptation," selected for by evolution.

The immaturity and persistence young children demonstrate are often accompanied by being overconfident, even foolhardy. Some of this comes from underestimating how hard it is do something really well, some from the fact that they don't yet compare themselves with others. Preschoolers are immune to relative failure compared with their buddies. Even when they can't get that beanbag to reach the target, they see their better-performing peers and show no hit to their self-esteem.[8]

They think they excel both in physical and intellectual tasks.[9] A child who watches Superman may think that she can jump off a great height too. Another child thinks that he can easily write a book. Some kids' bodies look like they are covered with zippers, given the number of scars in various stages of healing. Why do some kids have so many accidents? Jodie Plumert at the University of Iowa looked at the relationship between the number of injuries for which 6-year-olds needed medical treatment and these same kids' estimates of their physical capabilities.[10] Kids were shown a toy at varying heights on a high shelf, for example, and asked whether they would be able to reach it. Picture a tall bookcase with a shiny new [fill in the blank]. What is the likelihood that a kid would pull it down trying to play with that new temptation? Plumert's study turned out as might be expected: The more kids overestimated how good they were at this (and other physical tasks), the more likely they were to have had injuries in their homes. A 3-year-old we know was taken to an urban pool and just walked straight in, clothes and all! Fished out by his fully clothed mother who went in right after him, he said he knew how to swim.

Confidence is also manifest in our social interactions. A certain level of confidence is needed to interact with people we don't know. When we go to a party in another city, we have to have the confidence to go up to people and look for common ground. We all know how it feels to enter a room where we know no one. Some of us find this a torturous prospect. We have a highly intelligent friend who used to sweat profusely in these circumstances. Being smart is different from having social confidence; new social situations were hard for him.

Barreling-on confidence can continue to play a role throughout the lifespan, empowering people to think they know more than they really do. How much do you know about how your toilet works? We use it every day and the mechanism seems fairly straightforward. On a scale from 1 to 7, how would you rank your comprehension of the flush? Most adults would tick off the high end of the scale. We understand what makes the toilet empty and fill up again, but ask adults to actually write a description and their ratings plummet. Good thing there are plumbers. Why did we initially think we knew how toilets worked? Rozenblit and Keil at Yale University think that this kind of initial overconfidence is also useful to us. We live in a complex world and it is impossible for us to search out all the causal explanations we might want for how things work. By having the illusion that we understand, we can move on and only focus on things we really care about. As they wrote, "It may therefore be quite adaptive to have the illusion that we know more than we do so that we settle for what is enough."[11]

Barreling on can be a big problem. There is a reason the term *know-it-all* is in common parlance. And barreling on can get you in serious trouble if you are a CEO or a CFO of a company. Some have called it *hubris* and it was seen in profusion around the time of the great recession of 2008. Few captains of industry could even imagine that the economy could tank so deeply.[12] Ironically, companies may actually select executives who have more confidence than is healthy for the company. In general, barreling on is best captured by Mark Twain who said, "It ain't what you don't know that gets you into trouble. It's what you know for sure that just ain't so."[13]

LEVEL 2: WHERE DO I STAND?

When we start comparing ourselves with others, we are asking, 'Where do I stand?' Psychologists call this *social comparison*. One of us remembers spending lots of mental energy in grade school: "I am smarter than Harry but not as smart as Sylvia; I am a better runner than Cynthia but not as fast as Barry." This exercise leads us to make more realistic assessments about what we are good at and what we aren't so good at. Confidence becomes "where do I stand" when we compare our performances with others with similar characteristics. If as children we thought we were good in math, it made sense for us to compare our math skill with someone in the same grade than with someone in a higher or lower grade.[14] Children—as well as adults—look for people who are like us when we make social comparisons. And we tend to look at people who do better than we do. That's a good thing: Comparing ourselves with the best reader in the class motivates us to read more and try harder.[15]

However, "where do I stand" doesn't lead to great confidence in one's abilities because it is a fundamentally conservative way to think about what we can do. If we are motivated by "where do I stand," we are always looking over our shoulder to compare ourselves with others rather than trying that new approach. If we are worried about our relative position vis-à-vis our peers and what they might think of us, we are not likely to take those big, bold steps that might cause failure. 'Failure? No way. I select tasks that I am sure I can do so that I look good,' as research by Carol Dweck, a professor at Stanford University, has found.[16]

There is one period in development—adolescence—when children take enormous risks, risks that sometimes have grave consequences. Because so much of this has a social component—the need to impress one's friends or fit in—we place adolescent risk taking in "where do I stand?" We know that peers matter a lot because adolescent risk taking tends to occur in groups.[17] Put more boys in the car? Risk more accidents. Engage in sexual activity? Much more likely for adolescents if they think their peers are having sex too. Larry Steinberg of Temple University has investigated how adolescent brains develop and attributes their rise in risky behavior and the false confidence it entails to biologically driven remodeling of the part of the brain that processes social and emotional information.[18] The reader will be relieved to know—or will have observed in their own children—that risky behavior declines as adolescents move into adulthood. Eventually, the smarter cognitive part of the brain takes control over the more volatile emotional and social part. This means that "where do I stand" no longer rules adolescents' behavior.

Carol Dweck has led the way in our understanding of confidence.[19] For decades, she has been studying how to foster the confidence children and adults need to learn. In her laboratory you might be given analogies to solve like those on the old SATs: *light* is to *dark* as *naked*, *green*, or *illuminated* is to *dressed*, for example. You work away for 30 minutes and turn in the sheet. You do well, and she tells you how brilliant you are. You hold your head a little higher, bolstered by that good feeling of confidence. But when she gives you another set of problems that are much harder, you might give up sooner or find an excuse not to continue. Why? Dweck's findings suggest that you would try less if she told you that you were brilliant than if she had praised you instead for your effort. If she had ignored your obvious brilliance and told you instead that you had put out an amazing effort on the first set of problems, you would likely persevere much longer on the second, harder set. This is because you wouldn't worry about maintaining your "brilliant" reputation. Praising smarts has the paradoxical effect of reducing confidence. Praising effort keeps us going. Maybe it's because it removes the pressure: We don't have to keep showing how brilliant we are. Praising effort tells us that what matters is how hard we tried; getting the right answers is not what the task is all about.

When people are concerned about where they stand, they are likely to avoid tasks and situations they believe exceed their capabilities. In other words, they do not possess the confidence to break new ground. These people only select the problems they think they can do. It is tied up in the concept of *self-esteem*, or one's own feelings of self-worth. The overconfidence of preschoolers is self-esteem at its highest. It then declines in the school years as a result of the social comparisons we start to make. From about fourth grade, it rises again, but for a dip in the transition to junior high and high school. There are different types of self-esteem.[20] We have a notion of our academic self-esteem from how we do in school; our social self-esteem is our feeling of competence in getting along with peers and parents; physical or athletic self-esteem comes from being chosen first or last when teams form or from that home run you hit in camp. Another type of self-esteem comes from our feelings about our physical appearance. Our general self-esteem feeds into our confidence, but somewhat differently depending on the domain.

What self-esteem profile characterizes individuals at the where-do-I-stand level of confidence? Leave it to two brilliant psychologists—Brown and Dutton—to come up with an answer.[21] Undergraduate students were brought into the lab and told about a bogus problem-solving ability called *integrative orientation*. Say I give you three words: *car, swimming, cue.* Your job is to find a single word that links all three of these words. Try it! Give up yet? Maybe *pool* would work. This is called the Remote Associates Test.[22] The undergraduates were then given 10 problems like this to solve in 5 minutes. What they didn't know was that half of them received really hard problems and half really easy problems. Because the hard set was so hard and the easy set so easy, when the computer scored the undergraduates' performance it could give real scores. Students then completed a happiness scale about how they felt after getting their score and a scale related to their feelings of self-worth. That scale contained the words *proud, pleased with myself, ashamed,* and *humiliated.*

What did Brown and Dutton find? Whether students had high or low self-esteem in general didn't influence the feelings of happiness they reported about their scores. Of course, all students were happier if they did well on this test. But self-esteem really mattered on the scale that measured students' feelings of self-worth. Students who had low self-esteem felt ashamed and humiliated if they did poorly. After failure, the low self-esteem students' self-worth ratings fell off the cliff. Think about what this means. A person with low self-esteem is likely to pick tasks they know they can do because the effects of failure are devastating to them. If failure really hurts people with low self-esteem, they are much less likely to reach out beyond their level of comfort and take chances. People with low self-esteem are much less likely to try risky things, to branch out, or to stick their necks out. Why take a chance and fail if failure felt so awful in the past?

Where does this self-esteem concept come from, and how does it feed into the confidence to take risks? Kids need the space to practice risk taking and figure out their limits. And they need to succeed *and* fail to discover their own boundaries. "Helicopter parenting," like that practiced by Lynn and Joel, backfires for helping kids develop strong self-esteem. Lynn and Joel are rarely out of reach of their kids, whether their children need them or not. They try to make everything smooth and easy for their kids, insisting that Harry is assigned to the better after-school soccer team. Lynn and Joel are the parents who try to "sweep all obstacles out of the paths of their children," even when their children don't think there is a problem. They mean well; who wants their child to suffer? But these parents are not doing their children any favors. Why does Harry always have to be on the best team? Shouldn't he also learn how to deal with failure? This often continues with the parents doing Harry's homework and making him think he is entitled to that *A* grade. As we tell the occasional parent who calls us at our university offices, your child (really, an adult) did not fail because of anything you did; your child failed because of what he or she did not do. Parents who intervene in this way are not building confidence; they are implicitly conveying the message that "you can't do this without me," a message that will not well serve Harry and other helicopter children who need to learn to take off and land on their own.

One of us has a huge pile of boulders reaching to about 20 feet high at the back of her house. All the little cousins under age 12 have a blast climbing up the rocks as their parents sit complacently watching. What are the kids learning? This is a situation of controlled risk—high rocks, it's true, but parents are watching. Kids happily climb and find their height of comfort and practice placing a foot here or there to see what works. These lucky kids are learning their own limits, their own parameters for what can safely be climbed and what is too high for them. If a persnickety parent had not let their children do this, those children would have lost an opportunity to take a controlled risk, to learn about their own capabilities, to learn about what they could and couldn't do. This activity allowed the kids to make more realistic assessments of their limits, in turn feeding into their self-esteem.

In her bestselling book, *The Blessing of a Skinned Knee*, author and clinical psychologist Wendy Mogel makes the same point.[23] Parents' getting out of the way helps children build confidence. One of the helpful hints she offered is that parents should let children explore more and sometimes even get a skinned knee. We are not very good at that. We are so bent on ensuring our children's success that we finish their sentences, do their homework for them, rewrite their first written reports, and even hire folks to craft their college admissions essays. We have to turn failures into invitations for learning.

Another way to encourage confidence is to convey the idea that there is more than one way to do a task. All too often, we meet children who are rewarded for the "right" answer but not encouraged to try solving the problem another way. We can help our children see this in the simplest ways. Lara is headed to Grandma's house with her 7- and 9-year-old in tow. Living near two highways in the city, Lara can ask her kids to help plan the route. When routes are suggested and factors such as time and traffic are mentioned, they are talking about all the variables that feed into the decision. And without ever using the word, the kids are building confidence for making their way in the world.

Another way to feed children's confidence is through the arts, where there is no one right answer. As Ellen Winner and her colleagues have shown, the arts build habits of the mind.[24] One of these habits is to "engage and persist"—learning to persevere builds confidence and fuels the development of executive function skill. Two more are "envision" and "express." If you can picture mentally what you can't see and learn to convey this through some form of art, you are then in a position to "reflect"—to judge your own work and the work of others. These habits of mind are unique to the arts, whether visual, musical, theater, or anything else we can think of that is a form of self-expression. These studio habits also encourage "stretching and exploring" as they foster the creativity and confidence needed to encourage experimentation. Whether Justina writes a poem, sketches her dream house, or makes up a dance, the arts build confidence.

When Justina learns to talk about her work to others and to reflect on it, she will receive feedback that will help her to feel pride in her artistic achievements. Some children wouldn't finish high school if it weren't for their involvement in the arts at school.

Confidence is needed to take informed risks, but not just in the arts. In fact, our economic viability relies on it. This is why business writers like Chris Musselwhite have suggested that CEOs become coaches rather than bosses.[25] Unless the environment supports risk taking and innovation, a business is likely to flounder as it remains stuck in its ways. Musselwhite argued that companies should be fostering "smart-risks" by rewarding innovation—even when there is failure—and by encouraging small risks on a frequent basis. If failures are swept under the rug or if a postmortem includes assigning blame, knowledge workers will stay only at the where-do-I-stand level of confidence, reluctant to suggest innovation. Thus, a knowledge worker's environment can promote any of the levels of confidence we discuss in this chapter.

LEVEL 3: CALCULATED RISKS

The term *calculated risk* is defined by an online dictionary as taking a chance after careful analysis of the likely outcome, as in "Taking their dispute to arbitration was definitely a calculated risk."[26] *Calculated* here means "planned with forethought," and the phrase itself dates from World War II when the likelihood of losing bombers was taken into account before a bombing mission was initiated. In general, the term is used to describe the situation in which taking a chance to succeed is weighed against the costs of failure—a kind of risk–benefit analysis. We generally take calculated risks in every area of our lives, from picking a spouse, to accepting a college's admission, to changing jobs, to buying a car, even crossing a street. Our third level of confidence involves taking calculated risks and learning from our mistakes. Inevitably, we do not always make the right choices; however, a failure to take risks would leave us paralyzed, stuck with being single even if we loved deeply, stuck with the college that was not a "stretch," stuck to the career we failed to find satisfying, and stuck with our old, unreliable clunker of a car. Failing to take calculated risks in our own lives would lead to our economy and educational system becoming stagnant as well.

Having the confidence to make change can be shaped by one's home, school, or even by society at large. What if we told you that fully 50% of the population exhibits lower confidence than they should have? Those 50% are women. Making women into sex objects with the measurements of Barbie[27] and sexualizing little girls to look like hookers[28] does little to build the type of confidence that girls and women will need to reach the next level, dare to fail. Society has an impact very early. Aurora Sherman and Eileen Zurbiggen, two psychologists at the University of California, Santa Cruz, gave girls from 4 to 7 years of age either Doctor Barbie or Fashion Barbie or Mrs. Potato Head to play with.[29] They then showed the girls pictures of 10 workplaces and asked them who could do the jobs pictured: Could girls do them? Could boys do them? The results were scary. Regardless of whether girls play with Doctor Barbie or Fashion Barbie, they reported that girls could do only 6.6 of the jobs, whereas boys could do 9.5. That is a big difference for 20 minutes of playtime. What did the girls who played with Mrs. Potato Head think? If they said yes more often to the question of whether girls could do a job, it might be something about the stereotypes that Barbies reflect. Sure enough, the girls who played with Mrs. Potato Head said girls could do 8.3 of the careers, compared with a score of 9 for boys. What children play with matters for their confidence in the short term and for what they think others like them can accomplish.

Does encountering gender stereotypes in childhood matter in the long term for women's success and feelings of confidence? Apparently, even among women who reach the highest levels in our society there is a large confidence gap. Katty Kay and Claire Shipman noted that women are still woefully unrepresented at the highest levels.[30] Their claim is that this is a product of women's lack of confidence. Still, there are many women out there who dare to fail. But we sure don't make it easy for them. Consider Angela Merkel, German Chancellor; Nancy Pelosi, Minority Leader of the House of Representatives; Oprah Winfrey, who owns her own TV channel; and Diane Sawyer, who has been giving us the news for years. And did you know that the gorgeous Austrian actress Hedy Lamarr created a wireless communication invention that helped us win World War II and that was the forerunner of modern GPS and Wi-Fi? Or that a woman, Mary Anderson, invented the windshield wiper in 1903? Or that in the 1970s Patricia Billings invented GeoBond, an indestructible building material?

The Role of School, Family, and Temperament in Shaping Confidence

Erik Erikson, the world-renowned psychologist who built on the work of Sigmund Freud, suggested that there were eight stages in human development.[31] The one most relevant to confidence is marked by a tension between what he called "industry versus inferiority." During the school years, children become able to do more and more tasks, leading them to master new skills and try even more new things. Just consider what children learn: Reading, math, how to cross a street by themselves, how to ride a two-wheel bicycle, and how to tie their shoes and do household chores. Although psychoanalytic thinking is not prominent anymore in the United States, Erikson discovered something profound. As children become more competent in their everyday lives, they become better at knowing what they can and cannot do. This is calculating risk.

The classroom often encourages a where-do-I-stand approach (Level 2), comparing us with our classmates rather than asking that we achieve a personal best. In an educational system that thrives on getting one correct answer rather than on the process of learning, students lose their motivation to take risks because outperforming their classmates is sufficient. This works when students have well-defined problems (e.g., arithmetic), but it doesn't work so well when students are tackling less constrained problems (e.g., writing a paper on Angela Merkel). When children learn how to take calculated risks, they learn to think independently, embrace novelty, and question their intellectual, social, and cultural world.[32]

As clinical psychologists Nancy Eppler-Wolff and Susan Davis argued in their book, *Raising Children Who Soar*, there is an upside to taking risks: Success breeds feelings of self-confidence and competence.[33] Those kids climbing on the high rocks in the backyard are learning that failure won't destroy them and that they can recover from a misstep. Parents play a big role here because if they encourage children to keep trying when they encounter hard tasks—like homework—children will continue to try new things and not shut down to experimentation. Grit is nurtured by not letting kids give up but encouraging them to see what they can do. Sometimes breaking big tasks up into little ones is all your children need to know they can succeed.

We cannot minimize, however, temperamental differences between children. Some children are born risk takers (to the point that parents worry about what their child will do next), whereas some wait for others to try it first, even in the most encouraging homes. Picture one of us at a crowded public pool in Florence, Italy. We lost the 6-year-old and were frantic, looking everywhere. The only place we didn't look was at the top of the diving platform. There he was, with six men who were encouraging this intrepid child to jump off. Meanwhile, the 6-year-old's older brother wouldn't enter the pool without holding the hands of both his parents, worried about being separated from them.

It has been suggested that parents who are risk-averse with their children make it less rather than more likely that their children will attend college.[34] You can see how a risk-averse parent might influence a child's choices. Have a peek at this conversation between Rachel, a sixth grader, and her dad:

> *Rachel*: Should I write my essay for biology on frogs? I know a lot about frogs. Or should I write it on honey badgers? I really want to learn about them.
> *Dad*: [Genuinely attempting to be helpful.] Why not stick to what you know, honey?

Dad is explicitly discouraging Rachel from learning about a new animal. Why might Dad do that? Perhaps he is concerned that Rachel won't do as well on the assignment. Why take a chance? But not encouraging Rachel to embrace a new interest may have a long-term downside effect on her confidence and willingness to move beyond what she knows. Of course, one conversation like this will not make Rachel averse to risk. But a pattern like this might. Rachel might come to calculate that the risk she takes in writing about a new animal is greater than its possible benefit: "Could my grade be as good if I write about an animal I know less about?"

Taking Calculated Risks Is Gritty

We recognize that one way to meet our long-term goal (e.g., being a good student or running an excellent company) is to take chances to try new things. The confidence to change "business as usual" by studying in that new, more time-consuming way or buying that new, expensive machine is the only way we can better our current status.

Calculated risk—and the confidence associated with it—is found in every industry. A simple example is something that happens virtually every day. A treasured employee requests a raise that puts her out of the range of others in her tier and blows the entrepreneur's budget. Just "barreling on" and giving her the raise without much forethought might not have a happy ending for a variety of reasons. Calculating risk is involved when the entrepreneur considers the likelihood he will lose her if he does not give her the raise or offer to give her half of what she requested. As W. Brett Wilson, a business writer, put it, entrepreneurs are not just risk takers; they thrive on calculated risk. Entrepreneurs "have to be confident and tenacious but they also need to do their homework."[35] Savvy entrepreneurs will ask themselves what the likely consequences are of granting the request, granting a portion of the request, or turning the employee down completely.

Even calculated risks will occasionally lead to failures. The key is being able to learn from them. Professor Amy Edmondson of Harvard Business School argued that everyone *says* they want to learn from failure, but mostly this doesn't happen.[36] Companies have to first avoid the "blame game." Instead of "shoot the messenger," the messenger should be embraced and not chastised or blown off. Apparently, executives are concerned that if they don't blame someone, people will think that anything goes and standards will be lowered. We can identify with this because we both run laboratories that involve lots of people, some who try new things. Some in our labs have the grit to challenge procedures we have been using for a long time or to persist with that new method until we get it right (or not!). The research assistants who try new things and persevere are the ones we cherish because their confidence often pays off. And most of these have the wherewithal to distinguish between good risks and bad risks—important for figuring out which to take.

LEVEL 4: DARE TO FAIL

Go out on a limb. That's where the fruit is.
—Jimmy Carter, as quoted in K. Petras and R. Petras,
Age Doesn't Matter Unless You're a Cheese:
Wisdom From Our Elders

The final level of confidence is achieved when one *dares to fail*, knowing that the greatest advancement happens at the edges of our safety zone. In fact, those who take calculated risks at the edge often fail along the way and then climb back to success. They manage to succeed because they learn from their failures and have the grit to move beyond them. They exemplify grit; they have the passion for a single mission with an unswerving dedication to achieve that mission, whatever the obstacles and however long it might take.[37]

Angela Duckworth and her colleagues developed the Grit Scale to measure this quality.[38,39] For students at the University of Pennsylvania, scores on this simple 12-item test were more predictive of college GPA than SAT scores. At West Point, Duckworth gave the Grit Scale to 1,200 incoming cadets embarking on their grueling first summer training. The Grit Scale was better than the military's own complex Whole Candidate Score at predicting who would drop out and who would persevere.

Counterintuitively, one key component of the Grit Scale is the belief that failure is necessary to conquer challenges. The Grit Scale has been adapted for use with children, assessing attributes such as how hard children work and whether they complete tasks they started. If we are to prepare students to enter the frontier of ideas in a fast changing world, our educational system must include lessons on experimenting, hypothesizing, asking questions, and failing, so that students learn from mistakes. There is a fine line between perseverance and overconfidence. Sometimes our ideas are wrongheaded.

However, sufficient *content* knowledge and *critical thinking*—two of the other Cs—are checks that help us evaluate whether an idea has merit. Failures give us a metric of comparison for what works. If we only care about getting the right answer, we never experiment with a different way of solving a problem.

Indeed, learning opportunities are available in every failure. There is even research on how making mistakes during learning helps us to better remember new information. Why would that be so? And why are people so reluctant to fail? Two researchers in Britain, Potts and Shanks, asked adults to either generate responses in trying to remember the meaning of a new word (e.g., "What does *aboulomania* mean?") versus just picking between two possible meanings (e.g., *pathological indecisiveness* versus *intense desire for open spaces*).[40] They found that we learn more when we generate wrong answers (e.g., *likes to bowl*) than when we are more passive, choosing between the two choices. Actively making mistakes helped people remember more words in the end. This is because generating an answer—even when it is wrong—requires deeper thought than just selecting between possible answers. Also, getting something wrong makes people pay more attention; no one likes to be wrong. (By the way, *aboulomania* means pathological indecisiveness.)

Parents often have trouble praising the process of learning because they are so focused on the outcome. One of us remembers proudly presenting her report card to her dad with a shiny 95%. He said as a joke, "What happened to the other 5%?" This response devalued the hard work put into getting that amazing grade. Focusing on outcome seemed to wipe out all her effort. And such behavior has the strange and paradoxical effect of undermining the confidence we need to keep trying. A recent study told us that reducing academic pressure has the puzzling effect of helping children succeed. But perhaps this isn't so puzzling in light of Carol Dweck's research. She reminded us that when children are told how smart they are, they are more likely to give up in the face of difficult tasks than children who are praised for their effort.

Two French researchers, Frederique Autin and Jean-Claude Croizet, tried a really interesting experiment with sixth graders that wound up having a big payoff for the children's confidence—and their performance.[41] The researchers first gave all the children a set of difficult anagrams to solve. Here's an easy one if you know French: Make *nechi* into a real French word.[42] The researchers then told one group of sixth graders that these anagrams were hard, but with practice—just like riding a bike—they could improve. That same researcher asked another group of children how they had solved the anagrams with no discussion of the role of practice or difficulty level. What happened next is where the big differences showed up.

Both groups of children were asked to perform a "working memory" test requiring them to hold information in mind—like when you repeat a phone number to yourself so as not to forget it. Working memory is important for problem solving; failure to keep the premises of the problem in mind will hinder performance if you have to keep going back and forth. The children who were told that practice makes perfect did much better on this unrelated memory test than those who were told nothing about how people can work to improve their performance. Maybe the children who weren't told that they could get better with practice thought they were dumb. Maybe they were demoralized. The children who were told about the importance of practice apparently put in their full effort and didn't give up. Knowing that effort and practice matters motivated them to keep going. In other words, when children understand that learning is not instantaneous, that it is hard and takes grit, and that natural smarts are not enough, they actually do better on a hard task.

When interviewed, the researchers made clear that high-stakes tests and emphasis on grades—just what the United States is doing now—is the exact opposite of what their research supported. Children have to be given space to struggle and not to expect that if they don't understand immediately, they should just give up. In Autin's words, "Teachers and parents should emphasize children's progress rather than focusing solely on grades and test scores. Learning takes time and each step in the process should be rewarded, especially at early stages when students most likely will experience failure."[43] In other words, and as Carol Dweck argued, if we help students understand that the brain is like a muscle that gets better with exercise, students are much more likely to keep trying when they hit obstacles.[44] Being realistic about the effort involved in learning builds confidence. Helping students understand that failure is an inevitable part of the learning process invites their determination and perseverance. But, as these scientists are hinting, confidence can be manipulated and shaped by children's home and school environment. Emphasis on the process is fundamental.

Confidence can really make a difference in performance. Scott Barry Kaufman of New York University has also noticed the phenomenon that our French researchers noted: Expectations have everything to do with achievement. If people are put into situations in which they are expected to fail, "their performance does plummet. They turn into different people. Their head literally shuts down, and they end up confirming the expectations."[45] But if people are put into a situation where they are expected to do well, they do. In a study by Moè and Pazzaglia, women were asked to engage in a "mental rotation task," like the one in Figure 10.1.[46] Which of the four designs matches the standard?

Half the women and men were told that men did this task better and half were told that women did it better. Women did much worse after being told men were better; men did much worse after being told that women were better at it. These findings tell us that our confidence can be manipulated, that it's malleable. If we believe

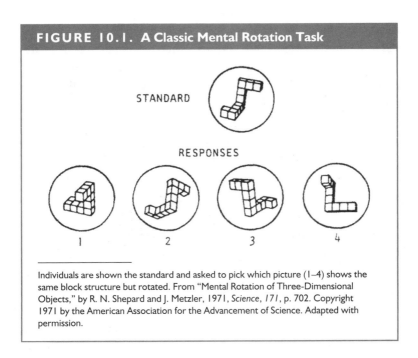

FIGURE 10.1. A Classic Mental Rotation Task

STANDARD

RESPONSES

1 2 3 4

Individuals are shown the standard and asked to pick which picture (1–4) shows the same block structure but rotated. From "Mental Rotation of Three-Dimensional Objects," by R. N. Shepard and J. Metzler, 1971, *Science, 171*, p. 702. Copyright 1971 by the American Association for the Advancement of Science. Adapted with permission.

that members of our group—whatever that group is—should not do well, we create a self-fulfilling prophecy and do poorly. If we believe that members of our group should do well, we increase our performance. There is a silver lining in this: We can help our children develop confidence with the right messages. If we want people to operate at the dare-to-fail level, we have to help insulate them against prevailing myths in our society about how they are expected to perform. Girls do just fine at math! We have to encourage children to play with toys that broaden their horizons rather than narrow them. And we have to help students persevere when learning is hard.

"Dare to fail" also implies *courage*. Peter Drucker was convinced that CEOs of corporations had it in their power to make even a failing company succeed. What was required was a broad view of the company's strengths and weaknesses and a willingness to ask hard questions about where the company was headed, even if that meant daring to fail. Edersheim used the example of Frances Hesselbein who took over the Girl Scouts in 1976 to make the point that it was either dare to fail or obscurity for the Girl Scouts.[47] If you were a member of the Girl Scouts in the '50s or '60s (we were!), you might have earned a merit badge for sewing or cooking. Hesselbein recognized that the world was moving fast and created merit badges that were unheard of in that earlier generation, such as for accounting and math.

There are numerous examples of dare to fail. Consider the phenomenon of Barack Obama. His confidence allowed a man of color, with no natural political base, to enter the White House as president. Or think of Eleanor Roosevelt. Up to her tenure in the White House, first ladies played wife and hostess. Their biggest worries were about the White House china and serving tea. Eleanor Roosevelt was criticized mightily for breaking the mold by becoming an activist for civil rights, for women's rights, and for factory jobs to be given to women in World War II. But where did she get the confidence to work so tirelessly for such unpopular causes? She wrote,

> You gain strength, courage and confidence by every experience in which you really stop to look fear in the face. You are able to say to yourself, "I have lived through this horror. I can take the next thing that comes along." You must do the thing you think you cannot do.[48]

Ms. Roosevelt can be a model for each of us and our children to look serious problems in the face and forge ahead while keeping in mind that not everyone will appreciate our efforts, as the next tale illustrates.

Do you own something made of Gore-Tex? It was invented in 1957 in a basement in Newark, Delaware, by Bob Gore and his son

Robert. At the time, the elder Gore was working for DuPont. When he offered them his invention and they turned it down, he started his own company. It now has annual sales of $3.2 billion and, as the world's first breathable and waterproof fabric, is used for everything from medical devices to shoes. Gore sums up one of the company's basic principles,

> We want our associates to feel maximum freedom in doing their job. There is also the expectation that there will be failure, and no one should be afraid of it. You are not going to accomplish much if you are.[49]

And what about Michael DeBakey, who invented the first artificial heart and transformed the treatment of cardiac patients? He was the first to perform bypass surgery, and even while he was in medical school he invented a key component of the heart–lung machine. This was high-risk stuff, from both a medical and ethical perspective.

Lest our readers think that only people with graduate degrees can dare to fail, consider Rosa Parks. An African American seamstress in Montgomery, Alabama, Parks refused on December 1, 1955, to give up her seat on a bus to a White man and started the civil rights movement. She said, in a 1992 interview with National Public Radio's Lynn Neary,

> I did not want to be mistreated, I did not want to be deprived of a seat that I had paid for. It was just time . . . there was opportunity for me to take a stand to express the way I felt about being treated in that manner.[50]

That took guts. Of course, she was arrested, and that set off a chain of events that changed our society significantly.

We could go on and on. The key to dare to fail, our last level of confidence, is to have the passion to realize what is needed, whether it is equal treatment for African Americans or a way to allow people to live on with heart disease or capitalizing on a chance invention as Gore did on the fabric that bears his name. When Vaughan celebrated the anniversary of that serum to Nome, he celebrated a team of 20 mushers who had bravely set forth on the expedition to chart untouched wilderness in Antarctica, mushers who dared to fail so that we would better understand the far reaches of our planet. Greatness emerges from what appear to be failures, and these failures become the opportunities for change and growth. If we don't reach for the stars, we will never fail but neither will we develop the grit it takes to achieve something new that will change our lives.

TAKING ACTION

Confidence. To dream big. To keep trying in the face of failure. To dare to fail. What the experiments we've described have shown us is that at least some of what creates confidence is the experiences we have and the expectations that others have for us. Those experiences and expectations can be powerful in shaping how confident we turn out to be.

In Yourself

How would you rate yourself on our confidence report card? Do you think you are often impulsive and just "barrel on" at Level 1, despite warning signs you somehow choose to ignore? Or are you timid about what you put forth, looking over your shoulder to see how you are being evaluated by others? "Where do I stand" at Level 2, can paralyze us into inaction. Perhaps you are the type of person who does your "homework" by studying all the angles and taking a Level 3 "calculated risk" to put forward that plan that changes the way a project will be carried out. Or are you the kind of person who "dares to fail" by proposing a new plan that questions the premises on which the project is founded? Wherever you fall on the report card, it is useful to reflect on your level of confidence and think about what you might want to change. And as you think about yourself, ask what kind of a model you want to be for your children. Those who barrel on beget those who barrel on. And those who give up in the face of difficulty are setting the stage for children who do not persevere.

As Eleanor Roosevelt said, challenge yourself, "Look fear in the face!" Say yes to things you might not have said yes to before! Push yourself to use your knowledge to take leadership in developing that new plan. Taking on new challenges will likely prove very rewarding. Friends of ours picked up new hobbies that they are now devoted to. Have you always wanted to do yoga? Go for it! How about that drama club you've been too shy to join? Check out their next meeting. When you tell your kids you are trying something new, they will support you and be inspired by your actions. When they see that first down dog, they will be intrigued.

In Your Children

Not all children are the same. Some seem to have been born confident and some have to develop it. Think about your own childhood. Were you the one who climbed that tree or went into that tunnel? Or were you the one who hung back, waiting to hear that it was safe? Kids will move at their own pace, but we all want our kids to have enough confidence to meet friends and to try to solve hard problems. We can help them increase their confidence quotient. Take social situations: Some kids try to melt into the woodwork when meeting new people (especially grown-ups), and others look new people in the eye and extend their hand for a shake. One of us had a babysitter who did this, and we thought it was a really nice practice. You can teach your children to do this. You can teach them to look new people in the eye and extend their hand. Having a practiced routine when they meet a new adult will help them get through it!

One way to build confidence is to make sure you are not praising children for their smarts. Praise for effort. Children will avoid trying new things if they think they might fail, especially if they think you will be upset by their failure. We want to encourage them to try and to move on even if they fail. When your child does something wrong or fails in a task, scolding will not be half as effective for building confidence as asking what happened in a truly neutral tone. Why did the babysitter trip on your truck? What happened on your spelling test? Think about the effect these questions have on children's responses. If you had just scolded him, he would not have to consider what went wrong. Whenever we can make children think (remember deep processing?), they are less likely to make the same mistake next time. A follow-up of, "What can you do differently next time?" puts the onus of the problem on the child, and the child has to think it through. Confidence comes from seeing that you could have done better and that you know the route to take!

In the Places You Go

Thomas Edison had a summer home in Fort Myers, Florida, that is open to the public. Share the story of Edison and how many blind alleys he encountered until he invented the lightbulb or the phonograph (you will have to explain that to your children!). Short of going to visit his home in Florida, go to the library and take out some books on Edison. Help your kids understand that success does not come overnight, despite what they see on TV. Hard work, perspiration, effort, and grit are characteristics you want your kids to have. You want them to understand that learning, inventing, and succeeding is hard, even for that footrace at school and certainly for that history project.

If you think your child has to develop more confidence, figure out what they like and try to provide more of it. Does she enjoy ice-skating? Go more often. Can you afford the occasional lesson? Help your children develop a zone of competence that will help them feel more confident all around. Next time when they say, "I can't," remind them how it took them time to learn to ice-skate but how good they are at it now.

Try not to evaluate but to question. When your child makes a drawing, ask her what she drew rather than saying, "Is that a drawing of the dog?" Ask your child to tell you why the dog's fur is green. Invite conversation; ditch the evaluation. This kind of interaction builds confidence and fuels children's attempts to keep trying. Remember, it's all about the process. Insisting on evaluating the outcome will not build your children's confidence in their abilities.

How Do We Create Environments That Foster Confidence?

It starts at home, but it doesn't end there. Recently, a story in *The New York Times* talked about how anxiety about doing math can be passed through generations.[51] But don't picture a math gene! Picture parents who make faces and groan when it is time to help their children tackle the math homework, even in the third grade. Yet knowing mathematics is essential for many highly paid careers; children will be shut out of those without competency in mathematics. At least one mother described in the article had the insight to know that she shouldn't let her children see her distress. She hid her grimaces by holding a piece of paper in front of her face. But she knew she wasn't successful because she would have outbursts when she said things like, "What are these teachers thinking? Are they nuts?" Remember that people perform worse when there are expectations that they will do poorly. As sure as if it were a cold, this mom was transmitting the germ for math anxiety to her kids. We need to create environments that foster confidence in our offspring, not breeding grounds for doubt and fear.

Outside your home, consider what your children can do to build their confidence and persistence. Are they old enough to have a chore they can carry out? Are they old enough to get a part-time job on weekends? Could they help an ailing neighbor or relative? Can they volunteer to help an organization? If we let them learn how good it feels to help others, they will surely feel good about themselves.

Some children are in classrooms where teachers make them feel great: "Oh Danny, don't worry! You'll get that problem right next time." Other teachers may not be as supportive. We won't know how our children's teachers react to failure if we don't talk to our kids. Take the time to talk about the pressures teachers are under and how learning is not instantaneous. Opening the door to such conversations can only help your child understand how confidence is built—hard work, perseverance, and grit are necessary for anyone to make their way. Nothing comes easy and our children have to know that.

CHAPTER 11

A REPORT CARD FOR THE 21ST CENTURY

The child is not a citizen of the future; he [sic] is a citizen from the very first moment of life and also the most important citizen because he represents and brings the "possible" . . . a bearer, here and now of rights, of values, of culture.

—Carla Rinaldi, *In Dialogue With Reggio Emilia: Listening, Researching and Learning*

Carla Rinaldi is a visionary. The president of the Loris Malaguzzi Centre Foundation, Rinaldi embodies the Reggio Emilia philosophy of education that started in the small Italian village situated between Bologna and Milan. Reggio Emilia is not just a method for teaching children; it is more a way of life. Children are seen as capable of constructing their own learning, driven by their own interests. Adults serve in the role of coaches, not directors. And children are described as "speaking" 100 languages through art, song, storytelling, and dance, to name a few.

In Reggio, children do not sit passively at desks waiting for information to be delivered and consumed. They are active explorers of their world, constantly interacting and creating, discovering and testing, as parents and teachers shift their focus from *what* children learn to *how* they learn. Children who grow up in these kinds of settings become deeply curious thinkers and grow into considerate and collaborative neighbors. As Rinaldi so eloquently told us, children living in a Reggio community are imbued with rights, values, and culture while learning how to become citizens in their community and of the world at large. The children show adults possibilities they might never discover themselves.

The 6Cs that we have presented in the pages of this book offer a glimpse of how we—parents and educators, app developers, and museum designers—can reimagine learning as a dynamic way of thinking that happens both in and out of school. It is a vision that applies to all children from ages 0 to 99 (and beyond) and that easily crosses geographic boundaries. It adapts to the ways we construct the habitats for children in our homes, schools, and communities.

We began to sketch our ideas for the 6Cs in 2009 in our book *A Mandate for Playful Learning in Preschool.* That same year, the Partnership for 21st Century Skills proposed a model of future skills that could transform the classroom.[1] The urgency was apparent. We were among a small congress of writers, scientists, and educators who unfurled scrolls listing their favorite candidates for a cadre of 21st-century skills. As the lists proliferated, it came as no surprise that collaboration, creative innovation, and critical thinking appeared on everyone's scroll.

The brainstorming, although productive, often settled on sets of inert lists rather than on coherent, science-based, integrated models for how we should think about success and its corollary, educational reform. Could we knit the skill sets together into a well-woven tapestry that would offer a panoramic view of learning, a view that respected learning differences and that offered measurable growth? Yes, we could. The 6Cs emerged as a 21st-century report card. Fully grasping the potential of the report card required that we think hard about what might count as success in a global world and about the skills our children would need to achieve that success. We have never met parents who did not want their child to soar. Across the globe, people are defining success in the same ways. As we said in Chapter 1 of this volume, society thrives when we craft environments in and out of school that support happy, healthy, thinking, caring, and social children who become collaborative, creative, competent, and responsible citizens tomorrow. The 6Cs are proposed as a science-based way to reach this vision of success and to fashion societies in ways that support families and children. We've seen it work in places as diverse as Canada, Finland, and Reggio Emilia—and even in exemplar schools in the United States.

THE 6Cs IN CONCERT: REALIZING THE BROADER VISION

Making this vision work for all requires that we adopt a more Reggio-like approach, with full recognition that we are raising a whole child and that education is as much about how you learn as it is about what you learn. The 6Cs capture this flavor as a set of skills that are inextricably linked. In our grid, Table 11.1, which first appeared in Chapter 1, we see the interplay as we move from left to right and from bottom to top. With our figurative 3-D glasses, we can also imagine the entire model in dynamic interaction as our children grow. How can we make this rich image in our minds a reality?

CALLING THE SKILLS BY THEIR NAMES

Believe it or not, the 6Cs advance our thinking just by calling attention to skills that often go unnoticed. Remember those so-called social "soft skills" that were the foundation for the "hard skills" like math and reading? If we do not think of a "soft skill" such as collaboration as central to learning, we will never plan our curricula to have group activities. And group activities, whether using building blocks or writing a science report, teach us to work together and to hear one another's views. Collaboration—a skill that rests on social relationships and the ability to regulate emotions—is central. In fact, kindergarten teachers say that children's ability to work together is one of the most important avenues for learning. Yet, our laser focus on reading and math often blinds us to the role of social competence in education.

TABLE 11.1. The 6Cs: A Second Look

	Collaboration	Communication	Content	Critical Thinking	Creative Innovation	Confidence
Level 4	Building it together	Tell a joint story	Expertise	Evidence	Vision	Dare to fail
Level 3	Back and forth	Dialogue	Making connections	Opinions	Voice	Calculated risks
Level 2	Side by side	Show and tell	Wide breadth/ Shallow understanding	Truths differ	Means–end	Where do I stand?
Level 1	On my own	Raw emotion	Early learning/ Situation specific	Seeing is believing	Experimentation	Barrel on

The same applies for areas like critical thinking. If a classroom is fashioned to give the facts—just the facts—and never gives a chance for debate, we are implicitly training students to achieve "seeing is believing," the lowest level of critical thinking. Even the study of history should be more about trends than facts. Our children have to see that the facts, like words on a page, can be rearranged to tell a different story. In a wonderful and enlightening example of this phenomenon, a student of ours from Berlin recounted what it was like to live through the destruction of the Berlin wall. "Most remarkably," he mentioned, "after the wall came down, the history books all changed." The "facts" from the East had now given way to the narrative from the West. Lenin who?

THE 6Cs BUILD ON EACH ANOTHER: MOVING ALONG THE GRID FROM LEFT TO RIGHT

The 6Cs are rooted in decades of research in psychological science. Each skill builds on the one before it and unfolds just as it naturally unfolds in the child. Communication is simply impossible without collaboration. Communication rests on recognizing that there are others around you with whom you seek to collaborate, even if it as primitive as vocalizing in sequence together. Another way to think about this is imagining the fictional character Robinson Crusoe's life. Living on an isolated island, he was hard pressed to communicate with anyone but himself. Communication is not a solo sport. That accomplished writer who writes only for herself is producing a diary. And a personal diary doth not a blog make. Unless she envisions an audience at the other end of her pen, she is not successfully communicating.

Then there is content, which relies essentially on communication. Although toddlers learn about the world through their own exploration, we know that they learn tons from their language-laced

251

communications with the adults around them. Later on, if you cannot listen to your elders or read deftly from a textbook, you will surely have trouble mastering world knowledge. This fact is the impetus behind the now popular Campaign for Grade-Level Reading. Introduced by the Casey Foundation, this initiative has become law in many states that want to ensure that children in third grade read at a third-grade level. Politicians know that children who do not read at grade level and who cannot read to learn are at risk of dropping out before they finish formal schooling. Third grade is a benchmark year, and content learning is crucially dependent on communication skills.

It should come as little surprise that critical thinking is intrinsically dependent on content. Content is also essential for critical thinking. It is hard to navigate information if you have no information to begin with! Lawyers and debaters must gather the evidence before they can weigh it. Entrepreneurs must do their "due diligence," examining companies' finances before they make offers to buy them. Researchers must critique existing studies and figure out what the authors missed before they can design a new and better study.

Content and critical thinking become key pillars for creative innovation. Remember that 10,000-hour rule? Creative geniuses are first and foremost masters of their trade. Equipped with enough strategic information, they become the tinkerers who create new products from old parts—or they create the new parts themselves. These creators also need practice in combining and recombining the elements. Dale Dougherty initiated an entire movement called the Maker Faire to bring this point to life. In his TED talk from 2011, Dougherty put it this way:

> All of us are makers. We're born makers. . . . Our next generation should be makers. . . . And we've got to get this into schools, or into communities in many ways—the ability to tinker, to shape and reshape the world around us.[2]

Finally, confidence depends on content, critical thinking, and creative innovation. Being willing to fail and try again is essential to success. As Tony Wagner, educator, author, and founder of Harvard's Change Leadership Group put it, "The most innovative companies celebrate failure."[3] But Randy Pausch, author of *The Last Lecture*, urged us to think about failures differently: "The brick walls are there to give us a chance to show how badly we want something."[4] Or as we once heard a local say when we were traveling in Israel, "Impossible? Impossible? Impossible simply means it will take a little longer."

In sum, the 6Cs are not merely an independent list of skills. They form an integrated whole in which all the skills are intrinsically linked. And they are central for learning and success. Although our grid captures the general thrust of development in each C, we recognize it as a convenient caricature. The Cs can influence one another in multiple ways: Reading more books gives you more *content* and more ability to criticize plot and story line (i.e., *critical thinking*), but studying the presidential debates may feed into your becoming more of an expert on *communication* and *confidence*. The 6Cs are thus like a spiral rather than a rigid stepwise trajectory. Think of the spiral as representing you or your child. Now put on your 3-D glasses and look at the spiral in your mind's eye. It is composed of six strands that correspond to each of the 6Cs. It has thickness as well as height and breadth. It's a rope whose fibers are continually twisting into thicker and thinner strands. The rope gets stronger over time. Maybe it even frays a bit. Some of the strands composing the rope will be wider than others because some of us are better at collaborating and some at critical thinking. But they will continue to actively change as we are exposed to new environments and new information.

If we imagine the 6Cs in motion, we see a dynamic system of learning that is visited and revisited according to different learning goals. The goals we set for ourselves change throughout life. Marcia can be a novice learner in orchestral conducting. As a novice conductor, she has to learn to collaborate with an orchestra in an entirely new way—perhaps even starting again in parallel play before she learns how to "read" the social cues from the violinists. Learning the score to first understand what Beethoven intended and how Ormandy interpreted his markings requires critical thinking. We are all growing and learning anew as we approach different areas throughout our lives.

THE 6Cs FROM NOVICE TO EXPERT: MOVING ALONG THE GRID FROM BOTTOM TO TOP

Our vision of the 6Cs captures general trends that can help us mark learning. The science of learning has given us real yardsticks for assessing our progress. The bottom to top structure of our model (that is, the successive levels from 1 to 4) captures real growth, but in most cases these skills don't just mature on their own; they need carefully prepared environments to nurture them. The point is that progress depends on a person's age and level and then exposure to just the right sort of experiences that will allow children to move up the proverbial ladder.

Consider language development, an integral part of communication. Babies cry, coo, smile, and laugh. But providing children with lots of language just when they are learning it and talking with them about what they are interested in is likely to help them move up the ladder sooner. It will also help them learn the vocabulary they need for learning content to succeed in school.

Or take critical thinking: As Professor Deanna Kuhn taught us, you can become a better critical thinker if you practice thinking from different perspectives.[5] Interfaith dialogue groups create

Kuhn-type experiments in the real world. If Christians and Jews and Muslims all sit down together and discuss their varied points of view, they are more likely to appreciate their differences and put ethnic biases aside. So, for any given topic—be it historical debates about slavery or defending the choice of a new car—we can measure how people move from a simplistic state of "seeing is believing" to one in which they weigh the evidence to support a position. Just as we can measure progress in communication and critical thinking, we can do so for each of the Cs offering us a qualitative view of our achievements in each area.

In our college classes, we have been using the 6Cs model for classroom pedagogy for over a decade. At the beginning of the school year, we ask our students to analyze their skills in terms of the 6Cs and they derive a profile of where each student sits within each of the skill sets. Our classes are then designed to include opportunities to practice working together on group reports and group projects (collaboration) and offer students a chance to post commentary about each article read. We make strong writing skills a priority in midterms and finals, require oral presentations of research, and judge students on their classroom participation (communication). Students must read primary journal articles on topics such as *the digital you* or *the psychology of morality* (both fall under content). Students are required to write exams designed to evaluate the arguments they have read (critical thinking) and to develop their own creative take on the research. We encourage them to find their voice in the safe place we set up in our classroom, and we encourage them to take intellectual risks and to persist in the face of failure (confidence).

True, students who grew up in a No Child Left Behind school system were a bit shocked by this vision of education. They had to learn that success was more about being well-rounded; regurgitating facts on a wide-ranging set of topics to get an *A* would no longer suffice. They had to be able to evaluate, communicate, integrate, and share their views. But they adapted. They thanked us—some even hugged us!—for the experience that filtered into all their other classes and flowed into their thinking beyond the university. At the end of the year, we asked those same students to rate themselves yet again on the 6Cs. They saw their own growth, and many told us, "This was a totally new way of learning. I cannot believe how much I have grown." They beamed even more when they were the ones picking up the choice jobs in a tight labor market. They achieved success at a deep level.

REFLECTING ON OUR OWN PROFILE
OF LEARNING AND SUCCESS

Just as we ask our students to fill out their own report card on the 6Cs to derive a profile, each of us, as parents and others who guide children, can engage in a self-evaluation of where we are and where we can go. At the end of each chapter on a different C, we challenged you to think about what level you fall into on the 6Cs grid with respect to your capabilities or your children's. This profile we create for ourselves, for others, and even for the organizations we join (how would our local PTA do on this grid?) represents a first step in our rethinking learning and reimagining education—broadly conceived. It encourages us to redesign our classrooms, homes, communities, and workplaces.

We are not saying that each person has to be at the top in each C, although we think that this is what we should strive for. Each of us does have to adapt to new situations when they arise, and an education that is "[fill in the blank]-content only" will never get us there. Looking at learning as a suite of skills on which we can build a profile will help us set goals and achieve them.

THE 6Cs IN PRACTICE: COMING TO YOUR HOMES, VILLAGES, CITIES, AND SCHOOLS

In the beginning, we promised you a new way of looking at learning. We also challenged our society's vision of success. Is success really about getting more stars on our homework sheets or getting all As, or is there something more? We suggested that just focusing on the learning that happens in school was insufficient for the children of the 21st century. First, children don't spend all that much time in school; we have to think about what they do the rest of the time. And second, learning in school may not be supporting children in all the other areas in which they need to develop.

Success includes content, but it is so much more. Don't we want our kids to be happy and to approach lifelong learning with joie de vivre? Don't we want them to have friends and to learn how to navigate the social mazes that confront them on the playground and in the workplace? And surely we want good citizens to propel our society and economy forward. If we want this type of success, we are going to have to think about education—in and out of school—in a more holistic way. And one way to achieve that end is to view the 6Cs through the metaphor of play.

GROWING THE 6Cs THROUGH PLAYFUL LEARNING

Somehow, somewhere in our society, we divorced play and learning as if one was the antithesis of the other. Indeed, in one of our papers, we likened the split between play and learning as analogous to the Capulets and Montagues from Shakespeare's *Romeo and Juliet*. The unfortunate mantra goes: If you are playing, you cannot be working. But Rinaldi and many other psychologists and educators caution us to think differently. "Play and learning are completely interdependent," she suggested, "like the wings of a butterfly where

257

play is one wing and work the other" (personal communication, August 2015). The butterfly will never be free without both.

Nested within play, Rinaldi added, are the seeds of citizenship and democracy. What might she mean? Rinaldi suggested that in play we have freedom. Children—the owners of their own play—become the drivers of the system and the stewards of what they create. But in play that freedom is not total; it is constrained by the rules of the group. That is, we cannot do anything we want to in that soccer game because it would not be fair to the others playing with us. So we must learn to work with others (*collaboration*) to move that ball down the field and to *communicate* our desire to pass to Sherry while seeing the field from others' perspectives' too. We have to understand the game and the evolving rules (*content*), *think critically* about solutions to any disputes, *create* new solutions to problems on and off the field among our teammates, and have the *confidence* and grit to first propose and then follow through on these solutions. This sounds a bit like a lesson in democracy and in how to be a good citizen. The games we played as children set the stage for us to understand how democracies work. Play is powerful.

But surely, you may be thinking, play has little place in school. And certainly all learning can't be fun. What about algebra? Our point of view is that there are actually two kinds of learning. Free play is the butterfly; children don't even realize how much they are learning when they are playing. The Toy Industry Association put out a fantastic series of YouTube videos called the "Genius of Play" (see https://www.youtube.com/user/TIAssociation). The videos illustrate what children are learning as they play. They show how make-believe builds communication and collaboration, for example, and how playing with blocks builds content about space and number. Imagine if we didn't let children play. When researchers keep animals in isolation, not permitting them to play with others of their ilk, they fail to produce many of the behaviors expected of their species.[6] Did you know that rats "laugh?" And even octopi play!

Free play is crucial for children's progress at all points on the 6Cs grid because it is through play that they acquire and practice these skills—as we illustrated earlier with a soccer game. Free play, whether alone or with peers or adults, allows kids to find their voice, to figure out what they like and don't like, and to pick up lots of content they will need for school. And let's not forget the important "soft skills" they pick up in play. Negotiation—which involves communication, collaboration, creativity, and confidence—is ubiquitous in play. Free play is wonderful. But what we call *guided play* helps children learn when adults want to teach them something specific.

Parents, grandparents, caregivers, and the other adults in our children's lives are their best teachers. But don't think "teachy-preachy"—we don't mean just telling and children listening. Think of following children's interests, answering their questions, and telling them what they want to know or helping them find the answers—all in the context of playing that board game or walking around the zoo. This is guided play. We have tested it scientifically. We compared children's learning when they were engaged in guided play versus when they were with a kind adult who just told them the same information. Children learn more in guided play than didactic instruction (sitting and listening). Whether children are learning new vocabulary or about what makes a triangle a triangle, they do better when they can be engaged and active.[7,8] This is when children are using their brains to think and transform. Sitting and listening are what many schools are like now, with big people telling little people how it is. The irony is that the little people don't retain what they are told. This is too passive a way to learn. The kind of learning children can use and take out of their schools happens more effectively when they are engaged and not passive. Free and guided play become metaphors for engaged and active learning, even for kids learning algebra! But how do we go about creating such environments? Are there any models for transforming our schools, homes, and communities as places to grow the 6Cs? Although we made many suggestions at the end of each of the 6Cs chapters, let's take a broader look now.

BUILDING PLAYFUL CONTEXTS FOR LEARNING AT SCHOOL

In Friends' Central School in Philadelphia, the lower school practices what is called *theme-based education*. Each summer, the teachers choose a theme for the coming year that they then all work on. One year they made up a fictional planet: *Orbis*, which is as equidistant from the sun as we are but in a galaxy on the other side of it. Each classroom becomes a different country on Orbis and must figure out how to survive fiscally and give their members a high quality of life. Lunaguavia is situated near a large ocean with ports. Its sunny climate is good for growing produce that can be shared around Orbis. Landlocked Interstasis is rich in minerals but needs to make collaborative deals with other countries to receive goods. These raw materials will be manufactured into products that are shipped elsewhere on Orbis. You get the idea. The children have to do collaborative and communicative work throughout the school day to help their country survive. But they also learn content. Math? If you have to build a boat to travel across the ocean before the produce spoils, you have to calculate the size of the boat, the kind of motor you need, and the miles you can travel. Does that mean second- and third graders are thinking algebraically and don't even know it? This is deeply impressive. Children are taught the core curriculum through a narrative that makes it exciting and accessible.

Or we could travel to San Diego's High Tech High, where a diverse student body from kindergarten to Grade 12 are solving real-world problems together as they learn, play, and create. There you can see a student-derived math curriculum called "origami math" or what was called "scenes of destruction," a series of plays designed to learn about the historical events and interpretations of those momentous lava-filled moments in Pompeii. Here, 58 eighth graders worked for months on the Pompeii project, answering questions such as, "What can you learn about the values of a society from the artifacts they carry with them into exile?" What began as a single charter school in the year 2000 has become an integrated network of 13 schools serving over 5,000 students.

These students are outperforming their peers in traditional outcome measures and have a love of learning and an ownership of their creations. Remarkably, this kind of education works equally well for nontraditional students. In Public School 94 in Manhattan, children with a host of developmental disabilities are demonstrating success by learning through the arts. Their teachers have them performing musicals like *Aladdin*, and children on the autism spectrum are developing collaborative and communicative skills that even their parents did not think possible! Children previously thought to be mute speak during the play! This initiative and High Tech High have both shown results with very diverse children in public schools. In scientific and educational parlance, this means that learning through play and discovery can "scale up." It also demonstrates how schools can be thoughtful about how we create contexts to support the 6Cs and to nurture and examine growth in each skill.

BUILDING PLAYFUL CONTEXTS FOR LEARNING AT HOME

Here is where parents can also enter into the fun. There are so many ways to transform your home into exciting 6C environments that nurture children in collaboration, communication, content, critical thinking, creativity, and confidence. The chapters in this book are dotted with ways to reflect on the 6Cs in yourself and your children while taking action with respect to the activities you do. When children join in dinner prep or cleanup, they are learning about collaboration and, often, communication. What happens at your dinner table? Do you talk about the events of the day? Can we be more mindful in the discussion that takes place? How might we make time—just 10 or 15 minutes after dinner—to do a puzzle, solve a riddle, sing favorite songs, or formulate an argument for the school debate? And can we then reinforce the lessons learned? The puzzle teaches spatial skills and the riddle is critical thinking at work.

BUILDING PLAYFUL CONTEXTS FOR LEARNING IN THE COMMUNITY

There are even ways to build playful smart zones into the community. Working with architect Itai Palti from Tel Aviv, we are designing new experiential architecture, dubbed UrbanThinkScape, to spruce up old bus stops by creating lights that project animations on the ground and benches equipped with puzzles that frame the back of the seat. The William Penn Foundation is working with us to turn imagination into reality.

Think of what you can do with signage in supermarkets to turn the ordinary into the extraordinary. In Tulsa, Oklahoma, we are working with the Kaiser Foundation to dress up supermarkets with adventures and games that get children looking for different kinds of apples, doing critical thinking and math as they inspect the towers of canned veggies.

How about taking a trip to the local park or children's museum? Kids love these places where they follow their noses and learn freely. How might we design exhibits and activities with the 6Cs in mind? We did exactly that when we conducted the Ultimate Block Party in Central Park in New York City. Twenty-eight activities born from the science of learning sprang up in the usually pristine park that day. We were shocked when over 50,000 people participated, hungry for new and less punishing ways for their children to learn! From LEGO building with a master designer to the robot exhibit from Columbia University, children learned content and so much more. In fact, after visiting three or more activities, parents reported that they changed their lens on learning and now saw the spatial development in the LEGO set and the science in the robots. Perhaps they even saw the world around them as replete with math, reading, social studies, and science.

Once you are conscious of the skills children need to succeed, once you drop the idea that learning only happens in schools and textbooks, once we recognize that play and talk fuel endless learning, we can see the connection between play and education through the 6Cs. The possibilities are endless, and learning abounds in every crevice of your experience. We need only share these teachable moments with our children and watch them blossom into happy, healthy, inquisitive humans.

AND IT'S NOT JUST ABOUT PLAY

Although playful learning is an apt metaphor for optimal learning generally, we all know that optimal learning occurs whenever we are engrossed in a task that captures our time and imagination. For the avid gardener, the 6Cs sprout when we are planting cooperatively with the neighbors or planning a crop that will yield tomatoes at the time we arrive home from summer vacation. For the athlete, collaboration can be learned on the field. Knowing when to take calculated risks can be the difference in winning or losing. For the musician, playing violin in that orchestra requires us to be deeply aware of the woodwinds and to have the technical skills to project our sound during the solos.

We see that many activities can serve as grist for the 6Cs to flourish. Perhaps that was what Carla Rinaldi wanted us to see in her Reggio program when she asked us to talk to trees. In many ways, the Reggio approach to learning is a perfect example of the 6Cs at work in a school environment. Like the 6Cs, it was born from the science that views children not just as heads but as whole, active, engaged people with social sides too. In the town of Emilia Romagna, children are viewed as the collective responsibility of the community. The children they educate and nurture today will be the leaders and citizens of the community 30 years from now. No doubt, the families in Italy want smart children just as we do, but as Rinaldi is the first to say, success will not be judged by a grade on a test. It is a bigger idea; it is about how we raise happy, healthy, thinking, caring, and social children who become collaborative, creative, competent, and responsible citizens tomorrow. At the core of this big idea are the ways in which we help our children learn to be collaborative, communicative, content rich, critical thinkers who are creative and who have the confidence and grit to make a difference in the world in which they live. As Rinaldi is fond of saying, this is our central job. We must all reinvent an education that is worthy of our children.

EPILOGUE: WHAT IF?
THE REPRISE

The LEGO Ideas Conference was abuzz with excitement. In a small town in Billund, Denmark, 300 like-minded people had gathered to start an educational movement. There was the man who dreamed up the creative Blue School in Manhattan; the woman charged with jump-starting an early childhood program for the King of Jordan; the scientist from Hong Kong who envisioned a new way to revamp Chinese education so that all children would be creative, critical thinkers; the principal of High Tech High in Seattle; the head of Harvard's Frontiers of Innovation; and Wendy Kopp, the dreamer who brought us Teach for America and, more recently, Teach for All. And that's just a slice of the assembled crowd. They were meeting because they recognized the disconnect between the way we are educating our children around the world and the needs of a modern society.

The conference opened with a simple exercise. "Please open the small plastic bag on your desk containing six multicolored LEGO bricks. How many unique combinations can you make from these six bricks?" Mathematicians in the audience started to calculate combinations and permutations. Six blocks, eight studs on each block—could it be 720? Could it be 48,000? Nope, the answer is just shy of one billion: 981,456,127—almost one billion combinations from six little bricks.

This exercise revealed the looming problem. We are educating children to build towers and to carefully place the red brick atop the blue and the blue atop the yellow. What if we started to teach in a way that revealed the infinite possibilities? Our children would still build towers, but they would also see a world ripe with potential.

This book uses the science of how people learn to suggest a new way to move beyond building towers and to equip our children—replete with minds *and* hearts—with the tools they need to become collaborative, creative, competent, and responsible citizens tomorrow. Doing this will require rethinking how children learn, appreciating that there is more than content, that the social child is best equipped to be the smart child, that creativity is the currency of our time, and that the best learning occurs when we fail along the way.

What if we transformed our homes, schools, and communities to foster this new kind of learning? The 6Cs could be our road map, our report card for how to nurture success. Our children would be groomed to envision and to build the society of their future. And our education—in and out of school—would finally be worthy of our children.

What if?

NOTES

CHAPTER I

1. Global Education First Initiative. (n.d.). *Priorities*. Retrieved from http://globaleducationfirst.org/priorities.html, para. 4.
2. Child and Youth Network. (2015). *What is CYN?* Retrieved from http://londoncyn.ca/about/, para. 1.
3. Bornstein, D. (2015, July 24). Teaching social skills to improve grades and lives. *The New York Times*. Retrieved from http://opinionator.blogs.nytimes.com/2015/07/24/building-social-skills-to-do-well-in-math/
4. James, W. (1890). *The principles of psychology*. New York, NY: Henry Holt & Company. http://dx.doi.org/10.1037/11059-000
5. Golinkoff, R. M., & Hirsh-Pasek, K. (1999). *How babies talk: The magic and mystery of language in the first three years of life*. New York, NY: Dutton.
6. Gopnik, A., Meltzoff, A. N., & Kuhl, P. K. (2000). *The scientist in the crib: What early learning tells us about the mind*. New York, NY: William Morrow.
7. Hirsh-Pasek, K., Golinkoff, R. M., & Eyer, D. (2003). *Einstein never used flashcards: How our children really learn—and why they need to play more and memorize less*. Emmaus, PA: Rodale Press.
8. Gardner, H. (2009). *Five minds for the future*. Boston, MA: Harvard Business Review Press.
9. Kuhn, D. (1999). A developmental model of critical thinking. *Educational Researcher, 28*(2), 16–25. http://dx.doi.org/10.3102/0013189X028002016

10. Siegler, M. G. (2010, August 4). Eric Schmidt: Every 2 days we create as much information as we did up to 2003. *TechCrunch.* Retrieved from http://techcrunch.com/2010/08/04/schmidt
11. Biech, E. (2007). *Thriving through change: A leader's practical guide to change.* Alexandria, VA: ASTD Press, p. 4.
12. Tomasco, S. (2010, May). *IBM 2010 global CEO study: Creativity selected as most crucial factor for future success.* Retrieved from IBM website: https://www-03.ibm.com/press/us/en/pressrelease/31670.wss

CHAPTER 2

1. Bracey, G. W. (2007, October 2). The Sputnik Effect: Why it endures, 50 years later. *Education Week.* Retrieved from http://www.edweek. org/ew/articles/2007/10/02/06bracey_web.h27.html, para. 8.
2. A nation at risk. (1983, April). Retrieved from https://www2.ed.gov/ pubs/NatAtRisk/risk.html
3. National Commission on Excellence in Education. (1983). A nation at risk: The imperative for educational reform. *The Elementary School Journal, 84*(2). Retrieved from http://www.jstor.org/stable/1001303, para. 1.
4. U.S. Department of Education. (1994). *Goals 2000: Educate America Act.* Retrieved from http://www2.ed.gov/legislation/GOALS2000/ TheAct/index.html
5. U.S. Department of Education. (1994). *National education goals.* Retrieved from http://www2.ed.gov/legislation/GOALS2000/ TheAct/sec102.html, para. 5, 6.
6. Bronson, P., & Merryman, A. (2013, February 6). Why can some kids handle pressure while others fall apart? *The New York Times Magazine.* Retrieved from http://www.nytimes.com/2013/02/10/magazine/ why-can-some-kids-handle-pressure-while-others-fall-apart.html
7. Strauss, V. (2011, August 1). Darling-Hammond: The mess we are in. *The Washington Post.* Retrieved from http://www.washingtonpost. com/blogs/answer-sheet/post/darling-hammond-the-mess-we-are-in/2011/07/31/gIQAXWSIoI_blog.html, para. 3.
8. Ravitch, D. (2010). *The death and life of the great American school system: How testing and choice are undermining education.* New York, NY: Basic Books.

9. Organization for Economic Cooperation and Development. (2012). *Programme for International Student Assessment (PISA): Results from PISA 2012.* Retrieved from http://www.oecd.org/pisa/keyfindings/PISA-2012-results-US.pdf

10. Kohn, D. (2015, May 16). Let the kids learn through play. *The New York Times.* Retrieved from http://www.nytimes.com/2015/05/17/opinion/sunday/let-the-kids-learn-through-play.html?_r=0, para. 5.

11. National Center on Education and the Economy. (2007). *Tough choices or tough times: The report of the Commission on the Skills of the American Workforce.* San Francisco, CA: Jossey-Bass.

12. Marshall, K. (2014, April 1). Tutoring preschool children growing in popularity. *The Age.* Retrieved from http://www.theage.com.au/victoria/tutoring-preschool-children-growing-in-popularity-20140331-35u6b.html

13. Miner, B. (2004/2005, Winter). *Keeping public schools public: Testing companies mine for gold.* Retrieved from Rethinking Schools website: http://www.rethinkingschools.org/special_reports/bushplan/test192.shtml, para. 1.

14. Quart, A. (2006, August). Extreme parenting. *Atlantic Monthly, 298*(1). Retrieved from http://web.fmk.edu.rs/files/blogs/2009-10/I/Engleski/Extreme_Parenting.pdf

15. Little & King Co. (2010). *The transformational toy manufacturing industry.* Retrieved from http://www.littleandking.com/white_papers/toy_manufacturing_industry_today.pdf

16. Rideout, V. J., Foehr, U. G., & Roberts, D. F. (2010). *Generation M2: Media in the lives of 8- to 18-year-olds.* Menlo Park, CA: Kaiser Family Foundation.

17. Calman, L. J., & Tarr-Whelan, L. (2014). *Early childhood education for all.* Cambridge, MA: MIT Press.

18. Edersheim, E. H. (2006). *The definitive Drucker: Challenges for tomorrow's executives.* New York, NY: McGraw-Hill.

CHAPTER 3

1. Heckman, J. (2015, June). Keynote address. In R. Winthrop (Chair), *Soft skills for workforce success: From research to action.* Symposium conducted at the meeting of the Brookings Institution, Washington, DC.

Retrieved from http://www.brookings.edu/~/media/events/2015/06/17-soft-skills-workforce-success/0617_transcript_soft-skills.pdf, p. 67.

2. The New York Academy of Sciences. (2015). Global STEM Alliance. Retrieved from Global STEM Alliance website: http://globalstemalliance.org/, para. 1.

3. Cisco and The New York Academy of Science grow global STEM alliance to meet the demand for future scientists, entrepreneurs and innovators. (2013, November 18). *The Network: Cisco's Technology News Site.* Retrieved from http://newsroom.cisco.com/press-release-content?articleId=1290739, para. 13.

4. Hirsh-Pasek, K., Golinkoff, R. M., & Eyer, D. (2003). *Einstein never used flash cards: How our children really learn—and why they need to play more and memorize less.* Emmaus, PA: Rodale Press.

5. Ministry of Education, Singapore. (2015). *Desired outcomes of education.* Retrieved from https://www.moe.gov.sg/education/education-system/desired-outcomes-of-education, para. 2.

6. Ministry of Education, Singapore. (2015). *Our education system.* Retrieved from https://www.moe.gov.sg/education/, para. 6.

7. Organisation for Economic Co-Operation and Development. (2010). *Strong performers and successful reformers in education: Lessons from PISA for the United States.* Retrieved from http://www.oecd.org/pisa/pisaproducts/46581035.pdf, p. 121.

8. Sahlberg, P. (2011). *Finnish lesson: What the world can learn from educational change in Finland.* New York, NY: Teachers College Press.

9. Abrams, S. E. (2011, January 28). The children must play. *New Republic.* Retrieved from http://www.newrepublic.com/article/politics/82329/education-reform-Finland-US, para. 11.

10. See note 9.

11. Programme for International Student Assessment. (2012). *Country note: Results from PISA 2012.* Paris, France: OECD.

12. Pascal, C. E. (n.d.). *Every child, every opportunity: Curriculum and pedagogy for the early learning program.* Retrieved from https://www.cpco.on.ca/files/6213/8142/6952/Every_Child_Every_Opportunity.pdf, p. iii.

13. Pascal, C. E. (n.d.). *Every child, every opportunity: Curriculum and pedagogy for the early learning program.* Retrieved from https://www.cpco.on.ca/files/6213/8142/6952/Every_Child_Every_Opportunity.pdf

14. Hirsh-Pasek, K., Zosh, J. M., Golinkoff, R. M., Gray, J. H., Robb, M. B., & Kaufman, J. (2015). Putting education in "educational" apps: Lessons from the science of learning. *Psychological Science in the Public Interest, 16*, 3–34. http://dx.doi.org/10.1177/1529100615569721

15. Goldin, A. P., Hermida, M. J., Shalom, D. E., Elias Costa, M., Lopez-Rosenfeld, M., Segretin, M. S., . . . Sigman, M. (2014). Far transfer to language and math of a short software-based gaming intervention. *Proceedings of the National Academy of Sciences of the United States of America, 111*, 6443–6448. http://dx.doi.org/10.1073/pnas.1320217111

16. Heckman, J. (2015, June). Keynote address. In R. Winthrop (Chair), *Soft skills for workforce success: From research to action.* Symposium conducted at the meeting of the Brookings Institution, Washington, DC. Retrieved from http://www.brookings.edu/~/media/events/2015/06/17-soft-skills-workforce-success/0617_transcript_soft-skills.pdf

CHAPTER 4

1. Lippman, L. H., Ryberg, R., Carney, R., & Moore, K. A. (2015). *Workforce connections—Key "soft skills" that foster youth workforce success: Towards a consensus across fields.* Washington, DC: Child Trends, p. 4.

2. Lippman, L. H., Ryberg, R., Carney, R., & Moore, K. A. (2015). *Workforce connections—Key "soft skills" that foster youth workforce success: Towards a consensus across fields.* Washington, DC: Child Trends.

3. The choice: Getting into college and paying for it (2013, June 14). *The New York Times.* Retrieved from http://thechoice.blogs.nytimes.com/?module=BlogMain&action=Click&region=Header&pgtype=Blogs&version=Blog%20Main&contentCollection=U.S

4. Sifting your Harvard questions, looking for parenting (and other) lessons. (2009, September 21). *The New York Times.* Retrieved from http://thechoice.blogs.nytimes.com/2009/09/21/harvardquestions/?_php=true&_type=blogs&_r=0#more-8381, para. 19.

5. Edersheim, E. H. (2006). *The definitive Drucker: Challenges for tomorrow's executives.* New York, NY: McGraw-Hill.

6. Ritchie, R. (2013, October 12). *History of the iPad (original): Apple makes the tablet magical and revolutionary.* Retrieved from http://www.imore.com/history-ipad-2010

7. Pink, D. (2005). *A whole new mind.* New York, NY: Riverhead Books, p. 1.

8. Pink, D. (2019). *Drive.* New York, NY: Riverhead Books.

9. Casner-Lotto, J., & Barrington, L. (2006). *Are they really ready to work? Employers' perspectives on the basic knowledge and applied skills of new entrants to the 21st century US workforce.* Retrieved from http://www.p21.org/storage/documents/FINAL_REPORT_PDF09-29-06.pdf

10. Casner-Lotto, J., & Barrington, L. (2006). *Are they really ready to work? Employers' perspectives on the basic knowledge and applied skills of new entrants to the 21st century US workforce.* Retrieved from http://www.p21.org/storage/documents/FINAL_REPORT_PDF09-29-06.pdf, p. 24.

11. Bond, T. J., Galinsky, E., Kim, S. S., & Brownfield, E. (2005, September). *2005 national study of employers.* Retrieved from http://familiesandwork.org/site/research/reports/2005nse.pdf

12. Adams, S. (2013, October 11). The 10 skills employers most want in 20-something employees. *Forbes Magazine.* Retrieved from http://www.forbes.com/sites/susanadams/2013/10/11/the-10-skills-employers-most-want-in-20-something-employees/

13. Partnership for 21st Century Learning. (n.d.). *Framework for 21st century learning.* Retrieved from http://www.p21.org/about-us/p21-framework

14. See note 13.

15. Hirsh-Pasek, K., Golinkoff, R. M., Singer, D., & Berk, L. (2009). *A mandate for playful learning in preschool: Presenting the evidence.* New York, NY: Oxford University Press.

16. Sifting your Harvard questions, looking for parenting (and other) lessons. (2009, September 21). *The New York Times.* Retrieved from http://thechoice.blogs.nytimes.com/2009/09/21/harvardquestions/?_php=true&_type=blogs&_r=0#more-8381

17. Galinsky, E. (2010). *Mind in the making: Seven essential life skills every child needs.* New York, NY: HarperCollins.

18. Organisation for Economic Co-Operation and Development. (2015). *Skills for social progress: The power of social and emotional skills.* Washington, DC: Author, p. 2.
19. Dalton, D. (2013, September 23). *The hard truth about soft skills.* Retrieved from http://dorothydalton.com/2013/09/23/professional-summary-soft-skills/, para. 1.
20. Mathews, J. (2009, January 5). The latest doomed pedagogical fad: 21st-century skills. *The Washington Post.* Retrieved from http://www.washingtonpost.com/wp-dyn/content/article/2009/01/04/AR2009010401532.html
21. Meltzoff, A. N., Kuhl, P. K., Movellan, J., & Sejnowski, T. J. (2009). Foundations for a new science of learning. *Science, 325,* 284–288.
22. Zernike, K. (2000, December 7). Ease up: Top colleges tell stressed applicants. *The New York Times.* Retrieved from http://www.nytimes.com/2000/12/07/us/ease-up-top-colleges-tell-stressed-applicants.html?pagewanted=all, para. 6.
23. Jones, D. E., Greenberg, M., & Crowley, M. (2015). Early social–emotional functioning and public health: The relationship between kindergarten social competence and future wellness. *American Journal of Public Health, 105,* 2283–2290. http://dx.doi.org/10.2105/AJPH.2015.302630
24. Carnegie, D. (1936). *How to win friends and influence people.* New York, NY: Pocket Books.

CHAPTER 5

1. Radsky, J. S., Kiston, C. J., Zuckerman, B., Nitzberg, K., Gross, J., Kaplan-Sanoff, M., . . . Silverstein, M. (2014). Patterns of mobile device use by caregivers and children during meals in fast food restaurants. *Pediatrics, 133,* e843. http://dx.doi.org/10.1542/peds.2013-3703
2. Tomasello, M. (2014). The ultra-social animal. *European Journal of Social Psychology, 44,* 187–194. http://dx.doi.org/10.1002/ejsp.2015
3. Wade, N. (2011, March 14). Supremacy of a social network. *The New York Times.* Retrieved from http://www.nytimes.com/2011/03/15/science/15humans.html?pagewanted=all&_r=0
4. Tomasello, M. (2009). *Why we cooperate.* Boston, MA: Boston Reviews Books.

5. Tomasello, M. (2001). *The cultural origins of human cognition.* Cambridge, MA: Harvard University Press.

6. Tomasello, M. (2001). *The cultural origins of human cognition.* Cambridge, MA: Harvard University Press, p. 202.

7. Chase, Z. (2011, March). *Want a job? You ought to be a tech geek.* Retrieved from the National Public Radio website: http://www.npr.org/templates/transcript/transcript.php?storyId=134236010, para. 24.

8. Daly, M., Delaney, L., Egan, M., & Baumeister, R. F. (2015). Childhood self-control and unemployment throughout the life span: Evidence from two British cohort studies. *Psychological Science, 26,* 709–723. http://dx.doi.org/10.1177/0956797615569001

9. Mischel, W., Ayduk, O., Berman, M. G., Casey, B. J., Gotlib, I. H., Jonides, J., . . . Shoda, Y. (2011). "Willpower" over the life span: Decomposing self-regulation. *Social Cognitive and Affective Neuroscience, 6,* 252–256. http://dx.doi.org/10.1093/scan/nsq081

10. Meltzoff, A. N. (1995). Understanding the intentions of others: Re-enactment of intended acts by 18-month-old children. *Developmental Psychology, 31,* 838–850. http://dx.doi.org/10.1037/0012-1649.31.5.838

11. Rummler, G., & Brache, A. P. (1991, January). Managing the white space. *Training.* Retrieved from http://www.performancedesignlab.com/wp-content/uploads/2012/04/43.-Managing-The-White-Space.pdf

12. Rosen, E. (2010, February 5). Smashing silos. *Bloomberg Business.* Retrieved from http://www.businessweek.com/managing/content/feb2010/ca2010025_358633.htm, para. 2.

13. Rezac, D. (n.d.). Silo syndrome: When leadership alone is not enough. *Rezac's Engaged Leadership Matrix.* Retrieved from http://rdmmatrix.blogspot.ca/2009/02/silo-syndrome-when-leadership-alone-is_10.html

14. See note 10.

15. Warneken, F., & Tomasello, M. (2006, March 3). Altruistic helping in human infants and young chimpanzees. *Science, 311,* 1301–1303. http://dx.doi.org/10.1126/science.1121448

16. Warneken, F., Chen, F., & Tomasello, M. (2006). Cooperative activities in young children and chimpanzees. *Child Development, 77,* 640–663. http://dx.doi.org/10.1111/j.1467-8624.2006.00895.x

17. Warneken, F., Hare, B., Melis, A. P., Hanus, D., & Tomasello, M. (2007). Spontaneous altruism by chimpanzees and young children. *PLoS Biology, 5,* 184. http://dx.doi.org/10.1371/journal.pbio.0050184

18. Warneken, F., Lohse, K., Melis, A. P., & Tomasello, M. (2011). Young children share the spoils after collaboration. *Psychological Science*, 22, 267–273, http://dx.doi.org/10.1177/0956797610395392, p. 271.

19. Bakan, J. (2011, August 21). The kids are not all right. *The New York Times*. Retrieved from http://www.nytimes.com/2011/08/22/opinion/corporate-interests-threaten-childrens-welfare.html, para. 1.

20. Dahl, R. (1996). *James and the giant peach*. New York, NY: Random House.

21. Deslauriers, L., Schelew, E., & Wieman, C. (2011, May 13). Improved learning in a large-enrollment physics class. *Science*, 332, 862–864. http://dx.doi.org/10.1126/science.1201783

22. Schrage, M. (1990). *Shared minds: The new technologies for collaboration*. New York, NY: Random House.

23. Denise, L. (1999). Collaboration vs. C-Three (Cooperation, Coordination, and Communication). *Innovating*, 7(3). Retrieved from http://www.keeppabeautiful.org/downloads/communicationattachments/collaborationstri.pdf

24. Merrill, P. (2008). *Innovation generation: Creating an innovation process and an innovative culture*. Milwaukee, WI: Quality Press, p. 184.

25. Mantle, M. L., & Lichty, R. (2013). *Managing the unmanageable: Rules, tools, and insights for managing software people and teams*. Boston, MA: Addison Wesley, p. 196.

26. Ramachandran, V. S. (n.d.). *The astonishing Francis Crick*. Retrieved from http://cbc.ucsd.edu/The_Astonishing_Francis_Crick.htm, para. 4.

27. Parten, M. B. (1932). Social participation among pre-school children. *The Journal of Abnormal and Social Psychology*, 27, 243–269. http://dx.doi.org/10.1037/h0074524

28. Gladwell, M. (2006). *Blink: The power of thinking without thinking*. New York, NY: Back Bay Books.

29. Wikipedia. (2015, March). In *Wikipedia*. Retrieved from http://wikieducator.org/Wikipedia, para. 3.

30. Tapscott, D., & Williams, A. D. (2008). *Wikinomics: How mass collaboration changes everything*. London, England: Penguin.

31. Tapscott, D. (n.d.). *TomPeters!* Retrieved from http://tompeters.com/cool-friends/tapscott-don/

32. Tomasco, S. (2010, May). *IBM 2010 global CEO study: Creativity selected as most crucial factor for future success.* Retrieved from IBM website: https://www-03.ibm.com/press/us/en/pressrelease/31670.wss

33. Edersheim, E. H. (2006). *The definitive Drucker.* New York, NY: McGraw-Hill, p. 135.

CHAPTER 6

1. A quote by Edward R. Murrow, 1908–1965. (2015). *Qotd.* Retrieved from http://www.qotd.org/search/single.html?qid=25925

2. Joseph Priestley. (n.d.). *BrainyQuote.* Retrieved from http://www.brainyquote.com/quotes/quotes/j/josephprie335782.html

3. Richtel, M. (2011, December 17). Reframing the debate over using phones behind the wheel. *The New York Times.* Retrieved from http://www.nytimes.com/2011/12/18/us/reframing-the-debate-over-using-phones-while-driving.html?_r=0, para. 19.

4. Smith, A. (2011, September 19). How Americans use texting. Retrieved from Pew Research Center website: http://www.pewinternet.org/2011/09/19/how-americans-use-text-messaging/

5. Worthen, B. (2012, September 12). The perils of texting while parenting. *The Wall Street Journal.* Retrieved from http://online.wsj.com/news/articles/SB10000872396390444772404577589683644202996

6. Bissonnette, Z. (2009, September 18). Looking for a job? Study Shakespeare. *Daily Finance.* Retrieved from http://www.dailyfinance.com/2009/09/18/looking-for-a-job-study-shakespeare/

7. Carnegie, D. (1998). *How to win friends and influence people.* Ann Arbor, MI: Gallery Books.

8. Dale Carnegie. (2015). *Wikipedia.* Retrieved from https://en.wikipedia.org/wiki/Dale_Carnegie

9. Cross cultural business blunders. (2014). *Kwintessential.* Retrieved from http://bit.ly/1M4ACRn

10. See note 9.

11. Frodi, A. M., & Lamb, M. E. (1980). Child abusers' responses to infant smiles and cries. *Child Development, 51,* 238–241. http://dx.doi.org/10.2307/1129612

12. Dunstan Baby (Producer). (2006). *Dunstan baby language* [DVD]. Available from http://www.dunstanbaby.com/the-gift-of-a-calm-baby-now-on-dvd/, Program One.

13. Roseberry, S., Hirsh-Pasek, K., & Golinkoff, R. M. (2014). Skype me! Socially contingent interactions help toddlers learn language. *Child Development, 85,* 956–970. http://dx.doi.org/10.1111/cdev.12166

14. Shure, M. (1993). *I can problem solve.* Champaign, IL: Research Press.

15. Greenberg, M. T., Kusche, C. A., & Riggs, N. (2004). The PATHS curriculum: Theory and research on neuro-cognitive development and school success. In J. E. Zins, R. P. Weissberg, M. C. Wang, & H. J. Walberg (Eds.), *Building academic success on social and emotional learning: What does the research say?* (pp. 170–188). New York, NY: Teachers College Press.

16. NACE Research. (2012). *Job outlook 2012.* Retrieved from https://www.uwsuper.edu/career/students/upload/Job-Outlook-2012-Member-Version-1.pdf, p. 28.

17. National Assessment Governing Board. (2010). *Writing framework for the 2011 National Assessment of Educational Progress.* Retrieved from https://www.nagb.org/content/nagb/assets/documents/publications/frameworks/writing/2011-writing-framework.pdf, p. 3.

18. Zimmerman, M. (2010, October 29). Losing your temper at work: How to survive it? *CBS MoneyWatch.* Retrieved from http://www.cbsnews.com/news/losing-your-temper-at-work-how-to-survive-it/

19. Frost, S. (n.d.). Top ten communication problems in the workplace. *eHow.* Retrieved from http://www.ehow.com/info_12099516_top-ten-communication-problems-workplace.html

20. Hallowell, E. M., & Ratey, J. J. (2011). *Driven to distraction: Recognizing and coping with attention deficit disorder.* New York, NY: Anchor Books.

21. Bender, L. (Producer), & Tarantino, Q. (Director). (1994). *Pulp fiction* [Motion picture]. United States: Miramax.

22. Diamond, A., Barnett, W. S., Thomas, J., & Munro, S. (2007, November 30). Preschool program improves cognitive control. *Science, 318,* 1387–1388. http://dx.doi.org/10.1126/science.1151148

23. Blair, C., & Raver, C. C. (2014). Closing the achievement gap through modification of neurocognitive and neuroendocrine function: Results from a cluster randomized controlled trial of an innovative approach

to the education of children in kindergarten. *PLoS ONE, 9*(11), e112393. http://dx.doi.org/10.1371/journal.pone.0112393

24. Brooks, J. G., & Brooks, M. G. (1999). *In search of understanding: The case for constructivist classrooms.* Alexandria, VA: ASCD.

25. Goodlad, J. I. (1984). A place called school: Prospects for the future. New York, NY: McGraw-Hill.

26. Fisher, K. R., Hirsh-Pasek, K., Newcombe, N., & Golinkoff, R. M. (2013). Taking shape: Supporting preschoolers' acquisition of geometric knowledge through guided play. *Child Development, 84,* 1872–1878. http://dx.doi.org/10.1111/cdev.12091

27. Strauss, V. (2012, June 3). The flip: Turning a classroom upside down. *The Washington Post.* Retrieved from http://www.washingtonpost. com/local/education/the-flip-turning-a-classroom-upside-down/ 2012/06/03/gJQAYk55BV_story.html

28. Joint Commission Resources. (n.d.). *Joint Commission guide to improving staff communication.* Retrieved from http://ebooks.dibaj.org/ product/joint-commission-guide-to-improving-staff-communication

29. Drucker, P. F. (1974). *Management: Risks, responsibilities, practices.* New York, NY: Harper & Row, p. 485.

30. Nulty, P., de Llosa, P., & Skelly von Brachel, J. (1992, March 23). The National Business Hall of Fame. *Fortune Magazine.* Retrieved from http://archive.fortune.com/magazines/fortune/fortune_archive/ 1992/03/23/76198/index.htm

31. Tannen, D. (2001). *Talking from 9 to 5: Men and women at work.* New York, NY: William Morrow.

32. Shonkoff, J., Phillips, D. A., Committee on Integrating the Science of Early Childhood Development. (2007). *From neurons to neighborhoods: The science of early child development.* Washington, DC: National Academies Press, p. 1.

33. Hirsh-Pasek, K., Adamson, L. B., Bakeman, R., Owen, M. T., Golinkoff, R. M., Pace, A., . . . Suma, K. (2015). Quality of early communication matters more than quantity of word input for low-income children's language success. *Psychological Science, 26,* 1071–1083. http://dx.doi.org/10.1177/0956797615581493

34. Goode, J. (2010, January 25). *Cute conversation between 3-year olds* [Video file]. Retrieved from https://www.youtube.com/watch? v=sL3vqlHabck

35. Caulkins, L., & Bellino, L. (1998). *Raising lifelong learners: A parent's guide.* Cambridge, MA: Da Capo Press.

36. Ames, G., & Murray, F. B. (1982). When two wrongs make a right: Promoting cognitive change by social conflict. *Developmental Psychology, 18,* 892–895. http://dx.doi.org/10.1037/0012-1649.18. 6.894

37. Lillard, A. S., Lerner, M. D., Hopkins, E. J., Dore, R. A., Smith, E. D., & Palmquist, C. M. (2013). The impact of pretend play on children's development: A review of the evidence. *Psychological Bulletin, 139,* 1–34. http://dx.doi.org/10.1037/a0029321

38. Dickinson, D. K., & Tabors, P. O. (2001). *Beginning literacy with language.* Baltimore, MD: Brookes.

39. Rudnick, M., & Kouba, W. (2006). *How the "Google effect" is transforming employee communications and driving employee engagement.* Retrieved from https://robertoigarza.files.wordpress.com/2008/11/ rep-how-the-google-effect-is-transforming-employee-communications-ww-2006.pdf, p. 5.

40. Schmidt, E., & Varian, H. (2005, December 2). Google: Ten golden rules. *Newsweek.* Retrieved from http://analytics.typepad.com/ files/2005_google_10_golden_rules.pdf, para. 12.

41. Banker, S. (2010, January 27). Multichannel logistics: Walmart.com's site-to-store strategy. *Logistic Viewpoints.* Retrieved from http:// logisticsviewpoints.com/2010/01/27/multichannel-logistics-walmart-coms-site-to-store-strategy/

42. Grice, H. P. (1975). Logic and conversation. In P. Cole & J. L. Morgan (Eds.), *Speech acts* (pp. 41–58). New York, NY: Academic Press.

43. Sunstein, C. (2009). *On rumors: How falsehoods spread, why we believe them, what can be done.* New York, NY: Farrar, Straus & Giroux.

44. Enemark, D. (2006, May 15). It's all about me: Why emails are so easily misunderstood. *The Christian Science Monitor.* Retrieved from http://www.csmonitor.com/2006/0515/p13s01-stct.html

45. Lobel-Sojeski, K. (2009). *Leading the virtual workforce: How great leaders transform organizations in the 21st century.* Mahwah, NJ: Wiley.

46. Rohn, J. (2012, February 9). [Facebook post]. Retrieved from https:// www.facebook.com/OfficialJimRohn/posts/10151254021005635

47. Golinkoff, R. M., Hirsh-Pasek, K., & Eyer, D. (2004). *Einstein never used flashcards: How our children really learn—and why they need to play more and memorize less.* New York, NY: Rodale Books, p. 79.

48. Garrison, M. M., & Christakis, D. A. (2005, December). *A teacher in the living room? Educational media for babies, toddlers, and preschoolers.* Menlo Park, CA: Henry J. Kaiser Family Foundation.

CHAPTER 7

1. Great Schools Staff. (n.d.). *The Florida Comprehensive Assessment Test and State Standards: An overview.* Retrieved from http://www.greatschools.org/gk/articles/testing-in-florida-fcat/

2. IBM Big Data Hub. (n.d.). *The four V's of big data.* Retrieved from http://www.ibmbigdatahub.com/sites/default/files/infographic_file/4-Vs-of-big-data.jpg

3. Plutarch. (1992). *Essays by Plutarch* (R. Waterfield, Trans.). London, England: Penguin Classics, p. 50.

4. Hammonds, B. (2009). *Quotes from Frank Smith and John Taylor Gatto.* Retrieved from http://leading-learning.blogspot.ca/2009/05/quotes-from-frank-smith-and-john-taylor.html?, para. 2.

5. Craik, F. I., & Lockhart, R. S. (1972). Levels of processing: A framework for memory research. *Journal of Verbal Learning & Verbal Behavior, 11,* 671–684. http://dx.doi.org/10.1016/S0022-5371(72)80001-X

6. *Prodromal* is used to describe early symptom indicating the onset of an attack or a disease. In schizophrenia, the prodromal phase includes social isolation and anxiety.

7. Markoff, J. (2009, July 25). Scientists worry machines may outsmart man. *The New York Times.* Retrieved from http://www.nytimes.com/2009/07/26/science/26robot.html, para. 8.

8. Turkle, S. (2011). *Alone together: Why we expect more from technology and less from each other.* New York, NY: Basic Books, p. 12.

9. National Center on Education and the Economy. (2007). *Tough choices or tough times: The report of the Commission on the Skills of the American Workforce.* San Francisco, CA: Jossey-Bass, p. 50.

10. This paraphrases something Darwin is reputed to have said in his book, *Origin of Species.* It appears in Megginson, L. C. (1963). Lessons

from Europe for American business, *Southwestern Social Science Quarterly, 44*, 3–13, p. 4.

11. James, W. (1890). *The principles of psychology*. New York, NY: Henry Holt & Company. http://dx.doi.org/10.1037/11059-000, p. 462.

12. Golinkoff, R. M., & Hirsh-Pasek, K. (1999). *How babies talk: The magic and mystery of language in the first three years of life*. New York, NY: Dutton.

13. Saffran, J. R., Aslin, R. N., & Newport, E. L. (1996). Statistical learning by 8-month-old infants. *Science, 274*, 1926–1928. http://dx.doi.org/10.1126/science.274.5294.1926

14. McElroy, M. (2013, October 30). A first step in learning by imitation, baby brains respond to another's actions. *University of Washington: UW Today*. Retrieved from http://www.washington.edu/news/2013/10/30/a-first-step-in-learning-by-imitation-baby-brains-respond-to-anothers-actions/, para. 4.

15. Bortfeld, H., Morgan, J. L., Golinkoff, R. M., & Rathbun, K. (2005). Mommy and me: Familiar names help launch babies into speech-stream segmentation. *Psychological Science, 16*, 298–304. http://dx.doi.org/10.1111/j.0956-7976.2005.01531.x

16. Gopnik, A., Meltzoff, A. N., & Kuhl, P. K. (2000). *The scientist in the crib: What early learning tells us about the mind*. New York, NY: William Morrow Paperbacks.

17. Chi, M. T. H. (2013). Learning from observing experts. In J. J. Staszewski (Ed.), *Expertise and skill acquisition: The impact of William G. Chase* (pp. 1–28). New York, NY: Psychology Press.

18. Trebesh, L. (2011, December 29). *Admitting you're wrong: Getting it right in business*. Retrieved from Better Business Bureau website: http://www.bbb.org/blog/2011/12/admitting-youre-wrong-getting-it-right-in-business/

19. Hsu, S. S., & Glasser, S. B. (2005, September 6). FEMA director singled out by response critics. *Washington Post*, p. A1.

20. Hatton, S. (2011, December 27). Stella the dinosaur expert [Video file]. Retrieved from https://www.youtube.com/watch?v=jM4nomPWQ88

21. Chi, M. T., & Koeske, R. D. (1983). Network representation of a child's dinosaur knowledge. *Developmental Psychology, 19*, 29–39. http://dx.doi.org/10.1037/0012-1649.19.1.29

22. Pranava. (2012, December 16). Re: Child correcting other children and adults—What to do? [Online forum comment]. Retrieved from http://www.mothering.com/forum/370-parenting-gifted-child/1370335-child-correcting-other-children-adults-what-do.html, para. 1.

23. Blewitt, P., Golinkoff, R. M., & Alioto, A. (2000). Do toddlers have label preferences? A possible explanation for word refusals. *First Language, 20,* 253–272.

24. Keil, F. (1996). *Concepts, kinds, and cognitive development.* Cambridge, MA: MIT Press.

25. Gelman, S. A., & Markman, E. M. (1985). Implicit contrast in adjectives vs. nouns: Implications for word-learning in preschoolers. *Journal of Child Language, 12,* 125–143. http://dx.doi.org/10.1017/S0305000900006279

26. Gentner, D. (1983). Structure mapping: A theoretical framework for analogy. *Cognitive Science, 7,* 155–170. http://dx.doi.org/10.1207/s15516709cog0702_3

27. Gentner, D., & Toupin, C. (1986). Systematicity and surface similarity in the development of analogy. *Cognitive Science, 10,* 277–300. http://dx.doi.org/10.1207/s15516709cog1003_2

28. Oakes, L. M., & Rakison, D. H. (2003). Issues in the early development of concepts and categories: An introduction. In D. H. Rakison & L. M. Oakes (Eds.), *Early category and concept development: Making sense of the blooming, buzzing confusion* (pp. 3–23). New York, NY: Oxford University Press. http://dx.doi.org/10.1207/s15327078in0701_7

29. See note 27.

30. Asch, S. E., & Nerlove, H. (1960). The development of double function terms in children: An exploratory investigation. In B. Kaplan & S. Wapner (Eds.), *Perspectives in psychological theory* (pp. 47–60). New York, NY: International Universities Press.

31. Darling-Hammond, L. (2007, May 21). Evaluating "No Child Left Behind." *The Nation.* Retrieved from http://www.thenation.com/article/evaluating-no-child-left-behind/, para. 11.

32. Venugopal Ramaswamy, S. (2015, April 2). State tests: Stakes are even higher for teachers. *Lohud.* Retrieved from http://www.lohud.com/story/news/local/2015/04/01/teachers-face-penalty-poor-student-performance/70798718/

33. Shavelson, R. J., Linn, R. L., Baker, E. L., Ladd, L. F., Darling-Hammond, L., Shepard, L. A., Barton, . . . Rothstein, R. (2010, August 27). Problems with the use of student test scores to evaluate teachers. *Economic Policy Institute.* Retrieved from http://www.epi.org/publication/bp278/, para. 6.

34. Parker-Poke, T. (2009, February 24). The 3 R's? A fourth is crucial, too: Recess. *The New York Times.* Retrieved from http://www.nytimes.com/2009/02/24/health/24well.html

35. Fausset, R., & Blinder, A. (2015, April 14). Atlanta school workers sentenced in test score cheating case. *The New York Times.* Retrieved from http://www.nytimes.com/2015/04/15/us/atlanta-school-workers-sentenced-in-test-score-cheating-case.html

36. Perlstein, L. (2008). *Tested: One American school struggles to make the grade.* New York, NY: Holt Paperbacks.

37. Sullivan, M. (2011, November 21). Behind America's tutor boom. *MarketWatch.* Retrieved from http://www.marketwatch.com/story/behind-americas-tutor-boom-1318016970246

38. Sawyer, R. K. (Ed.). (2006). *The Cambridge handbook of the learning sciences: Vol. 2., No. 5.* New York, NY: Cambridge University Press.

39. Oliver, H., & Utermohlen, R. (1995). *An innovative teaching strategy: Using critical thinking to give students a guide to the future.* Holly Springs, MS: Rust College.

40. Dunlosky, J., Rawson, K. A., March, E. J., Nathan, M. J., & Willingham, D. T. (2013). Improving students' learning with effective learning techniques: Promising directions from cognitive and educational psychology. *Psychological Science in the Public Interest, 14*, 4–58.

41. Sara. (n.d.). I used to believe: The childhood beliefs site [Web log message]. Retrieved from http://www.iusedtobelieve.com/animals/, para. 17.

42. Operator Lady. (n.d.). I used to believe: The childhood beliefs site [Web log message]. Retrieved from http://www.iusedtobelieve.com/science/telephones/, para. 7.

43. Major Dan. (2015, August 1). 10 famous bridge collapses. *History & Headlines.* Retrieved from http://www.historyandheadlines.com/10-famous-bridge-collapses/

44. Kohn, D. (2015, May 16). Let the kids learn through play. *The New York Times.* Retrieved from http://www.nytimes.com/2015/05/17/opinion/sunday/let-the-kids-learn-through-play.html, para. 4.

45. Newman, J. (2000, October 1). 20 of the greatest blunders in science in the last 20 years. *Discover*. Retrieved from http://discovermagazine. com/2000/oct/featblunders/

46. Karmiloff-Smith, K. (1992). *Beyond modularity*. Cambridge, MA: MIT Press.

47. Shonkoff, J. A. (2011). *Building the brain's "air traffic control" system: How early experiences shape the development of executive function*. Retrieved from Harvard University Center on the Developing Child website: http://developingchild.harvard.edu/resources/building-the-brains-air-traffic-control-system-how-early-experiences-shape-the-development-of-executive-function/, p. 1.

48. Rimm-Kaufman, S. E., Pianta, R. C., & Cox, M. J. (2000). Teachers' judgment of problems in the transition to kindergarten. *Early Childhood Research Quarterly*, *15*, 147–166. http://dx.doi.org/10.1016/ S0885-2006(00)00049-1

49. McClelland, M. M., Cameron, C. E., Connor, C. M., Farris, C. L., Jewkes, A. M., & Morrison, F. J. (2007). Links between behavioral regulation and preschoolers' literacy, vocabulary, and math skills. *Developmental Psychology*, *43*, 947–959. http://dx.doi. org/10.1037/0012-1649.43.4.947

50. Blair, C., & Razza, R. P. (2007). Relating effortful control, executive function, and false belief understanding to emerging math and literacy ability in kindergarten. *Child Development*, *78*, 647–663. http://dx.doi.org/10.1111/j.1467-8624.2007.01019.x

51. Alloway, T. P., & Alloway, R. G. (2010). Investigating the predictive roles of working memory and IQ in academic attainment. *Journal of Experimental Child Psychology*, *106*, 20–29. http://dx.doi. org/10.1016/j.jecp.2009.11.003

52. Diamond, A., Barnett, W. S., Thomas, J., & Munro, S. (2007, November 30). Preschool program improves cognitive control. *Science*, *318*, 1387–1388. http://dx.doi.org/10.1126/science.1151148

53. Goldstein, T., & Winner, E. (2012). Enhancing empathy and theory of mind. *Journal of Cognition and Development*, *13*, 19–37. http:// dx.doi.org/10.1080/15248372.2011.573514

54. Hardiman, M., Magsamen, S., McKhann, G., & Eilber, J. (2009). *Neuroeducation: Learning, arts, and the brain: Findings and challenges for educators and researchers from the 2009 Johns Hopkins University Summit*. New York, NY: Dana Press.

55. Anderson, Z. (2011, October 11). Rick Scott wants to shift university funding away from some degrees. *Sarasota Herald-Tribune.* Retrieved from http://politics.heraldtribune.com/2011/10/10/rick-scott-wants-to-shift-university-funding-away-from-some-majors/

56. Hirsh-Pasek, K., Zosh, J., Golinkoff, R. M., Gray, J., Kaufman, J., & Robb, M. (2015). Harnessing the science of learning to promote real educational apps. *Psychological Science in the Public Interest, 16,* 3–34. http://dx.doi.org/10.1177/1529100615569721

57. Hirsh-Pasek, K., Golinkoff, R. M., Singer, D., & Berk, L. (2009). *A mandate for playful learning in preschool: Presenting the evidence.* New York, NY: Oxford University Press.

58. Pashler, H., McDaniel, M., Rohrer, D., & Bjork, R. (2008). Learning styles concepts and evidence. *Psychological Science in the Public Interest, 9,* 105–119. http://dx.doi.org/10.1111/j.1539-6053.2009.01038.x

59. Penn Medicine. (2014, February 26). *New study suggests evidence-based narratives help emergency medicine doctors improve recall of opioid prescribing guidelines.* Retrieved from http://www.uphs.upenn.edu/news/News_Releases/2014/02/meisel/

60. Kilaru, A. S., Perrone, J. Auriemma, C. L. Shofer, F. S., Barg, F. K., & Meisel, Z. F. (2014). Evidence-based narratives to improve recall of opioid prescribing guidelines: A randomized experiment. *Academic Emergency Medicine, 21,* 244–249. http://dx.doi.org/10.1111/acem.12326

61. Hanford, E. (2012, January 1). *Physicists seek to lose the lecture as teaching tool.* Retrieved from the National Public Radio website: http://www.npr.org/2012/01/01/144550920/physicists-seek-to-lose-the-lecture-as-teaching-tool, para. 11.

62. Hanford, E. (2012, January 1). *Physicists seek to lose the lecture as teaching tool.* Retrieved from the National Public Radio website: http://www.npr.org/2012/01/01/144550920/physicists-seek-to-lose-the-lecture-as-teaching-tool, para. 20.

63. Mazur, E. (2009, January 2). Farewell, lecture? *Science, 323,* 50–51.

64. Grossman, L. (2008, November 13). Outliers: Malcolm Gladwell's success story. *Time.* Retrieved from http://content.time.com/time/magazine/article/0,9171,1858880-1,00.html

65. Chi, M. T. H. (1978). Knowledge structure and memory development. In R. Siegler (Ed.), *Children's thinking: What develops?* (pp. 73–96). Hillsdale, NJ: Erlbaum.

66. Chi, M. T. H. (2006). Two approaches to the study of experts' characteristics. In K. A. Ericsson, N. Charness, P. Feltovich, & R. Hoffman (Eds.), *Cambridge handbook of expertise and expert performance* (pp. 121–30). Cambridge, MA: Cambridge University Press.

67. The McGraw Center for teaching and Learning. (n.d.). *Novice v. expert problem solvers.* Retrieved from the Princeton University website: https://www.princeton.edu/mcgraw/library/for-students/problem-solvers/

68. Ericsson, K. A. (Ed.). (2009). *Development of professional expertise.* New York, NY: Cambridge University Press.

69. Vygotsky, L. (1978). *Mind in society: The development of higher mental processes.* Cambridge, MA: Harvard University Press

70. Wood, D. (1980). Teaching the young child: Some relationships between social interaction, language, and thought. In D. Olson (Ed.), *The social foundation of language and thought* (pp. 280–296). New York, NY: Norton.

71. Edersheim, E. H. (2006). *The definitive Drucker.* New York, NY: McGraw-Hill.

72. Krishnamurti, J. (n.d.). Jiddu Krishnamurti quotes. Retrieved from BrainyQuote.com website: http://www.brainyquote.com/quotes/quotes/j/jiddukrish395484.html

73. Benjamin, N., Haden, C. A., & Wilkerson, E. (2010). Enhancing building, conversation, and learning through caregiver–child interactions in a children's museum. *Developmental Psychology, 46,* 502–515. http://dx.doi.org/10.1037/a0017822

74. Haden, C. A. (2010). Talking about science in museums. *Child Development Perspectives, 4,* 62–67. http://dx.doi.org/10.1111/j.1750-8606.2009.00119.x

CHAPTER 8

1. Simon, M. H. (Producer), Simon, M. H., & Makar, M. (Directors). (2007). *Nursery university* [Motion picture]. United States: Docurama.

2. Bruni, F. (2015). *Where you go is not who you'll be: An antidote to the college admissions mania.* New York, NY: Grand Central.

3. Halpern, D. F. (1998). Teaching critical thinking for transfer across domains: Dispositions, skills, structure training, and metacognitive

monitoring. *American Psychologist, 53,* 449–455. http://dx.doi.org/10.1037/0003-066X.53.4.449, p. 450.

4. Kander, J. (n.d.). *Missouri history: Why is Missouri called the "Show-Me" State?* Retrieved from http://www.sos.mo.gov/archives/history/slogan.asp, para. 2.

5. Beyer, B. K. (1995). *Critical thinking.* Bloomington, IN: Phi Delta Kappa Educational Foundation, p. 8.

6. Foundation for Critical Thinking. (2013). *Defining critical thinking.* Retrieved from http://www.criticalthinking.org/pages/defining-critical-thinking/766, para. 3.

7. Platform Committee. (2012). *2012 Republican Party of Texas.* Retrieved from http://www.texasgop.org/wp-content/themes/rpt/images/2012Platform_Final.pdf, p. 12.

8. Gergely, G., Bekkering, H., & Király, I. (2002, February 14). Developmental psychology: Rational imitation in preverbal infants. *Nature, 415,* 755–755. http://dx.doi.org/10.1038/415755a

9. Flavell, J. H. (1993). The development of children's understanding of false belief and the appearance–reality distinction. *International Journal of Psychology, 28,* 595–604.

10. Campaign for a Commercial-Free Childhood. (n.d.). *About CCFC.* Retrieved from http://www.commercialfreechildhood.org/about-ccfc, para. 3.

11. Moses, L. J., & Baldwin, D. A. (2005). What can the study of cognitive development reveal about children's ability to appreciate and cope with advertising? *Journal of Public Policy & Marketing, 24,* 186–201. http://dx.doi.org/10.1509/jppm.2005.24.2.186

12. Kuhn, D., & Weinstock, M. (2002). What is epistemological thinking and why does it matter? In B. Hofer & P. Pintrich (Eds.), *Epistemology: The psychology of beliefs about knowledge and knowing* (pp. 121–140). Mahwah, NJ: Erlbaum.

13. Flavell, J. H., Mumme, D. L., Green, F. L., & Flavell, E. R. (1992). Young children's understanding of different types of beliefs. *Child Development, 63,* 960–977. http://dx.doi.org/10.2307/1131247

14. Kuhn, D., Cheney, R., & Weinstock, M. (2000). The development of epistemological understanding. *Cognitive Development, 15,* 309–328. http://dx.doi.org/10.1016/S0885-2014(00)00030-7

15. Stack, L. (2013, June 26). *"That's not my job": The lamest excuse in business today.* Retrieved from http://theproductivitypro.com/blog/2013/06/thats-not-my-job-the-lamest-excuse-in-business-today/

16. Kuhn, D. (1999). A developmental model of critical thinking. *Educational Researcher, 28*(2), 16–46. http://dx.doi.org/10.3102/0013189X028002016

17. Parish-Morris, J., Hennon, E. A., Hirsh-Pasek, K., Golinkoff, R. M., & Tager-Flusberg, H. (2007). Children with autism illuminate the role of social intention in word learning. *Child Development, 78,* 1265–1287. http://dx.doi.org/10.1111/j.1467-8624.2007.01065.x

18. We thank one of our anonymous reviewers for this wonderful example.

19. Price, M. (2007, November). The joke's in you. *Monitor on Psychology, 38*(10), 18. Retrieved from http://www.apa.org/monitor/nov07/thejoke.aspx, para. 13.

20. Price, M. (2007, November). The joke's in you. *Monitor on Psychology, 38*(10), 18. Retrieved from http://www.apa.org/monitor/nov07/thejoke.aspx

21. See note 16.

22. Rodriguez, T. (2014, June 12). Rethink your thoughts about thinking. *Scientific American, 25.* Retrieved from http://www.scientificamerican.com/article/rethink-your-thoughts-about-thinking

23. Baldoni, J. (2010, January 20). How leaders should think critically. *Harvard Business Review.* Retrieved from http://blogs.hbr.org/2010/01/how-leaders-should-think-criti/, para. 2.

24. Pallardy, R. (2015). *Deepwater Horizon oil spill of 2010.* Retrieved from http://www.britannica.com/event/Deepwater-Horizon-oil-spill-of-2010

25. Gabler, N. (2011, August 13). The elusive big idea. *The New York Times.* Retrieved from http://www.nytimes.com/2011/08/14/opinion/sunday/the-elusive-big-idea.html?pagewanted=all, para. 5.

26. Khalifa, M. (2007, May). *International marketing mistakes related to culture.* Retrieved from http://www.slideshare.net/levi22usa/international-marketing-mistakes-related-to-culture

27. See note 16.

28. See note 3.

29. Piaget, J. (1952). *The origins of intelligence in children* (M. Cook, Trans.). Madison, CT: International Universities Press.

30. Mills, C. M. (2013). Knowing when to doubt: Developing a critical stance when learning from others. *Developmental Psychology, 49*, 404–418. http://dx.doi.org/10.1037/a0029500

31. Ma, L., & Ganea, P. A. (2009). Dealing with conflicting information: Young children's reliance on what they see versus what they told. *Developmental Science, 13*, 151–160. http://dx.doi.org/10.1111/j.1467-7687.2009.00878.x

32. See note 30.

33. Mills, C. M. (2013). Knowing when to doubt: Developing a critical stance when learning from others. *Developmental Psychology, 49*, 40–418. http://dx.doi.org/10.1037/a0029500, p. 413.

34. Brooks, X. (2013, June 2). Michael Douglas on Liberace, Cannes, cancer and cunnilingus. *The Guardian*. Retrieved from http://www.theguardian.com/film/2013/jun/02/michael-douglas-liberace-cancer-cunnilingus

35. Centers for Disease Control and Prevention. (2015). *Vaccines do not cause autism*. Retrieved from http://www.cdc.gov/vaccinesafety/concerns/autism/, para. 7.

36. Allday, R. (2015, March 7). Failure to vaccinate led to California's measles outbreak. *San Francisco Chronicle*. Retrieved from http://www.sfchronicle.com/bayarea/article/Failure-to-vaccinate-fueled-state-s-measles-6121401.php, para. 9.

37. See note 12.

38. Kuhn, D. (2009). The importance of learning about knowing: Creating a foundation for development of intellectual values. *Child Development Perspectives, 3*, 112–117. http://dx.doi.org/10.1111/j.1750-8606.2009.00089.x

39. Curtis, L. (2015). *Ten takeaway tips for teaching critical thinking*. Retrieved from Killeen Independent School District website: https://www.killeenisd.org/teachers/index.cfm?param1=13542

40. See note 30.

41. Wilson, E. O. (1999). *Consilience: The unity of knowledge* (Vol. 31). New York, NY: Random House, p. 294.

42. Pellegrino, J. W., & Hilton, M. L. (Eds.). (2013). *Education for life and work: Developing transferable knowledge and skills in the 21st century*. Washington, DC: National Academies Press.

43. Gardner, H. (2006). *Five minds for the future.* Boston, MA: Harvard Business School Press, p. 46.

44. Tough, P. (2012). *How children succeed.* New York, NY: Houghton Mifflin, Harcourt.

45. Gilbert, D. T. (1991). How mental systems believe. *American Psychologist, 46,* 107–119. http://dx.doi.org/10.1037/0003-066X.46.2.107, p. 111.

46. Darling-Hammond, L. (Ed.). (2008). *Powerful learning.* San Francisco, CA: Wiley.

47. de Icaza, M. A. (1991, November 6). U.S. Students memorize, but don't understand [Letter to the editor]. *The New York Times.* Retrieved from http://www.nytimes.com/1991/11/06/opinion/l-us-students-memorize-but-don-t-understand-740191.html, para. 2, 3.

48. de Icaza, M. A. (1991, November 6). U.S. Students memorize, but don't understand [Letter to the editor]. *The New York Times.* Retrieved from http://www.nytimes.com/1991/11/06/opinion/l-us-students-memorize-but-don-t-understand-740191.html, para. 5.

49. This example was inspired by the following reference: Paul, R., & Elder, L. (2012). *Critical thinking handbook: K–3rd grades.* Tomales, CA: Foundation for Critical Thinking Press.

50. Kuhn, D., & Weinstock, M. (2002). What is epistemological thinking and why does it matter? In B. Hofer & P. Pintrich (Eds.), *Epistemology: The psychology of beliefs about knowledge and knowing* (pp. 121–140). Mahwah, NJ: Erlbaum, p. 139.

51. Halpern, D. F. (1998). Teaching critical thinking for transfer across domains: Dispositions, skills, structure training, and metacognitive monitoring. *American Psychologist, 53,* 449–455. http://dx.doi.org/10.1037/0003-066X.53.4.449

52. Sternberg, R. J., & Grigorenko, E. L. (2007). *Teaching for successful intelligence: To increase student learning and achievement.* Newbury Park, CA: Corwin Press.

53. Edersheim, E. H. (2007). *The definitive Drucker.* New York, NY: McGraw-Hill.

54. Kantor, J., & Streitfeld, D. (2015, August 15). Amazon's bruising, thrilling workplace. *The New York Times.* Retrieved from http://www.nytimes.com/2015/08/16/technology/inside-amazon-wrestling-big-ideas-in-a-bruising-workplace.html, para. 29.

CHAPTER 9

1. Gardner, H. (2006). *Five minds for the future*. Boston, MA: Harvard Business School Press, p. 77.

2. Bronson, P., & Merryman, A. (2010, July 10). The creativity crisis. *Newsweek*. Retrieved from http://www.newsweek.com/creativity-crisis-74665

3. Kim, K. H. (2011). The creativity crisis: The decrease in creative thinking scores on the Torrance Tests of Creative Thinking. *Creativity Research Journal*, *23*, 285–295. http://dx.doi.org/10.1080/10400419.2011.627805

4. Guilford, J. P. (1967). *The nature of human intelligence*. New York, NY: McGraw-Hill, p. 213.

5. Robinson, K. (2011). *Out of our minds: Learning to be creative*. Oxford, England: Capstone.

6. Pink, D. H. (2005). *A whole new mind: Moving from the information age to the conceptual age*. New York, NY: Riverhead Books.

7. Florida, R. (2002, May). The rise of the creative class. *Washington Monthly*. Retrieved from http://www.washingtonmonthly.com/features/2001/0205.florida.html

8. Halpern, D., & Riggio, H. (2003). *Thinking critically about critical thinking* (4th ed.). Mahwah, NJ: Erlbaum, p. 211.

9. Runco, M. A. (2007). *Creativity*. New York, NY: Academic Press, p. 40.

10. Chiem, D., & Caswell, B. (2008). *The 3-mind revolution*. New York, NY: Marshall Cavendish.

11. Think different. (n.d.). In *Wikipedia*. Retrieved from http://en.wikipedia.org/wiki/Think_different

12. Russ, S. W. (2014). *Pretend play in childhood: Foundation of adult creativity*. Washington, DC: American Psychological Association. http://dx.doi.org/10.1037/14282-000, p. 25.

13. Kaufman, J. C., & Beghetto, R. A. (2009). Beyond big and little: The four C model of creativity. *Review of General Psychology*, *13*, 1–12. http://dx.doi.org/10.1037/a0013688, p. 3.

14. Hoicka, E., & Butcher, J. (2015). Parents produce explicit cues that help toddlers distinguish joking and pretending. *Cognitive Science*. Advance online publication. http://dx.doi.org/10.1111/cogs.12264

15. Leonardi, P. M. (2011, December). Early prototypes can hurt a team's creativity. *Harvard Business Review*. Retrieved from http://hbr.org/2011/12/early-prototypes-can-hurt-a-teams-creativity/ar/1

16. Weisberg, R. W. (1993). *Creativity: Beyond the myth of genius*. New York, NY: WH Freeman.

17. Gardner, H. (2006). *Five minds for the future*. Boston, MA: Harvard Business School Press, p. 89.

18. Bonawitz, E., Shafto, P., Gweon, H., Goodman, N. D., Spelke, E., & Schulz, L. (2011). The double-edged sword of pedagogy: Instruction limits spontaneous exploration and discovery. *Cognition, 120*, 322–330. http://dx.doi.org/10.1016/j.cognition.2010.10.001

19. Lucas, C. G., Bridgers, S., Griffiths, T. L., & Gopnik, A. (2014). When children are better (or at least more open-minded) learners than adults: Developmental differences in learning the forms of causal relationships. *Cognition, 131*, 284–299. http://dx.doi.org/10.1016/j.cognition.2013.12.010

20. Kaufman, J. C., & Beghetto, R. A. (2009). Beyond big and little: The four C model of creativity. *Review of General Psychology, 13*, 1–12. http://dx.doi.org/10.1037/a0013688, p. 2.

21. Goffin, S. G., & Tull, C. Q. (1985). Problem solving: Encouraging active learning. *Young Children, 40*, 28–32.

22. Wallis, C., & Steptoe, S. (2006, December 10). How to bring our schools out of the 20th century. *Time*. Retrieved from http://content.time.com/time/magazine/article/0,9171,1568480,00.html, para. 1.

23. Preus, B. (2007). Educational trends in China and the United States: Proverbial pendulum or potential for balance? *Phi Delta Kappa, 89*, 115–118, p. 116.

24. Zhao, Y. (2009). *Catching up or leading the way: American education in the age of globalization*. Alexandria, VA: ASCD.

25. Weisberg, R. W. (2006). Expertise and reason in creative thinking: Evidence from case studies and the laboratory. In J. C. Kaufman & J. Baer (Eds.), *Creativity and reason in cognitive development* (pp. 7–42). West Nyack, NY: Cambridge University Press. http://dx.doi.org/10.1017/CBO9780511606915.003

26. This analogy was inspired by the following paper: Kaufman, J. C., & Beghetto, R. A. (2009). Beyond big and little: The four C model of creativity. *Review of General Psychology, 13*, 1–12. http://dx.doi.org/10.1037/a0013688

27. Kaufman, J. C., & Beghetto, R. A. (2009). Beyond big and little: The four C model of creativity. *Review of General Psychology, 13*, 1–12. http://dx.doi.org/10.1037/a0013688

28. Sternberg, R. J., & Grigorenko, E. L. (2007). *Teaching for successful intelligence: To increase student learning and achievement.* Newbury Park, CA: Corwin Press.

29. See note 28.

30. Azzam, A. M. (2009). Why creativity now? A conversation with Sir Ken Robinson. *Educational Leadership.* Retrieved from http://www.ascd. org/publications/educational-leadership/sept09/vol67/num01/Why-Creativity-Now%C2%A2-A-Conversation-with-Sir-Ken-Robinson. aspx, para. 14.

31. Brynjolfsson, E., & McAfee, A. (2012). *Race against the machine: How the digital revolution is accelerating innovation, driving productivity, and irreversibly transforming employment and the economy.* Lexington, MA: Digital Frontier Press.

32. Partnership for 21st Century Skills. (2008). *21st century skills, education, and competitiveness: A resource and policy guide.* Retrieved from http://www.p21.org/storage/documents/21st_century_skills_ education_and_competitiveness_guide.pdf, p. 6, 10.

33. See note 27.

34. Williams, S. D. (2008). *Kid inventors: Brain children.* Retrieved from http://www.afterschooltreats.com/wfdata/frame1216-1158/ pressrel5.asp

35. Iwashina, K., & Pellegrini, T. (Producers), & Gelb, D. (Director). (2011). *Jiro Dreams of Sushi* [Motion picture]. United States: Preferred Content, Sundial Pictures.

36. High Line Park. (n.d.). Retrieved from New York Travel website: http://www.newyorktravel.gr/index.php/en/new-york-attractions/ new-york-parks/836-high-line-park, para. 21.

37. Brown. T. (2008, May). Tales of creativity and play [Video file]. Retrieved from https://www.ted.com/talks/tim_brown_on_creativity_ and_play?language=en

38. Friends of the High Line. (2008, May 30). *High Line history: Narrated by Ethan Hawke* [Video file]. Retrieved from https://www.youtube. com/watch?v=F1tVsezifw4&noredirect=1

39. Chow, B. (2011, August 1). IDEO: What's it like to work at IDEO? [Web log message]. Retrieved from http://www.quora.com/IDEO/ Whats-it-like-to-work-at-IDEO, para. 2.

40. Elkhorne, J. (1967, March 1). Edison—The fabulous drone. *73 Magazine.* Retrieved from http://www.arimi.it/wp-content/73/03_March_1967.pdf, p. 52.
41. Yamada, K. (2014). *What do you do with an idea?* Seattle, WA: Compendium.
42. See note 14.
43. Watters, A. (2015). *Lego mindstorms: A history of educational robots.* Retrieved from the Hack Education website: http://hackeducation.com/2015/04/10/mindstorms

CHAPTER 10

1. Vaughan, N. D. (1995). *My life of adventure.* Mechanicsburg, PA: Stackpole Books.
2. This was Wayne Gretzky's answer to Bob McKenzie's statement, "You have taken a lot of shots this year," in the January 16, 1983, edition of *Hockey News.*
3. Duckworth, A. L. (2013, April). *The key to success? Grit* [Video file]. Retrieved from http://www.ted.com/talks/angela_lee_duckworth_the_key_to_success_grit?language=en
4. William Edward Hickson. (n.d.). In *Wikipedia.* Retrieved from http://en.wikipedia.org/wiki/William_Edward_Hickson
5. Best, J. (2011). *Everyone's a winner: Life in our congratulatory culture.* Berkeley and Los Angeles: University of California Press.
6. Prendergast, M. (1994). *For God, country and Coca-Cola: The unauthorized history of the great American soft drink and the company that makes it.* New York, NY: Basic Books.
7. Bjorklund, D. (2007). *Why youth is not wasted on the young: Immaturity in human development.* Maiden, MA: Blackwell.
8. Ruble, D. (1983). The development of social comparison processes and their role in achievement-related self-socialization. In E. T. Higgins, D. N. Ruble, & W. W. Hartup (Eds.), *Social cognition and social development: A socio–cultural perspective* (pp. 134–157). New York, NY: Cambridge University Press.
9. Lipko, A. R., Dunlosky, J., & Merriman, W. E. (2009). Persistent overconfidence despite practice: The role of task experience in pre-

schoolers' recall predictions. *Journal of Experimental Child Psychology*, *103*, 152–166. http://dx.doi.org/10.1016/j.jecp.2008.10.002

10. Plumert, J. (1995). Relations between children's overestimation of their physical abilities and their accident proneness. *Developmental Psychology*, *31*, 866–876. http://dx.doi.org/10.1037/0012-1649.31.5.866

11. Rozenblit, L., & Keil, F. (2002). The misunderstood limits of folk science: An illusion of explanatory depth. *Cognitive Science*, *26*, 521–562. http://dx.doi.org/10.1207/s15516709cog2605_1, p. 558.

12. Thaler, R. H. (2010, August 21). The overconfidence problem in forecasting. *The New York Times*. Retrieved from http://www.nytimes.com/2010/08/22/business/economy/22view.html?_r=0

13. Kettering, C. F. (1937, May). Research and industry. *Scientific American*, *156*, 285–288, p. 282.

14. Goethals, G. R., & Darley, J. (1977). Social comparison theory: An attributional approach. In J. Suls & R. L. Miller (Eds.), *Social comparison processes: Theoretical and empirical perspectives* (pp. 259–278). Washington, DC: Hemisphere.

15. Blanton, H., Buunk, B. P., Gibbons, F. X., & Kuyper, H. (1999). When better-than-others compare upward: Choice of comparison and comparative evaluation as independent predictors of academic performance. *Journal of Personality and Social Psychology*, *76*, 420–430. http://dx.doi.org/10.1037/0022-3514.76.3.420

16. Dweck, C. (2006). *Mindset: The new psychology of success*. New York, NY: Random House.

17. Steinberg, L. (2008). A social neuroscience perspective on adolescent risk-taking. *Developmental Review*, *28*, 78–106. http://dx.doi.org/10.1016/j.dr.2007.08.002

18. Steinberg, L. (2014). *Age of opportunity*. Boston, MA: Houghton Mifflin Harcourt.

19. See note 16.

20. Berk, L. E. (2003). *Child development* (6th ed.). New York, NY: Pearson.

21. Brown, J. D., & Dutton, K. A. (1995). The thrill of victory, the complexity of defeat: Self-esteem and people's emotional reactions to success and failure. *Journal of Personality and Social Psychology*, *68*, 712–722. http://dx.doi.org/10.1037/0022-3514.68.4.712

22. Mednick, S. A. (1962). The associative basis of the creative process. *Psychological Review*, 69, 220–232. http://dx.doi.org/10.1037/h0048850

23. Mogel, W. (2001). *The blessing of a skinned knee: Using Jewish teachings to raise self-reliant children*. New York, NY: Penguin.

24. Hetland, L., Winner, E., Veenema, S., & Sheridan, K. (2007). *Studio habits: The real benefits of visual arts education*. New York, NY: Teachers College Press.

25. Musselwhite, C. (n.d.). *Author archives*. Retrieved from Discovery Learning website: https://www.discoverylearning.com/author/chrismusselwhite/page/2/

26. Ammer, C. (2013). *The American heritage dictionary of idioms* (2nd ed.). Boston, MA: Houghton Mifflin Harcourt.

27. Goldstein, S. (2013, April 14). Barbie as a real woman is anatomically impossible and would have to walk on all fours, chart shows. *New York Daily News*. Retrieved from http://www.nydailynews.com/life-style/health/barbie-real-womaan-anatomically-impossible-article-1.1316533

28. Zurbriggen, E. L., Collins, R. L., Lamb, S., Roberts, T.-A., Tolman, D. L., Ward, L. M., & Blake, J. (2008). *Report of the APA task force on the sexualization of girls*. Retrieved from American Psychological Association website: http://www.apa.org/pi/women/programs/girls/report.aspx

29. Jackson, D. Z. (2014, March 14). Barbie, crusher of aspirations. *Boston Globe*. Retrieved from http://www.bostonglobe.com/opinion/editorials/2014/03/13/anything-barbie-may-actually-dumb-down-girl-career-aspirations/NSP0EScntNa8ZtbiHP9YrL/story.html

30. Kay, K., & Shipman, C. (2014). *The confidence code: The science and art of self-assurance—What women should know*. New York, NY: HarperCollins.

31. Davis, S., & Eppler-Wolff, N. (2009). *Raising children who soar: A guide to healthy risk-taking in an uncertain world*. New York, NY: Teachers College Press.

32. See note 31.

33. See note 31.

34. Elmore, T. (2012, December 10). Kids-need-risk [Web log message]. Retrieved from http://growingleaders.com/blog/kids-need-risk/medium_7081636/

35. Wilson, W. B. (2013, May 8). Why you shouldn't fear a calculated risk. *Financial Post*. Retrieved from http://business.financialpost.com/2013/05/08/a-calculated-risk-isnt-something-to-be-feared/, para. 2.

36. Edmondson, A. C. (2011, April). Strategies for learning from failure. *Harvard Business Review*. Retrieved from http://hbr.org/2011/04/strategies-for-learning-from-failure/ar/1

37. Duckworth, A. L., Peterson, C., Matthews, M. D., & Kelly, D. R. (2007). Grit: Perseverance and passion for long-term goals. *Journal of Personality and Social Psychology, 92*, 1087–1101. http://dx.doi.org/10.1037/0022-3514.92.6.1087

38. See note 37.

39. Duckworth, A. L., & Quinn, P. D. (2009). Development and validation of the short grit scale (grit-s). *Journal of Personality Assessment, 91*, 166–174. http://dx.doi.org/10.1080/00223890802634290

40. Potts, R., & Shanks, D. R. (2014). The benefit of generating errors during learning. *Journal of Experimental Psychology: General, 143*, 644–667. http://dx.doi.org/10.1037/a0033194

41. Autin, F., & Croizet, J. C. (2012). Improving working memory efficiency by reframing metacognitive interpretation of task difficulty. *Journal of Experimental Psychology: General, 141*, 610–618. http://dx.doi.org/10.1037/a0027478

42. The answer? *Chien* [dog]!

43. American Psychological Association. (2012, March 12). *Reducing academic pressure may help children succeed*. Retrieved from http://www.apa.org/news/press/releases/2012/03/academic-pressure.aspx, para. 7.

44. See note 16.

45. Kaufman, S. B. (2011, December 8). Confidence matters just as much as achievement. *Psychology Today*. Retrieved from http://www.psychologytoday.com/blog/beautiful-minds/201112/confidence-matters-just-much-ability, para. 1.

46. Moè, A., & Pazzaglia, F. (2006). Following the instructions! Effects of gender beliefs in mental rotation. *Learning and Individual Differences, 16*, 369–377. http://dx.doi.org/10.1016/j.lindif.2007.01.002

47. Edersheim, E. H. (2006). *The definitive Drucker: Challenges for tomorrow's executives.* New York, NY: McGraw-Hill.

48. Roosevelt, E. (1960). *You learn by living: Eleven keys for a more fulfilling life.* Philadelphia, PA: Westminster Press, p. 29.

49. Ward, A. (1985, November 10). An all-weather idea. *The New York Times Magazine.* Retrieved from http://www.nytimes.com/1985/11/10/magazine/an-all-weather-idea.html, p. 4.

50. Corley, C. (2005, October 25). *Civil rights icon Rosa Parks dies.* Retrieved from National Public Radio website: http://www.npr.org/templates/story/story.php?storyId=4973548

51. Hoffman, J. (August 24, 2015). Square root of kids' math anxiety: Their parents' help. *The New York Times.* Retrieved from http://well.blogs.nytimes.com/2015/08/24/square-root-of-kids-math-anxiety-their-parents-help/?_r=0

CHAPTER 11

1. Partnership for 21st Century Skills. (2009). *P21 framework definitions.* Retrieved from http://www.p21.org/storage/documents/P21_Framework_Definitions.pdf

2. Dougherty, D. (2011, January). *We are makers* [Video file]. Retrieved from https://www.ted.com/talks/dale_dougherty_we_are_makers?language=en

3. Wagner, T. (2012). *Calling all innovators.* Retrieved from http://www.tonywagner.com/resources/calling-all-innovators-3

4. Randy Pausch. (n.d.). *Goodreads.* Retrieved from http://www.goodreads.com/author/show/287960.Randy_Pausch

5. Kuhn, D., & Crowell, A. (2011). Dialogic argumentation as a vehicle for developing young adolescents' thinking. *Psychological Science, 22,* 545–552. http://dx.doi.org/10.1177/0956797611402512

6. Wenner, M. (2009). The serious need for play. *Scientific American Mind, 20,* 22–29.

7. Fisher, K. R., Hirsh-Pasek, K., Newcombe, N., & Golinkoff, R. M. (2013). Taking shape: Supporting preschoolers' acquisition of geo-

metric knowledge through guided play. *Child Development, 84,* 1872–1878. http://dx.doi.org/10.1111/cdev.12091

8. See also: Hadley, E. B., Dickinson, D. K., Golinkoff, R. M., & Hirsh-Pasek, K. (in press). Examining the acquisition of vocabulary knowledge depth among preschool-aged children. *Reading Research Quarterly.*

INDEX

ABOUT THE AUTHORS

Roberta Michnick Golinkoff, PhD, obtained her bachelor's degree at Brooklyn College, her PhD at Cornell University, and was awarded a postdoctoral fellowship at the Learning Research and Development Center of the University of Pittsburgh. She is the Unidel H. Rodney Sharp Professor of Education, Professor of Linguistics and Cognitive Science, and Professor of Psychological and Brain Sciences at the University of Delaware. She has won numerous awards for her work, including the John Simon Guggenheim Fellowship, the James McKeen Cattell Sabbatical Award, the Urie Bronfenbrenner Award for Lifetime Contribution to Developmental Psychology in the Service of Science and Society, and two awards from the American Psychological Association: the Award for Distinguished Service to Psychological Science and Distinguished Scientific Lecturer. With her long-standing colleague Kathy Hirsh-Pasek, Dr. Golinkoff was the 2015 recipient of the James McKeen Cattell Fellow Award for lifetime contributions to applied psychological science. She routinely travels worldwide to speak to academic as well as lay groups. Having written over 150 articles and 16 books, monographs, and special journal issues, she is an expert on language development, playful learning, and early spatial knowledge. Three of her books are directed at parents and practitioners because she is passionate about dissemination. To bring the science of learning to the streets, Dr. Golinkoff cofounded the Ultimate Block Party movement to celebrate the science of learning.

Kathy Hirsh-Pasek, PhD, is the Stanley and Debra Lefkowitz Distinguished Faculty Fellow in the Department of Psychology at Temple University and a Senior Fellow at the Brookings Institution. Her research examines the development of early language and literacy, as well as the role of play in learning. With her long-term collaborator, Roberta Michnick Golinkoff, she is the author of 14 books and hundreds of publications. She is the recipient of the American Psychological Association's Urie Bronfenbrenner Award for Lifetime Contribution to Developmental Psychology in the Service of Science and Society, Award for Distinguished Service to Psychological Science, and Distinguished Scientific Lecturer award, as well as the Association for Psychological Science's James McKeen Cattell Fellow Award. Dr. Hirsh-Pasek is a fellow of the American Psychological Association and the American Psychological Society and the president-elect of the International Society for Infant Studies. She has served as the associate editor of *Child Development*. Her book *Einstein Never Used Flashcards: How Children Really Learn and Why They Need to Play More and Memorize Less* won the prestigious Books for a Better Life Award as the best psychology book in 2003. Dr. Hirsh-Pasek received her bachelor's degree from the University of Pittsburgh and her PhD from the University of Pennsylvania.